W9-DAT-078

GREAT THEORIES IN
LITERARY CRITICISM

Great Theories in
LITERARY
CRITICISM

Edited by Karl Beckson

THE NOONDAY PRESS

a division of

FARRAR, STRAUS AND COMPANY

New York

Copyright © 1963 by Karl Beckson
Library of Congress catalog card number 63–8295
First Noonday Press Printing, 1963

Published simultaneously in Canada by
Ambassador Books, Ltd., Toronto
Manufactured in the United States of America
by H. Wolff, New York

TO
MACE AND ERIC

Foreword

The intention of this volume, within the restrictions of limited space, is to present a selection of great critical statements from Plato to Arnold, with the emphasis on English criticism, since most general readers or students will be chiefly interested in that tradition. In most cases, the selection is presented in its entirety, though I have not hesitated to omit passages which are excessively illustrative or which are concerned with technical matters of little relevance to central theory. Where lengthy omissions occur, I have summarized their contents briefly.

Since literary criticism, especially on its highest levels, presupposes knowledge of its historical context, the prefaces are designed to give the reader some understanding of the significant literary, philosophical, or historical forces which form the "background" of the work. Great violence has no doubt been done to the periods discussed in the process of making simple what is in reality extremely complex, but it is hoped that the outlines may serve some function.

KARL BECKSON

Brooklyn College,
The City University of New York
May 1, 1962

Contents

I

CLASSICAL ANTIQUITY: FOUR GREAT CRITICS

Preface

Of the earliest works revealing Greek attitudes towards literature, Homer's *Iliad* and *Odyssey* and Hesiod's *Theogony* (all of which date from about the eighth century B.C.) imply a theory which has long influenced and perplexed Western critical thought—namely, that the poet creates through the instrumentality of a god. In his epics, Homer seeks inspiration by appealing to the Muses for assistance in telling his tales, an invocation designed by the ancients to suggest the poet's source of creative energy and narrative truth. Unlike Homer, who actively sought divine aid, Hesiod, in the *Theogony,* a divine genealogy, relates that while tending sheep on Mount Helicon a Muse breathed into him the art with which to sing of the gods. (Our term *inspiration* is consequently derived from the Latin *inspirare,* meaning "to breathe into.")

This method of divine communication with man was not startlingly original in Homer's time, for the theory of literary creation by inspiration and the older prophetic tradition were closely identified: like the poet, the seer, or prophet, functioned as a receptacle for messages from the gods. Since the gods were presumably truthful, the poet also spoke truth, for was he not, like the prophet, in direct touch with Mount Olympus? Like many early philosophers, Plato was to cast doubt upon such an assumption, contending that inspiration was a source of error, not truth.

Though both Homer and Hesiod accept inspiration as the source of their creativity, they indicate different attitudes as to the primary function of poetry. For Homer, pleasure, produced by the enchantment of verse, was the end of the poetic experience, whereas Hesiod, in accordance with the tradition of prophecy, believed that the gods, in revealing themselves through the poet, wished to instruct men. This dispute between pleasure and didacticism as primary ends may be observed, in one form or another, throughout the history of Western literary criticism.

A further early suggestion on the nature of art occurs in Homer's *Iliad*. There, the poet, in describing the workmanship of Hephaistos, who has carved the image of a newly ploughed field on Achilles' shield, marvels at the lifelike blackness of the soil. The illusion of reality in art—a doctrine central to later discussions—was, like the theory of inspiration, to be subjected to Plato's rigorous dialectic.

II

By the sixth century B.C., the attempt on the part of such philosophers as Xenophanes, Pythagoras, and Heraclitus to establish a cosmos based on natural law led to an attack on Homer and Hesiod, who, in depicting the gods as jealous, revengeful, and quarrelsome, had filled the universe with capricious forces. The least attractive qualities of men, they said, were thus attributed to the great gods. Since Homer's epic world consisted not of rational order but of anthropomorphic chaos, philosophy, not poetry, was the only source of truth, hence the only suitable study. (At that time, Greek education was based primarily on the study of the ancient poets.)

Despite the attempts of these philosophers to discredit the older myths, others came to Homer's defense. Anaxagoras, for example, insisted that the myths, if interpreted allegorically, contained great truths, both moral and scientific. Thus, he said, the literal narrative concealed more significant meaning. Indeed, such an allegorical approach to literature was to have a profound, though sometimes disastrous, effect upon critics and theologians for centuries.

III

With a rationalistic tradition inherited from the previous century, literary criticism emerged, in the fifth century B.C., from the half-light of the obscure past into some prominence. Two extant speeches by Georgias, a fifth-century rhetorician, indicate the existence of a considerable body of poetic theory, now lost, concerned with style and structure. Happily, however, the critical judgments of the great poet Pindar and the comic dramatist Aristophanes have survived. Both subjected earlier theory and opinion to new examination.

Pindar insisted that inspiration was not a state in which the poet was "out of his mind," but the result of the deliberate exercise of inborn ability. The poet's technique, he maintained, that which he learns, is less significant than that which he "knows by nature." Consequently, the poet's excellence rests primarily upon his ability to use his natural gifts. In the hands of Pindar, the theory of inspiration, divested of divine significance, now made poets solely responsible for their creations, the gods only onlookers.

In four comic plays of Aristophanes, however, are to be found the most significant literary judgments of the fifth century. The most important, *The Frogs* (405 B.C.), both excellent comedy and major criticism, attempts to evaluate the tragic dramatists Euripides and Aeschylus. In the play, the god Dionysius, in whose honor drama festivals were held, decides to restore the recently deceased Euripides to life, for the future of tragedy is gravely threatened. Reaching Pluto's underworld, Dionysius discovers that the two playwrights are preparing to compete for the throne of tragedy. After arguments are heard, scales are employed to weigh their respective verse line by line. Satisfied with Aschylus', Dionysius leads him back to earth.

In awarding the victory to Aeschylus, Aristophanes decides that the great dramatist has embodied in his plays the noble virtues of manliness and valor, loyalty and courage—all of which were responsible for the greatness of Athens, whereas Euripides inculcates doubt, not certainty; cunning, not obedience. Thus, since the latter appeals to base motives, Aeschylus was the greater dramatist because of his skill in developing social virtue. In a period of political decline (Athens was, by Aristophanes' time, no longer the greatest city-state in Greece), such criticism attempted to strengthen social morality against growing skepticism and confusion in values. For Aristophanes, art must, in short, contribute to the health of the body politic, an attitude later reiterated by Plato.

IV

The "quarrel of long standing between philosophy and poetry," referred to by Plato in the *Republic,* continued into the fourth century B.C., a period of artistic and political confusion. The great Periclean democracy, weakened by prolonged warfare with oligarchical Sparta and its allies, had come to a disastrous end in 404 B.C., the final year of the Peloponnesian War. In the period that followed, Plato sought to establish intellectual order and stability through systematic inquiry into metaphysics, politics, ethics, education, and poetry. Part of his intention was to counteract the relativism of the Sophists, who popularized skeptical attitudes toward any absolute knowledge or morality. What emerged, from our point of interest, was an attempt to discredit, as had the sixth-century philosophers, poetry which was not salutary to moral and intellectual development. In short, poetry which could not directly contribute to the stability of the state must be suppressed.

Like Xenophanes and others before him, Plato, in the *Republic,* attacked the Homeric epics for portraying the weaknesses of men in the form of gods. In addition, he considered the current comedy dangerous to society, for it catered to man's lower appetites rather than his higher faculties, to a desire for sensationalism rather than moral improvement. In tragedy, Plato said, the audience identified too closely with heroes who displayed undesirable traits. Such literature could only debilitate moral stability.

Such is the ethical disapproval voiced by Plato. In support of his conclusions, he turned to his own metaphysics to condemn such poetry as he found unacceptable. Book X of the *Republic* contains the famous indictment of poetry that "lies," for the poet who "imitates" nature in his epic or tragedy, Plato says, produces a copy of a copy of reality—that which is absolute, immutable, eternal. In creating an even more imperfect version than the world he uses as his model, he is, in short, even less reliable as a source of truth than the world we actually see. Elsewhere in the *Republic* and later in the *Laws,* Plato does, however, concede that poetry which represents things as they ought to be rather than as they are could suggest ideal forms. Nevertheless, he is firm in his insistence that "hymns to the gods and praises of famous men are the only poetry which ought to be admitted into our State."

In effect, the banishment applies to all epic and tragedy, a rejection of the glories of Greece. Despite Plato's important qualification as to hymns and panegyrics, defenders of poetry, such as Sir Philip Sidney in his *Apology for Poetry* (1595), were to lament that Plato had "banished poets out of his Commonwealth." Indeed, Plato's utterances, taken to mean that all poetry spoke falsehoods, have become scripture to Puritans and Philistines, justifying either condemnation of or indifference to imaginative literature.

Often overlooked, a significant passage occurs in the *Laws,* one of Plato's last works, in which he admits the value of comedy and tragedy, though they must be, he insists, prudently censored. Here, in a dialogue concerned with the practical problems confronting an actual state, Plato is understandably less restrictive than he is in the *Republic,* which is concerned with an ideal state. Plato was, after all, a superb artist himself.

V

In one sense, Aristotle's *Poetics* may be considered a reply to Plato's expostulation that poetry was a source of error and moral debilitation, for now poetry was conceived as superior to history and a cathartic of undesirable emotions. For Aristotle, Plato's illustrious pupil at the Academy, the idea of imitation underwent considerable change, from the Platonic copying of nature to the

Aristotlean perfecting of nature. Reality, for Aristotle, consists of the world we apprehend, within which there is a continuous fulfillment of forms—in brief, a world of "Becoming," as opposed to the Platonic world of "Being," which is the static, unchanging reality of Ideas, or Forms, beyond the natural world. In creating character and action liberated from the accidents of nature—as they would be if permitted logical fulfillment, as Aristotle says, "according to the law of probability or necessity"—the poet provides the spectator with insight into the nature of reality, into its universal forms, whereas the historian deals with "unfulfilled" particulars.

In his concept of catharsis, never fully explained, Aristotle presents a solution to the Platonic contention that the audience, in identifying with character, subjects itself to undesirable emotions which debilitate morality. The characteristic emotional response to the tragic hero's situation—that of pity and fear—is finally purged, Aristotle suggests, so that the audience is not only restored to emotional stability but also made more intensely aware of the moral consequences of the hero's acts. In defending poetry, a term used for drama as well, Aristotle voiced the sentiments of his age, for men of letters generally held that art was morally valuable in the formation of character. Plato's rejection of most poetry was no doubt regarded as eccentric, but it is obvious that Plato took such a position precisely because he recognized its power.

VI

With the decline of Athens' intellectual and political supremacy, other Greek cities, notably Alexandria, became important as cultural centers, though no major critical theories or influences emerged. As early as the third century B.C., Greek art had begun to influence the Romans; Homer, for example, may have been known in 165 B.C. through Crates, who, like other Greek teachers, had traveled to Rome. After 146 B.C., when Greece became a Roman province, the thought and art of the Greeks permeated all areas of Roman culture. Scholarly and critical activity, by the beginning of the first century B.C., then shifted from Alexandria to Rome.

The prestige of earlier Greek art is evident in the *Art of Poetry,* in which Horace urges the study of the ancient Greek poets, though he has only scorn for the inspired, or "mad," poet. The source of the idea of "imitation," a central dogma of Renaissance neo-classicism, the *Art of Poetry* did not bring about a revival of Greek forms, but it later was of enormous significance to Renaissance critics who readily converted his advice concerning structure and style into absolute rules for drama and poetry.

In his urbanity and calculated ease, in his grace and refinement, Horace eludes those Renaissance commentators who made him a dogmatic authority. In the eighteenth century, Alexander Pope, who, like many English neo-classicists, was closer in temperament to Horace than to the Italian and French critics who yearned for certainty, writes in his *Essay on Criticism:*

> Horace still charms with graceful
>   negligence,
> And without method talks us into sense;
> Will, like a friend, familiarly convey
> The truest notions in the easiest way.

VII

Of the four great classical critics represented here, the one who most closely approximates the modern sensibility, both in temperament and in attitude, is "Longinus" (sometimes referred to as the "Pseudo-Longinus," for no one is certain of either author or date of the treatise), author of the *Peri Hupsous,* variously translated as *On Loftiness or Elegancy of Speech, Elevation of Style, On Literary Excellence,* but best known as *On the Sublime* since Boileau's translation in 1674, *Le traité du sublime.* During the eighteenth century, the term *sublime,* extended from its literary meaning, acquired philosophical importance as the basis for aesthetic speculation. Longinus, however, was primarily concerned with the effects of style and the mind of the writer, not with the effects of mountains, storms, waterfalls, or other phenomena that eighteenth-century critics and philosophers (Kant included) saw as sources of the sublime. (Indeed, Longinus himself does not make clear whether the sublime has its source in the artist or in style or both, since he shifts without clarifying his terms.)

An indication of Longinus' fame in the eighteenth-century may be seen in the numerous references to his name or work, the most famous of which is Pope's indirect allusion to the *Peri Hupsous* in his satire of poetasters and dunces entitled *Peri Bathous, or the Art of Sinking in Poetry* (1728), proceeding, one might say, from the sublime to the ridiculous. (Indeed, Pope introduced the word *bathos* into the language, by which he meant a sudden descent from the exalted to the ludicrous.) In *On Poetry: a Rhapsody* (1733), Swift comments on the fashionable use made by pedantic critics of Longinus, who had become the inevitable victim of cultists:

A forward Critick often dupes us
With sham Quotations *Peri Hupsous*
And if we have not read Longinus,
Will magisterially outshine us.
Then lest with Greek he over-run ye,
Procure this Book for Love or Money
Translated from Boileau's Translation,
And quote Quotation on Quotation.

Longinus was used, frequently by the neo-classicists themselves, in many other ways: to combat insistence on "rules" and "correctness," to locate the source of greatness not in slavish imitation of the ancients but in the individual genius of the poet. For Longinus, the primary value of the literary experience was its capacity to thrill the reader, to "transport" him, as some translators put it, out of himself. For the romantics in the nineteenth century, Longinus was the *one* critic in classical antiquity who had acknowledged the extraordinary power of poetry liberated from didacticism and generated by the brilliance of the artist's mind.

Plato

(c. 428–347 B.C.)

From THE REPUBLIC, BOOK X

The greatest of Plato's dialogues, *The Republic,* dates from about
385 B.C. Searching for an answer to the question "What is justice?"
Socrates reports several conversations that he had at Pireaeus,
near Athens, during which he outlined the ideal state.

In Book X, part of which is given here, Glaucon, Plato's brother,
is engaged in conversation on the nature of reality with Socrates,
who issues the famous banishment of those poets dangerous to the
state.

The translation is by Benjamin Jowett.

———◆———

Soc. Of the many excellences which I perceive in the order of our
State, there is none which upon reflection pleases me better than
the rule about poetry.

Gla. To what do you refer?

Soc. To the rejection of imitative poetry, which certainly ought not
to be received; as I see far more clearly now that the parts of the
soul have been distinguished.

Gla. What do you mean?

Soc. Speaking in confidence, for I should not like to have my words
repeated to the tragedians and the rest of the imitative tribe—
but I do not mind saying to you, that all poetical imitations are
ruinous to the understanding of the hearers, and that the knowledge of their true nature is the only antidote to them.

Gla. Explain the purport of your remark.

Soc. Well, I will tell you, although I have always from my earliest youth had an awe and love of Homer, which even now makes the words falter on my lips, for he is the great captain and teacher of the whole of that charming tragic company; but a man is not to be reverenced more than the truth, and therefore I will speak out.

Gla. Very good.

Soc. Listen to me then, or rather, answer me.

Gla. Put your question.

Soc. Can you tell me what imitation is? for I really do not know.

Gla. A likely thing, then, that I should know.

Soc. Why not? for the duller eye may often see a thing sooner than the keener.

Gla. Very true; but in your presence, even if I had any faint notion, I could not muster courage to utter it. Will you enquire yourself?

Soc. Well then, shall we begin the enquiry in our usual manner: Whenever a number of individuals have a common name, we assume them to have also a corresponding idea or form. Do you understand me?

Gla. I do.

Soc. Let us take any common instance; there are beds and tables in the world—plenty of them, are there not?

Gla. Yes.

Soc. But there are only two ideas or forms of them—one the idea of a bed, the other of a table.

Gla. True.

Soc. And the maker of either of them makes a bed or he makes a table for our use, in accordance with the idea—that is our way of speaking in this and similar instances—but no artificer makes the ideas themselves: how could he?

Gla. Impossible.

Soc. And there is another artist,—I should like to know what you would say of him.

Gla. Who is he?

Soc. One who is the maker of all the works of all other workmen.

Gla. What an extraordinary man!

Soc. Wait a little, and there will be more reason for your saying so. For this is he who is able to make not only vessels of every kind,

but plants and animals, himself and all other things—the earth
and heaven, and the things which are in heaven or under the
earth; he makes the gods also.

Gla. He must be a wizard and no mistake.

Soc. Oh! you are incredulous, are you? Do you mean that there is
no such maker or creator, or that in one sense there might be a
maker of all these things but in another not? Do you see that
there is a way in which you could make them all yourself?

Gla. What way?

Soc. An easy way enough; or rather, there are many ways in which
the feat might be quickly and easily accomplished, none quicker
than that of turning a mirror round and round—you would soon
enough make the sun and the heavens, and the earth and yourself, and other animals and plants, and all the other things of
which we were just now speaking, in the mirror.

Gla. Yes, but they would be appearances only.

Soc. Very good, you are coming to the point now. And the painter
too is, as I conceive, just such another—a creator of appearances, is he not?

Gla. Of course.

Soc. But then I suppose you will say that what he creates is untrue.
And yet there is a sense in which the painter also creates a bed?

Gla. Yes, but not a real bed.

Soc. And what of the maker of the bed? Were you not saying that
he too makes, not the idea which, according to our view, is the
essence of the bed, but only a particular bed?

Gla. Yes, I did.

Soc. Then if he does not make that which exists he cannot make
true existence, but only some semblance of existence; and if any
one were to say that the work of the maker of the bed, or of any
other workman, has real existence, he could hardly be supposed
to be speaking the truth.

Gla. At any rate, philosophers would say that he was not speaking
the truth.

Soc. No wonder, then, that his work too is an indistinct expression
of truth.

Gla. No wonder.

Soc. Suppose now that by the light of the examples just offered we enquire who this imitator is?

Gla. If you please.

Soc. Well then, here are three beds: one existing in nature, which is made by God, as I think that we may say—for no one else can be the maker?

Gla. No.

Soc. There is another which is the work of the carpenter?

Gla. Yes.

Soc. And the work of the painter is a third?

Gla. Yes.

Soc. Beds, then, are of three kinds, and there are three artists who superintend them: God, the maker of the bed, and the painter?

Gla. Yes, there are three of them.

Soc. God, whether from choice or from necessity, made one bed in nature and one only; two or more such ideal beds neither ever have been nor ever will be made by God.

Gla. Why is that?

Soc. Because even if He had made but two, a third would still appear behind them which both of them would have for their idea, and that would be the ideal bed and not the two others.

Gla. Very true.

Soc. God knew this, and He desired to be the real maker of a real bed, not a particular maker of a particular bed, and therefore He created a bed which is essentially and by nature one only.

Gla. So we believe.

Soc. Shall we, then, speak of Him as the natural author or maker of the bed?

Gla. Yes, inasmuch as by the natural process of creation He is the author of this and of all other things.

Soc. And what shall we say of the carpenter—is not he also the maker of the bed?

Gla. Yes.

Soc. But would you call the painter a creator and maker?

Gla. Certainly not.

Soc. Yet if he is not the maker, what is he in relation to the bed?

Gla. I think, that we may fairly designate him as the imitator of that which the others make.

Soc. Good; then you call him who is third in the descent from nature an imitator?

Gla. Certainly.

Soc. And the tragic poet is an imitator, and therefore, like all other imitators, he is thrice removed from the king and from the truth?

Gla. That appears to be so.

Soc. Then about the imitator we are agreed. And what about the painter?—I would like to know whether he may be thought to imitate that which originally exists in nature, or only the creations of artists?

Gla. The latter.

Soc. As they are or as they appear? You have still to determine this.

Gla. What do you mean?

Soc. I mean, that you may look at a bed from different points of view, obliquely or directly or from any other point of view, and the bed will appear different, but there is no difference in reality. And the same of all things.

Gla. Yes, the difference is only apparent.

Soc. Now let me ask you another question: Which is the art of painting designed to be—an imitation of things as they are, or as they appear—of appearance or of reality?

Gla. Of appearance.

Soc. Then the imitator is a long way off the truth, and can do all things because he lightly touches on a small part of them, and that part an image. For example: A painter will paint a cobbler, carpenter, or any other artist, though he knows nothing of their arts; and, if he is a good artist, he may deceive children or simple persons, when he shows them his picture of a carpenter from a distance, and they will fancy that they are looking at a real carpenter.

Gla. Certainly.

Soc. And whenever any one informs us that he has found a man who knows all the arts, and all things else that anybody knows, and every single thing with a higher degree of accuracy than any other man—whoever tells us this, I think that we can only imagine him to be a simple creature who is likely to have been deceived by some wizard or actor whom he met, and whom he thought all-knowing, because he himself was unable to analyse the nature of knowledge and ignorance and imitation.

Gla. Most true.

Soc. And so, when we hear persons saying that the tragedians, and Homer, who is at their head, know all the arts and all things human, virtue as well as vice, and divine things too, for that the good poet cannot compose well unless he knows his subject, and that he who has not this knowledge can never be a poet, we ought to consider whether here also there may not be a similar illusion. Perhaps they may have come across imitators and been deceived by them; they may not have remembered when they saw their works that these were but imitations thrice removed from the truth, and could easily be made without any knowledge of the truth, because they are appearances only and not realities? Or, after all, they may be in the right, and poets do really know the things about which they seem to the many to speak so well?

Gla. The question should by all means be considered.

Soc. Now do you suppose that if a person were able to make the original as well as the image, he would seriously devote himself to the image-making branch? Would he allow imitation to be the ruling principle of his life, as if he had nothing higher in him?

Gla. I should say not.

Soc. The real artist, who knew what he was imitating, would be interested in realities and not in imitations; and would desire to leave as memorials of himself works many and fair; and, instead of being the author of encomiums, he would prefer to be the theme of them.

Gla. Yes, that would be to him a source of much greater honour and profit.

Soc. Then, we must put a question to Homer; not about medicine, or any of the arts to which his poems only incidentally refer: we are not going to ask him, or any other poet, whether he has cured patients like Asclepius, or left behind him a school of medicine such as the Asclepiads were, or whether he only talks about medicine and other arts at second hand; but we have a right to know respecting military tactics, politics, education, which are the chiefest and noblest subjects of his poems, and we may fairly ask him about them. 'Friend Homer,' then we say to him, 'if you are only in the second remove from truth in what you say of virtue, and not in the third—not an image maker or imitator— and if you are able to discern what pursuits make men better or worse in private or public life, tell us what State was ever better governed by your help? The good order of Lacedaemon is due to Lycurgus, and many other cities great and small have been simi- larly benefited by others; but who says that you have been a good legislator to them and have done them any good? Italy and Sicily boast of Charondas, and there is Solon who is renowned among us; but what city has anything to say about you?' Is there any city which he might name?

Gla. I think not; not even the Homerids themselves pretend that he was a legislator.

Soc. Well, but is there any war on record which was carried on successfully by him, or aided by his counsels, when he was alive?

Gla. There is not.

Soc. Or is there any invention of his, applicable to the arts or to human life, such as Thales the Milesian or Anacharsis the Scythian, and other ingenious men have conceived, which is attributed to him?

Gla. There is absolutely nothing of the kind.

Soc. But, if Homer never did any public service, was he privately a guide or teacher of any? Had he in his lifetime friends who loved to associate with him, and who handed down to posterity an Homeric way of life, such as was established by Pythagoras who was so greatly beloved for his wisdom, and whose followers are to this day quite celebrated for the order which was named after him?

Gla. Nothing of the kind is recorded of him. For surely, Socrates,

Creophylus, the companion of Homer, that child of flesh, whose name always makes us laugh, might be more justly ridiculed for his stupidity, if, as is said, Homer was greatly neglected by him and others in his own day when he was alive?

Soc. Yes, that is the tradition. But can you imagine, Glaucon, that if Homer had really been able to educate and improve mankind —if he had possessed knowledge and not been a mere imitator— can you imagine, I say, that he would not have had many followers, and been honoured and loved by them? Protagoras of Abdera, and Prodicus of Ceos, and a host of others, have only to whisper to their contemporaries: 'You will never be able to manage either your own house or your own State until you appoint us to be your ministers of education'—and this ingenious device of theirs has such an effect in making men love them that their companions all but carry them about on their shoulders. And is it conceivable that the contemporaries of Homer, or again of Hesiod, would have allowed either of them to go about as rhapsodists, if they had really been able to make mankind virtuous? Would they not have been as unwilling to part with them as with gold, and have compelled them to stay at home with them? Or, if the master would not stay, then the disciples would have followed him about everywhere, until they had got education enough?

Gla. Yes, Socrates, that, I think, is quite true.

Soc. Then must we not infer that all these poetical individuals, beginning with Homer, are only imitators; they copy images of virtue and the like, but the truth they never reach? The poet is like a painter who, as we have already observed, will make a likeness of a cobbler though he understands nothing of cobbling; and his picture is good enough for those who know no more than he does, and judge only by colours and figures.

Gla. Quite so.

Soc. In like manner, the poet with his words and phrases may be said to lay on the colours of the several arts, himself understanding their nature only enough to imitate them; and other people, who are as ignorant as he is, and judge only from his words, imagine that if he speaks of cobbling, or of military tactics, or of anything else, in metre and harmony and rhythm, he speaks very well—such is the sweet influence which melody and rhythm by nature have. And I think that you must have observed again and again what a poor appearance the tales of poets make when stripped of the colours which music puts upon them, and recited in simple prose.

Gla. Yes.

Soc. They are like faces which were never really beautiful, but only blooming; and now the bloom of youth has passed away from them?

Gla. Exactly.

Soc. Here is another point: The imitator or maker of the image knows nothing of true existence; he knows appearances only. Am I not right?

Gla. Yes.

Soc. Then let us have a clear understanding, and not be satisfied with half an explanation.

Gla. Proceed.

Soc. Of the painter we say that he will paint reins, and he will paint a bit?

Gla. Yes.

Soc. And the worker in leather and brass will make them?

Gla. Certainly.

Soc. But does the painter know the right form of the bit and reins? Nay, hardly even the workers in brass and leather who make them; only the horseman who knows how to use them—he knows their right form.

Gla. Most true.

Soc. And may we not say the same of all things?

Gla. What?

Soc. That there are three arts which are concerned with all things: one which uses, another which makes, a third which imitates them?

Gla. Yes.

Soc. And the excellence or beauty or truth of every structure, animate or inanimate, and of every action of man, is relative to the use for which nature or the artist has intended them.

Gla. True.

Soc. Then the user of them must have the greatest experience of them, and he must indicate to the maker the good or bad qualities which develop themselves in use; for example, the flute-player will tell the flute-maker which of his flutes is satisfactory to the performer; he will tell him how he ought to make them, and the other will attend to his instructions?

Gla. Of course.

Soc. The one knows and therefore speaks with authority about the goodness and badness of flutes, while the other, confiding in him, will do what he is told by him?

Gla. True.

Soc. The instrument is the same, but about the excellence or badness of it the maker will only attain to a correct belief; and this he will gain from him who knows, by talking to him and being compelled to hear what he has to say, whereas the user will have knowledge?

Gla. True.

Soc. But will the imitator have either? Will he know from use whether or no his drawing is correct or beautiful? Or will he have right opinion from being compelled to associate with another who knows and gives him instructions about what he should draw?

Gla. Neither.

Soc. Then he will no more have true opinion than he will have knowledge about the goodness or badness of his imitations?

Gla. I suppose not.

Soc. The imitative artist will be in a brilliant state of intelligence about his own creations?

Gla. Nay, very much the reverse.

Soc. And still he will go on imitating without knowing what makes a thing good or bad, and may be expected therefore to imitate only that which appears to be good to the ignorant multitude?

Gla. Just so.

Soc. Thus far then we are pretty well agreed that the imitator has no knowledge worth mentioning of what he imitates. Imitation is only a kind of play or sport, and the tragic poets, whether they write in Iambic or in Heroic verse, are imitators in the highest degree?

Gla. Very true.

Soc. And now tell me, I conjure you, has not imitation been shown by us to be concerned with that which is thrice removed from the truth?

Gla. Certainly.

Soc. And what is the faculty in man to which imitation is addressed?

Gla. What do you mean?

Soc. I will explain: The body which is large when seen near, appears small when seen at a distance?

Gla. True.

Soc. And the same object appears straight when looked at out of the water, and crooked when in the water; and the concave becomes convex, owing to the illusion about colours to which the sight is liable. Thus every sort of confusion is revealed within us; and this is that weakness of the human mind on which the art of conjuring and of deceiving by light and shadow and other ingenious devices imposes, having an effect upon us like magic.

Gla. True.

Soc. And the arts of measuring and numbering and weighing come to the rescue of the human understanding—there is the beauty of them—and the apparent greater or less, or more or heavier, no longer have the mastery over us, but give way before calculation and measure and weight?

Gla. Most true.

Soc. And this, surely, must be the work of the calculating and rational principle in the soul?

Gla. To be sure.

Soc. And when this principle measures and certifies that some things are equal, or that some are greater or less than others, there occurs an apparent contradiction?

Gla. True.

Soc. But were we not saying that such a contradiction is impossible —the same faculty cannot have contrary opinions at the same time about the same thing?

Gla. Very true.

Soc. Then that part of the soul which has an opinion contrary to measure is not the same with that which has an opinion in accordance with measure?

Gla. True.

Soc. And the better part of the soul is likely to be that which trusts to measure and calculation?

Gla. Certainly.

Soc. And that which is opposed to them is one of the inferior principles of the soul?

Gla. No doubt.

Soc. This was the conclusion at which I was seeking to arrive when I said that painting or drawing, and imitation in general, when doing their own proper work, are far removed from truth, and the companions and friends and associates of a principle within us which is equally removed from reason, and that they have no true or healthy aim.

Gla. Exactly.

Soc. The imitative art is an inferior who marries an inferior, and has inferior offspring.

Gla. Very true.

Soc. And is this confined to the sight only, or does it extend to the hearing also, relating in fact to what we term poetry?

Gla. Probably the same would be true of poetry.

Soc. Do not rely on a probability derived from the analogy of painting; but let us examine further and see whether the faculty with which poetical imitation is concerned is good or bad.

Gla. By all means.

Soc. We may state the question thus:—Imitation imitates the actions of men, whether voluntary or involuntary, on which, as they imagine, a good or bad result has ensued, and they rejoice or sorrow accordingly. Is there anything more?

Gla. No, there is nothing else.

Soc. But in all this variety of circumstances is the man at unity with himself—or rather, as in the instance of sight there was confusion and opposition in his opinions about the same things, so here also is there not strife and inconsistency in his life? Though I need hardly raise the question again, for I remember that all this has been already admitted; and the soul has been acknowledged by us to be full of these and ten thousand similar oppositions occurring at the same moment?

Gla. And we were right.

Soc. Yes, thus far we were right; but there was an omission which must now be supplied.

Gla. What was the omission?

Soc. Were we not saying that a good man, who has the misfortune to lose his son or anything else which is most dear to him, will bear the loss with more equanimity than another?

Gla. Yes.

Soc. But will he have no sorrow, or shall we say that although he cannot help sorrowing, he will moderate his sorrow?

Gla. The latter is the truer statement.

Soc. Tell me: will he be more likely to struggle and hold out against his sorrow when he is seen by his equals, or when he is alone?

Gla. It will make a great difference whether he is seen or not.

Soc. When he is by himself he will not mind saying or doing many things which he would be ashamed of any one hearing or seeing him do?

Gla. True.

Soc. There is a principle of law and reason in him which bids him resist, as well as a feeling of his misfortune which is forcing him to indulge his sorrow?

Gla. True.

Soc. But when a man is drawn in two opposite directions, to and from the same object, this, as we affirm, necessarily implies two distinct principles in him?

Gla. Certainly.

Soc. One of them is ready to follow the guidance of the law?

Gla. How do you mean?

Soc. The law would say that to be patient under suffering is best, and that we should not give way to impatience, as there is no knowing whether such things are good or evil; and nothing is gained by impatience; also, because no human thing is of serious importance, and grief stands in the way of that which at the moment is most required.

Gla. What is most required?

Soc. That we should take counsel about what has happened, and when the dice have been thrown order our affairs in the way which reason deems best; not, like children who have had a fall, keeping hold of the part struck and wasting time in setting up a howl, but always accustoming the soul forthwith to apply a remedy, raising up that which is sickly and fallen, banishing the cry of sorrow by the healing art.

Gla. Yes, that is the true way of meeting the attacks of fortune.

Soc. Yes, and the higher principle is ready to follow this suggestion of reason?

Gla. Clearly.

Soc. And the other principle, which inclines us to recollection of our troubles and to lamentation, and can never have enough of them, we may call irrational, useless, and cowardly?

Gla. Indeed, we may.

Soc. And does not the latter—I mean the rebellious principle——furnish a great variety of materials for imitation? Whereas the wise and calm temperament, being always nearly equable, is not easy to imitate or to appreciate when imitated, especially at a public festival when a promiscuous crowd is assembled in a theatre. For the feeling represented is one to which they are strangers.

Gla. Certainly.

Soc. Then the imitative poet who aims at being popular is not by nature made, nor is his art intended, to please or to affect the rational principle in the soul; but he will prefer the passionate and fitful temper, which is easily imitated?

Gla. Clearly.

Soc. And now we may fairly take him and place him by the side of the painter, for he is like him in two ways: first, inasmuch as his creations have an inferior degree of truth—in this, I say, he is like him; and he is also like him in being concerned with an inferior part of the soul; and therefore we shall be right in refusing to admit him into a well-ordered State, because he awakens and nourishes and strengthens the feelings and impairs the reason. As in a city when the evil are permitted to have authority and the good are put out of the way, so in the soul of man, as we maintain, the imitative poet implants an evil constitution, for he indulges the irrational nature which has no discernment of greater and less, but thinks the same thing at one time great and at another small—he is a manufacturer of images and is very far removed from the truth.

Gla. Exactly.

Soc. But we have not yet brought forward the heaviest count in our accusation:—the power which poetry has of harming even the good (and there are very few who are not harmed), is surely an awful thing?

Gla. Yes, certainly, if the effect is what you say.

Soc. Hear and judge: The best of us, as I conceive, when we listen to a passage of Homer, or one of the tragedians, in which he represents some pitiful hero who is drawling out his sorrows in a long oration, or weeping, and smiting his breast—the best of us, you know, delight in giving way to sympathy, and are in raptures at the excellence of the poet who stirs our feelings most.

Gla. Yes, of course I know.

Soc. But when any sorrow of our own happens to us, then you may observe that we pride ourselves on the opposite quality—we would fain be quiet and patient; this is the manly part, and the other which delighted us in the recitation is now deemed to be the part of a woman.

Gla. Very true.

Soc. Now can we be right in praising and admiring another who is doing that which any one of us would abominate and be ashamed of in his own person?

Gla. No, that is certainly not reasonable.

Soc. Nay, quite reasonable from one point of view.

Gla. What point of view?

Soc. If you consider that when in misfortune we feel a natural hunger and desire to relieve our sorrow by weeping and lamentation, and that this feeling which is kept under control in our own calamities is satisfied and delighted by the poets;—the better nature in each of us, not having been sufficiently trained by reason or habit, allows the sympathetic element to break loose because the sorrow is another's; and the spectator fancies that there can be no disgrace to himself in praising and pitying any one who comes telling him what a good man he is, and making a fuss about his troubles; he thinks that the pleasure is a gain, and why should he be supercilious and lose this and the poem too? Few persons ever reflect, as I should imagine, that from the evil of other men something of evil is communicated to themselves. And so the feeling of sorrow which has gathered strength at the sight of the misfortunes of others is with difficulty repressed in our own.

Gla. How very true!

Soc. And does not the same hold also of the ridiculous? There are jests which you would be ashamed to make yourself, and yet on the comic stage, or indeed in private, when you hear them, you are greatly amused by them, and are not at all disgusted at their unseemliness;—the case of pity is repeated;—there is a principle in human nature which is disposed to raise a laugh, and this which you once restrained by reason, because you were afraid of being thought a buffoon, is now let out again; and having stimulated the risible faculty at the theatre, you are betrayed unconsciously to yourself into playing the comic poet at home.

Gla. Quite true.

Soc. And the same may be said of lust and anger and all the other affections, of desire and pain and pleasure, which are held to be inseparable from every action—in all of them poetry feeds and

Aristotle

(384–322 B.C.)

POETICS

It is generally agreed that the *Poetics,* like Aristotle's other surviving works, consists of lecture notes used at the Lyceum, which Aristotle founded and directed for thirteen years (335-322 B.C.). Internal evidence suggests that a "second book" on comedy may have existed at one time; moreover, in the *Rhetoric,* Aristotle states the *Poetics* contains a discussion of the kinds of laughter.

Apparently the *Poetics* had little or no influence in classical antiquity (neither Horace, Cicero, nor Quintilian mention it), but since the Renaissance, it has dominated all discussions of tragedy.

The translation used here is by S. H. Butcher. Brackets indicate passages believed inserted by later copyists; the whole of section XII, for example, Butcher considered spurious.

I

[*Imitation*]

I PROPOSE to treat of Poetry in itself and of its various kinds, noting the essential quality of each; to inquire into the structure of the plot as requisite to a good poem; into the number and nature of the parts of which a poem is composed; and similarly into whatever else falls within the same inquiry. Following, then, the order of nature, let us begin with the principles which come first.

2. Epic poetry and Tragedy, Comedy also and Dithyrambic poetry, and the music of the flute and of the lyre in most of their forms, are all in their general conception modes of imitation. 3. They differ, however, from one another in three respects,— the medium, the objects, the manner or mode of imitation, being in each case distinct.

4. For as there are persons who, by conscious art or mere habit, imitate and represent various objects through the medium of colour and form, or again by the voice; so in the arts above mentioned, taken as a whole, the imitation is produced by rhythm, language, or "harmony," either singly or combined.

Thus in the music of the flute and of the lyre, "harmony" and rhythm alone are employed; also in other arts, such as that of the shepherd's pipe, which are essentially similar to these. 5. In dancing, rhythm alone is used without "harmony"; for even dancing imitates character, emotion, and action, by rhythmical movement.

6. There is another art which imitates by means of language alone, and that either in prose or verse—which verse, again, may either combine different metres or consist of but one kind—but this has hitherto been without a name. 7. For there is no common term we could apply to the mimes of Sophron and Xenarchus and the Socratic dialogues on the one hand; and, on the other, to poetic imitations in iambic, elegiac, or any similar metre. People do, indeed, add the word "maker" or "poet" to the name of the metre, and speak of elegiac poets, or epic (that is, hexameter) poets, as if it were not the imitation that makes the poet, but the verse that entitles them all indiscriminately to the name. 8. Even when a treatise on medicine or natural science is brought out in verse, the name of poet is by custom given to the author; and yet Homer and Empedocles have nothing in common but the metre, so that it would be right to call the one poet, the other physicist rather than poet. 9. On the same principle, even if a writer in his poetic imitation were to combine all metres, as Chaeremon did in his Centaur, which is a medley composed of metres of all kinds, we should bring him too under the general term poet. So much then for these distinctions.

10. There are, again, some arts which employ all the means above mentioned,—namely, rhythm, tune and metre. Such are Dithyrambic and Nomic poetry, and also Tragedy and Comedy; but between them the difference is, that in the first two cases these means are all employed in combination, in the latter, now one means is employed, now another.

Such, then, are the differences of the arts with respect to the medium of imitation.

II
[*Character*]

Since the objects of imitation are men in action, and these men must be either of a higher or a lower type (for moral character mainly answers to these divisions, goodness and badness being the distinguishing marks of moral differences), it follows that we must represent men either as better than in real life, or as worse, or as they are. It is the same in painting. Polygnotus depicted men as nobler than they are, Pauson as less noble, Dionysius drew them true to life.

2. Now it is evident that each of the modes of imitation above mentioned will exhibit these differences, and become a distinct kind in imitating objects that are thus distinct. 3. Such diversities may be found even in dancing, flute-playing, and lyre-playing. So again in language, whether prose or verse unaccompanied by music. Homer, for example, makes men better than they are; Cleophon as they are; Hegemon the Thasian, the inventor of parodies, and Nicochares, the author of the Deiliad, worse than they are. 4. The same thing holds good of Dithyrambs and Nomes; here too one may portray different types, as Timotheus and Philoxenus differed in representing their Cyclopes. The same distinction marks off Tragedy from Comedy; for Comedy aims at representing men as worse, Tragedy as better than in actual life.

III
[*Manner of imitation*]

There is still a third difference—the manner in which each of these objects may be imitated. For the medium being the same, and the objects the same, the poet may imitate by narration—in which case he can either take another personality as Homer does, or speak in his own person, unchanged—or he may present all his characters as living and moving before us.

2. These, then, as we said at the beginning, are the three differences which distinguish artistic imitation—the medium, the objects and the manner. So that from one point of view, Sophocles is an imitator of the same kind as Homer—for both imitate higher types of character; from another point of view, of the same kind as Aristophanes—for both imitate persons acting and doing. 3. Hence, some say, the name of "drama" is given to such poems, as representing action. For the same reason the Dorians claim the invention both of Tragedy and Comedy. The claim to Comedy is put forward by the Megarians,—not only by those of Greece proper, who allege that it originated under their democracy, but also by the Megarians of Sicily, for the poet Epicharmus, who is much earlier than Chionides and Magnes, belonged to that country. Tragedy too is claimed by certain Dorians of the Peloponnese. . . .

IV
[Origin of poetry]

Poetry in general seems to have sprung from two causes, each of them lying deep in our nature. 2. First, the instinct of imitation is implanted in man from childhood, one difference between him and other animals being that he is the most imitative of living creatures; and through imitation he learns his earliest lessons; and no less universal is the pleasure felt in things imitated. 3. We have evidence of this in the facts of experience. Objects which in themselves we view with pain, we delight to contemplate when reproduced with minute fidelity: such as the forms of the most ignoble animals and of dead bodies. 4. The cause of this again is, that to learn gives the liveliest pleasure, not only to philosophers but to men in general; whose capacity, however, of learning is more limited. 5. Thus the reason why men enjoy seeing a likeness is, that in contemplating it they find themselves learning or inferring, and saying perhaps, "Ah, that is he." For if you happen not to have seen the original, the pleasure will be due not to the imitation as such, but to the execution, the colouring, or some such other cause.

6. Imitation, then, is one instinct of our nature. Next, there is the instinct for "harmony" and rhythm, metres being manifestly sections of rhythm. Persons, therefore, starting with this natural gift developed by degrees their special aptitudes, till their rude improvisations gave birth to Poetry.

7. Poetry now diverged in two directions, according to the individual character of the writers. The graver spirits imitated noble actions, and the actions of good men. The more trivial sort imitated the actions of meaner persons, at first composing satires, as the former did hymns to the gods and the praises of famous men. 8. A poem of the satirical kind cannot indeed be put down to any author earlier than Homer; though many such writers probably there were. But from Homer onward, instances can be cited,—his own *Margites,* for example, and other similar compositions. The appropriate metre was also here introduced; hence the measure is still called the iambic or lampooning measure, being that in which people lampooned one another. 9. Thus the older poets were distinguished as writers of heroic or of lampooning verse.

As, in the serious style, Homer is pre-eminent among poets, for he alone combined dramatic form with excellence of imitation, so he too first laid down the main lines of Comedy, by dramatising the ludicrous instead of writing personal satire. His *Margites* bears the same relation to Comedy that the Iliad and Odyssey do to Tragedy. 10. But when Tragedy and Comedy came to light, the two classes of poets still followed their natural bent: the lampooners became writers of Comedy, and the Epic poets were succeeded by Tragedians, since the drama was a larger and higher form of art.

11. Whether Tragedy has as yet perfected its proper types or not; and whether it is to be judged in itself, or in relation also to the audience,—this raises another question. 12. Be that as it may, Tragedy—as also Comedy—was at first mere improvisation. The one originated with the leaders of the Dithyramb, the other with

those of the phallic songs, which are still in use in many of our cities. Tragedy advanced by slow degrees; each new element that showed itself was in turn developed. Having passed through many changes, it found its natural form, and there it stopped.

13. Aeschylus first introduced a second actor; he diminished the importance of the Chorus, and assigned the leading part to the dialogue. Sophocles raised the number of actors to three, and added scene-painting. 14. Moreover, it was not till late that the short plot was discarded for one of greater compass, and the grotesque diction of the earlier satyric form for the stately manner of Tragedy. The iambic measure then replaced the trochaic tetrameter, which was originally employed when the poetry was of the satyric order, and had greater affinities with dancing. Once dialogue had come in, Nature herself discovered the appropriate measure. For the iambic is, of all measures, the most colloquial: we see it in the fact that conversational speech runs into iambic form more frequently than into any other kind of verse; rarely into hexameters, and only when we drop the colloquial intonation. 15. The additions to the number of "episodes" or acts, and the other improvements of which tradition tells, must be taken as already described; for to discuss them in detail would, doubtless, be a large undertaking.

V
[*Comedy and epic*]

Comedy is, as we have said, an imitation of characters of a lower type—not, however, in the full sense of the word bad, the Ludicrous being merely a subdivision of the ugly. It consists in some defect or ugliness which is not painful or destructive. To take an obvious example, the comic mask is ugly and distorted, but does not imply pain.

2. The successive changes through which Tragedy passed, and the authors of these changes, are well known, whereas Comedy has had no history, because it was not at first treated seriously. It was late before the Archon granted a comic chorus to a poet; the

performers were till then voluntary. Comedy had already taken definite shape when comic poets, distinctively so called, are heard of. 3. Who introduced masks, or prologues, or increased the number of actors—these and other similar details remain unknown. As for the plot, it came originally from Sicily; but of Athenian writers Crates was the first who, abandoning the "iambic" or lampooning form, generalised his themes and plots.

4. Epic poetry agrees with Tragedy in so far as it is an imitation in verse of characters of a higher type. They differ, in that Epic poetry admits but one kind of metre, and is narrative in form. They differ, again, in their length: for Tragedy endeavours, as far as possible, to confine itself to a single revolution of the sun, or but slightly to exceed this limit; whereas the Epic action has no limits of time. This, then, is a second point of difference; though at first the same freedom was admitted in Tragedy as in Epic poetry.

5. Of their constituent parts some are common to both, some peculiar to Tragedy. Whoever, therefore, knows what is good or bad Tragedy, knows also about Epic poetry: for all the elements of an Epic poem are found in Tragedy, but the elements of a Tragedy are not all found in the Epic poem.

VI

[*Tragedy*]

Of the poetry which imitates in hexameter verse, and of Comedy, we will speak hereafter. Let us now discuss Tragedy, resuming its formal definition, as resulting from what has been already said.

2. Tragedy then, is an imitation of an action that is serious, complete, and of a certain magnitude; in language embellished with each kind of artistic ornament, the several kinds being found in separate parts of the play; in the form of action, not of narrative; through pity and fear effecting the proper purgation of these emotions. 3. By "language embellished," I mean language into which rhythm, "harmony," and song enter. By "the several kinds in separate parts," I mean, that some parts are rendered through the medium of verse alone, others again with the aid of song.

4. Now as tragic imitation implies persons acting, it necessarily follows, in the first place, that Spectacular equipment will be a part of Tragedy. Next, Song and Diction, for these are the medium of imitation. By "Diction" I mean the mere metrical arrangement of the words: as for "Song," it is a term whose sense every one understands.

5. Again, Tragedy is the imitation of an action; and an action implies personal agents, who necessarily possess certain distinctive qualities both of character and thought; for it is by these that we qualify actions themselves, and these—thought and character—are the two natural causes from which actions spring, and on actions again all success or failure depends. 6. Hence, the Plot is the imitation of the action:—for by plot I here mean the arrangement of the incidents. By Character I mean that in virtue of which we ascribe certain qualities to the agents. Thought is required wherever a statement is proved, or, it may be, a general truth enunciated. 7. Every Tragedy, therefore, must have six parts, which parts determine its quality—namely, Plot, Character, Diction, Thought, Spectacle, Song. Two of the parts constitute the medium of imitation, one the manner, and three the objects of imitation. And these complete the list. 8. These elements have been employed, we may say, by the poets to a man; in fact, every play contains Spectacular elements as well as Character, Plot, Diction, Song, and Thought.

9. But most important of all is the structure of the incidents. For Tragedy is an imitation, not of men, but of an action and of life, and life consists in action, and its end is a mode of action, not a quality. 10. Now character determines men's qualities, but it is by their actions that they are happy or the reverse. Dramatic action, therefore, is not with a view to the representation of character: character comes in as subsidiary to the actions. Hence the incidents and the plot are the end of a tragedy; and the end is the chief thing of all. 11. Again, without action there cannot be a tragedy; there may be without character. The tragedies of most of our modern poets fail in the rendering of character; and of poets in general this is often true. It is the same in painting; and here

lies the difference between Zeuxis and Polygnotus. Polygnotus delineates character well: the style of Zeuxis is devoid of ethical quality. 12. Again, if you string together a set of speeches expressive of character, and well finished in point of diction and thought, you will not produce the essential tragic effect nearly so well as with a play which, however deficient in these respects, yet has a plot and artistically constructed incidents. 13. Besides which, the most powerful elements of emotional interest in Tragedy—Peripeteia or Reversal of Intention, and Recognition scenes—are parts of the plot. 14. A further proof is, that novices in the art attain to finish of diction and precision of portraiture before they can construct the plot. It is the same with almost all the early poets.

The Plot, then, is the first principle, and, as it were, the soul of a tragedy: Character holds the second place. 15. A similar fact is seen in painting. The most beautiful colours, laid on confusedly, will not give as much pleasure as the chalk outline of a portrait. Thus Tragedy is the imitation of an action, and of the agents, mainly with a view to the action.

16. Third in order is Thought,—that is, the faculty of saying what is possible and pertinent in given circumstances. In the case of oratory, this is the function of the political art and of the art of rhetoric: and so indeed the older poets make their characters speak the language of civic life; the poets of our time, the language of the rhetoricians.

17. Character is that which reveals moral purpose, showing what kind of things a man chooses or avoids. Speeches, therefore, which do not make this manifest, or in which the speaker does not choose or avoid anything whatever, are not expressive of character. Thought, on the other hand, is found where something is proved to be or not to be, or a general maxim is enunciated.

18. Fourth among the elements enumerated comes Diction; by which I mean, as has been already said, the expression of the meaning in words; and its essence is the same both in verse and prose.

19. Of the remaining elements Song holds the chief place among the embellishments.

The Spectacle has, indeed, an emotional attraction of its own, but, of all the parts, it is the least artistic, and connected least with the art of poetry. For the power of Tragedy, we may be sure, is felt even apart from representation and actors. Besides, the production of spectacular effects depends more on the art of the stage machinist than on that of the poet.

VII

[*Structure of the plot*]

These principles being established, let us now discuss the proper structure of the Plot, since this is the first and most important part of Tragedy.

2. Now, according to our definition, Tragedy is an imitation of an action that is complete, and whole, and of a certain magnitude; for there may be a whole that is wanting in magnitude. 3. A whole is that which has a beginning, a middle, and an end. A beginning is that which does not itself follow anything by causal necessity, but after which something naturally is or comes to be. An end, on the contrary, is that which itself naturally follows some other thing, either by necessity, or as a rule, but has nothing following it. A middle is that which follows something as some other thing follows it. A well constructed plot, therefore, must neither begin nor end at haphazard, but conform to these principles.

4. Again, a beautiful object, whether it be a picture of a living organism or any whole composed of parts, must not only have an orderly arrangement of parts, but must also be of a certain magnitude; for beauty depends on magnitude and order. Hence an exceedingly small picture cannot be beautiful; for the view of it is confused, the object being seen in an almost imperceptible moment of time. Nor, again, can one of vast size be beautiful; for as the eye cannot take it all in at once, the unity and sense of the whole is lost for the spectator; as for instance if there were a picture a thousand miles long. 5. As, therefore, in the case of animate bodies and pictures a certain magnitude is necessary, and a magnitude which may be easily embraced in one view; so in the plot, a

certain length is necessary, and a length which can be easily embraced by the memory. 6. The limit of length in relation to dramatic competition and sensuous presentment, is no part of artistic theory. For had it been the rule for a hundred tragedies to compete together, the performance would have been regulated by the water-clock—as indeed we are told was formerly done. 7. But the limit as fixed by the nature of the drama itself is this:—the greater the length, the more beautiful will the piece be by reason of its size, provided that the whole be perspicuous. And to define the matter roughly, we may say that the proper magnitude is comprised within such limits, that the sequence of events, according to the law of probability or necessity, will admit of a change from bad fortune to good, or from good fortune to bad.

VIII
[Unity of plot]

Unity of plot does not, as some persons think, consist in the unity of the hero. For infinitely various are the incidents in one man's life, which cannot be reduced to unity; and so, too, there are many actions of one man out of which we cannot make one action. 2. Hence the error, as it appears, of all poets who have composed a Heracleid, a Theseid, or other poems of the kind. They imagine that as Heracles was one man, the story of Heracles must also be a unity. 3. But Homer, as in all else he is of surpassing merit, here too—whether from art or natural genius—seems to have happily discerned the truth. In composing the Odyssey he did not include all the adventures of Odysseus—such as his wound on Parnassus, or his feigned madness at the mustering of the host—incidents between which there was no necessary or probable connexion: but he made the Odyssey, and likewise the Iliad, to centre round an action that in our sense of the word is one. 4. As therefore, in the other imitative arts, the imitation is one when the object imitated is one, so the plot, being an imitation of an action, must imitate one action and that a whole, the structural union of the parts being such that, if any one of them is displaced or removed, the whole will be disjointed and disturbed. For a thing whose presence or absence makes no visible difference, is not an organic part of the whole.

IX
[Poetry and history]

It is, moreover, evident from what has been said, that it is not the function of the poet to relate what has happened, but what may happen—what is possible according to the law of probability or necessity. 2. The poet and the historian differ not by writing in verse or in prose. The work of Herodotus might be put into verse, and it would still be a species of history, with metre no less than without it. The true difference is that one relates what has happened, the other what may happen. 3. Poetry, therefore, is a more philosophical and a higher thing than history: for poetry tends to express the universal, history the particular. 4. By the universal I mean how a person of a certain type will on occasion speak or act, according to the law of probability or necessity; and it is this universality at which poetry aims in the names she attaches to the personages. The particular is—for example—what Alcibiades did or suffered. 5. In Comedy this is already apparent: for here the poet first constructs the plot on the lines of probability, and then inserts characteristic names;—unlike the lampooners who write about particular individuals. 6. But tragedians still keep to real names, the reason being that what is possible is credible: what has not happened we do not at once feel sure to be possible: but what has happened is manifestly possible: otherwise it would not have happened. 7. Still there are some tragedies in which there are only one or two well known names, the rest being fictitious. In others, none are well known,—as in Agathon's Antheus, where incidents and names alike are fictitious, and yet they give none the less pleasure. 8. We must not, therefore, at all costs keep to the received legends, which are the usual subjects of Tragedy. Indeed, it would be absurd to attempt it; for even subjects that are known are known only to a few, and yet give pleasure to all. 9. It clearly follows that the poet or "maker" should be the maker of plots rather than of verses; since he is a poet because he imitates, and what he imitates are actions. And even if he chances to take an historical subject, he is none the less a poet; for there is no reason why some events that have actually happened should not conform to the law of the probable and possible, and in virtue of that quality in them he is their poet or maker.

10. Of all plots and actions the epeisodic are the worst. I call a plot "epeisodic" in which the episodes or acts succeed one another without probable or necessary sequence. Bad poets compose such pieces by their own fault, good poets, to please the players; for, as they write show pieces for competition, they stretch the plot beyond its capacity, and are often forced to break the natural continuity.

11. But again, Tragedy is an imitation not only of a complete action, but of events terrible and pitiful. Such an effect is best produced when the events come on us by surprise; and the effect is heightened when, at the same time, they follow as cause and effect. 12. The tragic wonder will then be greater than if they happened of themselves or by accident; for even coincidences are most striking when they have an air of design. We may instance the statue of Mitys at Argos, which fell upon his murderer while he was a spectator at a festival, and killed him. Such events seem not to be due to mere chance. Plots, therefore, constructed on these principles are necessarily the best.

X
[Simple and Complex plots]

Plots are either Simple or Complex, for the actions in real life, of which the plots are an imitation, obviously show a similar distinction. 2. An action which is one and continuous in the sense above defined, I call Simple, when the change of fortune takes place without Reversal of Intention and without Recognition.

A Complex action is one in which the change is accompanied by such Reversal, or by Recognition, or by both. 3. These last should arise from the internal structure of the plot, so that what follows should be the necessary or probable result of the preceding action. It makes all the difference whether any given event is a case of *propter hoc* or *post hoc* [the *post hoc, ergo propter* hoc fallacy in logic: "after this, therefore because of this"].

XI
[Reversal and recognition]

Reversal of Intention is a change by which the action veers round to its opposite, subject always to our rule of probability or necessity. Thus in the Oedipus, the messenger comes to cheer Oedipus and free him from his alarms about his mother, but by revealing who he is, he produces the opposite effect. Again in the Lynceus, Lynceus is being led away to his death, and Danaus goes with him, meaning to slay him; but the outcome of the action is, that Danaus is killed and Lynceus saved.

2. Recognition, as the name indicates, is a change from ignorance to knowledge, producing love or hate between the persons destined by the poet for good or bad fortune. The best form of recognition is coincident with a Reversal of Intention, as in the Oedipus. 3. There are indeed other forms. Even inanimate things of the most trivial kind may sometimes be objects of recognition. Again, we may recognise or discover whether a person has done a thing or not. But the recognition which is most intimately connected with the plot and action is, as we have said, the recognition of persons. 4. This recognition, combined with Reversal, will produce either pity or fear; and actions producing these effects are those which, by our definition, Tragedy represents. Moreover, it is upon such situations that issues of good or bad fortune will depend. 5. Recognition, then, being between persons, it may happen that one person only is recognised by the other—when the latter is already known—or it may be necessary that the recognition should be on both sides. Thus Iphigenia is revealed to Orestes by the sending of the letter; but another act of recognition is required to make Orestes known to Iphigenia.

6. Two parts, then, of the Plot—Reversal of Intention and Recognition—turn upon surprises. A third part is the Tragic Incident. The Tragic Incident is a destructive or painful action, such as death on the stage, bodily agony, wounds, and the like.

XII
[*Structure of tragedy*]

[The parts of Tragedy which must be treated as elements of the whole, have been already mentioned. We now come to the quantitative parts—the separate parts into which Tragedy is divided— namely, Prologue, Episode, Exodos, Choric song; this last being divided into Parodos and Stasimon. These are common to all plays: peculiar to some are the songs of actors from the stage and the Commoi.

2. The Prologos is that entire part of a tragedy which precedes the Parodos of the Chorus. The Episode is that entire part of a tragedy which is between complete choric songs. The Exodos is that entire part of a tragedy which has no choric song after it. Of the Choric part the Parodos is the first undivided utterance of the Chorus: the Stasimon is a Choric ode without anapaests or trochaic tetrameters: the Commos is a joint lamentation of Chorus and actors. 3. The parts of Tragedy which must be treated as elements of the whole have been already mentioned. The quantitative parts— the separate parts into which it is divided—are here enumerated.]

XIII
[*Plot and the tragic hero*]

As the sequel to what has already been said, we must proceed to consider what the poet should aim at, and what he should avoid, in constructing his plots; and by what means the specific effect of Tragedy will be produced.

2. A perfect tragedy should, as we have seen, be arranged not on the simple but on the complex plan. It should, moreover, imitate actions which excite pity and fear, this being the distinctive mark of

tragic imitation. It follows plainly, in the first place, that the change of fortune presented must not be the spectacle of a virtuous man brought from prosperity to adversity: for this moves neither pity nor fear; it merely shocks us. Nor, again, that of a bad man passing from adversity to prosperity: for nothing can be more alien to the spirit of Tragedy; it possesses no single tragic quality; it neither satisfies the moral sense, nor calls forth pity or fear. Nor, again, should the downfall of the utter villian be exhibited. A plot of this kind would, doubtless, satisfy the moral sense, but it would inspire neither pity nor fear; for pity is aroused by unmerited misfortune, fear by the misfortune of a man like ourselves. Such an event, therefore, will be neither pitiful nor terrible. 3. There remains, then, the character between these two extremes,—that of a man who is not eminently good and just, yet whose misfortune is brought about not by vice or depravity, but by some error or frailty. He must be one who is highly renowned and prosperous,—a personage like Oedipus, Thyestes, or other illustrious men of such families.

4. A well constructed plot should, therefore, be single in its issue, rather than double as some maintain. The change of fortune should be not from bad to good, but, reversely, from good to bad. It should come about as the result not of vice, but of some great error or frailty, in a character either such as we have described, or better rather than worse. 5. The practice of the stage bears out our view. At first the poets recounted any legend that came in their way. Now, the best tragedies are founded on the story of a few houses,—on the fortunes of Alcmaeon, Oedipus, Orestes, Meleager, Thyestes, Telephus, and those others who have done or suffered something terrible. A tragedy, then, to be perfect according to the rules of art should be of this construction. 6. Hence they are in error who censure Euripides just because he follows this principle in his plays, many of which end unhappily. It is, as we have said, the right ending. The best proof is that on the stage and in dramatic competition, such plays, if well worked out, are the most tragic in effect; and Euripides, faulty though he may be in the general management of his subject, yet is felt to be the most tragic of the poets.

7. In the second rank comes the kind of tragedy which some

place first. Like the Odyssey, it has a double thread of plot, and also an opposite catastrophe for the good and for the bad. It is accounted the best because of the weakness of the spectators; for the poet is guided in what he writes by the wishes of his audience. 8. The pleasure, however, thence derived is not the true tragic pleasure. It is proper rather to Comedy, where those who, in the piece, are the deadliest enemies—like Orestes and Aegisthus—quit the stage as friends at the close, and no one slays or is slain.

XIV
[Fear and pity]

Fear and pity may be aroused by spectacular means; but they may also result from the inner structure of the piece, which is the better way, and indicates a superior poet. For the plot ought to be so constructed that, even without the aid of the eye, he who hears the tale told will thrill with horror and melt to pity at what takes place. This is the impression we should receive from hearing the story of the Oedipus. 2. But to produce this effect by the mere spectacle is a less artistic method, and dependent on extraneous aids. Those who employ spectacular means to create a sense not of the terrible but only of the monstrous, are strangers to the purpose of Tragedy; for we must not demand of Tragedy any and every kind of pleasure, but only that which is proper to it. 3. And since the pleasure which the poet should afford is that which comes from pity and fear through imitation, it is evident that this quality must be impressed upon the incidents.

Let us then determine what are the circumstances which strike us as terrible or pitiful.

4. Actions capable of this effect must happen between persons who are either friends or enemies or indifferent to one another. If an enemy kills an enemy, there is nothing to excite pity either in the act or the intention,—except so far as the suffering in itself is pitiful. So again with indifferent persons. But when the tragic incident occurs between those who are near or dear to one another—if, for example, a brother kills, or intends to kill, a brother, a son his

father, a mother her son, a son his mother, or any other deed of the kind is done—these are the situations to be looked for by the poet. 5. He may not indeed destroy the framework of the received legends—the fact, for instance, that Clytemnestra was slain by Orestes and Eriphyle by Alcmaeon—but he ought to show invention of his own, and skilfully handle the traditional material. Let us explain more clearly what is meant by skilful handling.

6. The action may be done consciously and with knowledge of the persons, in the manner of the older poets. It is thus too that Euripides makes Medea slay her children. Or, again, the deed of horror may be done, but done in ignorance, and the tie of kinship or friendship be discovered afterwards. The Oedipus of Sophocles is an example. Here, indeed, the incident is outside the drama proper; but cases occur where it falls within the action of the play: one may cite the Alcmaeon of Astydamas, or Telegonus in the Wounded Odysseus. 7. Again, there is a third case,—<to be about to act with knowledge of the persons and then not to act. The fourth case is> when some one is about to do an irreparable deed through ignorance, and makes the discovery before it is done. These are the only possible ways. For the deed must either be done or not done,—and that wittingly or unwittingly. But of all these ways, to be about to act knowing the persons, and then not to act, is the worst. It is shocking without being tragic, for no disaster follows. It is, therefore, never, or very rarely, found in poetry. One instance, however, is in the Antigone, where Haemon threatens to kill Creon. 8. The next and better way is that the deed should be perpetrated. Still better, that it should be perpetrated in ignorance, and the discovery made afterwards. There is then nothing to shock us, while the discovery produces a startling effect. 9. The last case is the best, as when in the Cresphontes Merope is about to slay her son, but, recognising who he is, spares his life. So in the Iphigenia, the sister recognises the brother just in time. Again in the Helle, the son recognises the mother when on the point of giving her up. This, then, is why a few families only, as has been already observed, furnish the subjects of tragedy. It was not art, but happy chance, that led poets to look for such situations and so im-

press the tragic quality upon their plots. They are compelled, therefore, to have recourse to those houses whose history contains moving incidents like these.

Enough has now been said concerning the structure of the incidents, and the proper constitution of the plot.

XV
[*Character*]

In respect of Character there are four things to be aimed at. First, and most important, it must be good. Now any speech or action that manifests moral purpose of any kind will be expressive of character: the character will be good if the purpose is good. This rule is relative to each class. Even a woman may be good, and also a slave; though the woman may be said to be an inferior being, and the slave quite worthless. 2. The second thing to aim at is propriety. There is a type of manly valour; but valour in a woman, or unscrupulous cleverness, is inappropriate. 3. Thirdly, character must be true to life: for this is a distinct thing from goodness and propriety, as here described. 4. The fourth point is consistency: for though the subject of the imitation, who suggested the type, be inconsistent, still he must be consistently inconsistent. 5. As an example of motiveless degradation of character, we have Menelaus in the Orestes: of character indecorous and inappropriate, the lament of Odysseus in the Scylla, and the speech of Melanippe: of inconsistency, the Iphigenia at Aulis,—for Iphigenia the suppliant in no way resembles her later self.

6. As in the structure of the plot, so too in the portraiture of character, the poet should always aim either at the necessary or the probable. Thus a person of a given character should speak or act in a given way, by the rule either of necessity or of probability; just as this event should follow that by necessary or probable sequence. 7. It is therefore evident that the unravelling of the plot, no less than the complication, must arise out of the plot itself, it must not be brought about by the *Deus ex Machina*—as in the Medea, or in the Return of the Greeks in the Iliad. The *Deus ex*

Machina should be employed only for events external to the drama,—for antecedent or subsequent events, which lie beyond the range of human knowledge, and which require to be reported or foretold; for to the gods we ascribe the power of seeing all things. Within the action there must be nothing irrational. If the irrational cannot be excluded, it should be outside the scope of the tragedy. Such is the irrational element in the Oedipus of Sophocles.

8. Again, since Tragedy is an imitation of persons who are above the common level, the example of good portrait-painters should be followed. They, while reproducing the distinctive form of the original, make a likeness which is true to life and yet more beautiful. So too the poet, in representing men who are irascible or indolent, or have other defects of character, should preserve the type and yet ennoble it. In this way Achilles is portrayed by Agathon and Homer.

9. These then are rules the poet should observe. Nor should he neglect those appeals to the senses, which, though not among the essentials, are the concomitants of poetry; for here too there is much room for error. But of this enough has been said in the published treatises.

XVI

[*Kinds of recognition*]

What Recognition is has been already explained. We will now enumerate its kinds.

First, the least artistic form, which, from poverty of wit, is most commonly employed—recognition by signs. 2. Of these some are congenital,—such as "the spear which the earth-born race bear on their bodies," or the stars introduced by Carcinus in his Thyestes. Others are acquired after birth; and of these some are bodily marks, as scars; some external tokens, as necklaces, or the little ark in the Tyro by which the discovery is effected. 3. Even these admit of more or less skilful treatment. Thus in the recognition of Odysseus by his scar, the discovery is made in one way by the nurse, in another by the herdsmen. The use of tokens for the express purpose of proof—and, indeed, any formal proof with or without tokens—is a less artistic mode of recognition. A better kind is that which comes about by a turn of incident, as in the Bath Scene in the Odyssey.

4. Next come the recognitions invented at will by the poet, and on that account wanting in art. For example, Orestes in the Iphigenia reveals the fact that he is Orestes. She, indeed, makes herself known by the letter; but he, by speaking himself, and saying what the poet, not what the plot requires. This, therefore, is nearly allied to the fault above mentioned:—for Orestes might as well have brought tokens with him. . . .

5. The third kind depends on memory when the sight of some object awakens a feeling: as in the Cyprians of Dicaeogenes, where the hero breaks into tears on seeing the picture; or again in the "Lay of Alcinous," where Odysseus, hearing the minstrel play the lyre, recalls the past and weeps; and hence the recognition.

6. The fourth kind is by process of reasoning. Thus in the Choëphori:—"Some one resembling me has come: no one resembles me but Orestes: therefore Orestes has come." Such too is the discovery made by Iphigenia in the play of Polyidus the Sophist. It was a natural reflexion for Orestes to make, "So I too must die at the altar like my sister." So, again, in the Tydeus of Theodectes, the father says, "I came to find my son, and I lose my life." So too in the Phineidae: the women, on seeing the place, inferred their fate: —"Here we are doomed to die, for here we were cast forth." 7. Again, there is a composite kind of recognition involving false inference on the part of one of the characters, as in the Odysseus Disguised as a Messenger. A said <that no one else was able to bend the bow; . . . hence B (the disguised Odysseus) imagined that A would> recognise the bow which, in fact, he had not seen; and to bring about a recognition by this means—the expectation that A would recognise the bow—is false inference.

8. But, of all recognitions, the best is that which arises from the incidents themselves, where the startling discovery is made by natural means. Such is that in the Oedipus of Sophocles, and in the Iphigenia; for it was natural that Iphigenia should wish to dispatch

a letter. These recognitions alone dispense with the artificial aid of tokens or amulets. Next come the recognitions by process of reasoning.

XVII

[Constructing the plot]

In constructing the plot and working it out with the proper diction, the poet should place the scene, as far as possible, before his eyes. In this way, seeing everything with the utmost vividness, as if he were a spectator of the action, he will discover what is in keeping with it, and be most unlikely to overlook inconsistencies. The need of such a rule is shown by the fault found in Carcinus. Amphiaraus was on his way from the temple. This fact escaped the observation of one who did not see the situation. On the stage, however, the piece failed, the audience being offended at the oversight.

2. Again, the poet should work out his play, to the best of his power, with appropriate gestures; for those who feel emotion are most convincing through natural sympathy with the characters they represent; and one who is agitated storms, one who is angry rages, with the most life-like reality. Hence poetry implies either a happy gift of nature or a strain of madness. In the one case a man can take the mould of any character; in the other, he is lifted out of his proper self.

3. As for the story, whether the poet takes it ready made or constructs it for himself, he should first sketch its general outline, and then fill in the episodes and amplify in detail. The general plan may be illustrated by the Iphigenia. A young girl is sacrificed; she disappears mysteriously from the eyes of those who sacrificed her; she is transported to another country, where the custom is to offer up all strangers to the goddess. To this ministry she is appointed. Some time later her own brother chances to arrive. The fact that the oracle for some reason ordered him to go there, is outside the general plan of the play. The purpose, again, of his coming is outside the action proper. However, he comes, he is

seized, and, when on the point of being sacrificed, reveals who he is. The mode of recognition may be either that of Euripides or of Polyidus, in whose play he exclaims very naturally:—"So it was not my sister only, but I too, who was doomed to be sacrificed"; and by that remark he is saved.

4. After this, the names being once given, it remains to fill in the episodes. We must see that they are relevant to the action. In the case of Orestes, for example, there is the madness which led to his capture, and his deliverance by means of the purificatory rite. 5. In the drama, the episodes are short, but it is these that give extension to Epic poetry. Thus the story of the Odyssey can be stated briefly. A certain man is absent from home for many years; he is jealously watched by Poseidon, and left desolate. Meanwhile his home is in a wretched plight—suitors are wasting his substance and plotting against his son. At length, tempest-tost, he himself arrives; he makes certain persons acquainted with him; he attacks the suitors with his own hand, and is himself preserved while he destroys them. This is the essence of the plot; the rest is episode.

XVIII
[*Parts of the plot*]

Every tragedy falls into two parts,—Complication and Unravelling or *Dénouement*. Incidents extraneous to the action are frequently combined with a portion of the action proper, to form the Complication; the rest is the Unravelling. By the Complication I mean all that extends from the beginning of the action to the part which marks the turning-point to good or bad fortune. The Unravelling is that which extends from the beginning of the change to the end. Thus, in the Lynceus of Theodectes, the Complication consists of the incidents presupposed in the drama, the seizure of the child, and then again* * <The Unravelling> extends from the accusation of murder to the end.

2. There are four kinds of Tragedy, the Complex, depending

entirely on Reversal and Recognition; the Pathetic (where the motive is passion),—such as the tragedies on Ajax and Ixion; the Ethical (where the motives are ethical),—such as the Phthiotides and the Peleus. The fourth kind is the Simple <We here exclude the purely spectacular element>, exemplified by the Phorcides, the Prometheus, and scenes laid in Hades. 3. The poet should endeavour, if possible, to combine all poetic merits; or failing that, the greatest number and those the most important; the more so, in face of the cavilling criticism of the day. For whereas there have hitherto been good poets, each in his own branch, the critics now expect one man to surpass all others in their several lines of excellence.

In speaking of a tragedy as the same or different, the best test to take is the plot. Identity exists where the Complication and Unravelling are the same. Many poets tie the knot well, but unravel it ill. Both arts, however, should always be mastered.

4. Again, the poet should remember what has been often said, and not make a Tragedy into an Epic structure. By an Epic structure I mean one with a multiplicity of plots: as if, for instance, you were to make a tragedy out of the entire story of the Iliad. In the Epic poem, owing to its length, each part assumes its proper magnitude. In the drama the result is far from answering to the poet's expectation. 5. The proof is that the poets who have dramatised the whole story of the Fall of Troy, instead of selecting portions, like Euripides; or who have taken the whole tale of Niobe, and not a part of her story, like Aeschylus, either fail utterly or meet with poor success on the stage. Even Agathon has been known to fail from this one defect. In his Reversals of Intention, however, he shows a marvellous skill in the effort to hit the popular taste,—to produce a tragic effect that satisfies the moral sense. 6. This effect is produced when the clever rogue, like Sisyphus, is outwitted, or the brave villain defeated. Such an event is probable in Agathon's sense of the word: "it is probable," he says, "that many things should happen contrary to probability."

7. The Chorus too should be regarded as one of the actors; it

should be an integral part of the whole, and share in the action, in the manner not of Euripides but of Sophocles. As for the later poets, their choral songs pertain as little to the subject of the piece as to that of any other tragedy. They are, therefore, sung as mere interludes,—a practice first begun by Agathon. Yet what difference is there between introducing such choral interludes, and transferring a speech, or even a whole act, from one play to another?

XIX
[*Diction and Thought*]

It remains to speak of Diction and Thought, the other parts of Tragedy having been already discussed. Concerning Thought, we may assume what is said in the Rhetoric, to which inquiry the subject more strictly belongs. 2. Under Thought is included every effect which has to be produced by speech, the subdivisions being,—proof and refutation; the excitation of the feelings, such as pity, fear, anger, and the like; the suggestion of importance or its opposite. 3. Now, it is evident that the dramatic incidents must be treated from the same points of view as the dramatic speeches, when the object is to evoke the sense of pity, fear, importance, or probability. The only difference is, that the incidents should speak for themselves without verbal exposition; while the effects aimed at in speech should be produced by the speaker, and as a result of the speech. For what were the business of a speaker, if the Thought were revealed quite apart from what he says?

4. Next, as regards Diction. One branch of the inquiry treats of the Modes of Expression. But this province of knowledge belongs to the art of Delivery, and to the masters of that science. It includes, for instance,—what is a command, a prayer, a narrative, a threat, a question, an answer, and so forth. 5. To know or not to know these things involves no serious censure upon the poet's art. For who can admit the fault imputed to Homer by Protagoras,— that in the words, "Sing, goddess, of the wrath," he gives a command under the idea that he utters a prayer? For to tell some one

to do a thing or not to do it is, he says, a command. We may, there-fore, pass this over as an inquiry that belongs to another art, not to poetry.

[Sections XX, XXI, XXII are here omitted, since a knowledge of ancient Greek is necessary to follow Aristotle's discussion of tech-nical matters in grammar, diction, and style.]

XXIII
[Narrative poetry]

As to that poetic imitation which is narrative in form and employs a single metre, the plot manifestly ought, as in a tragedy, to be con-structed on dramatic principles. It should have for its subject a sin-gle action, whole and complete, with a beginning, a middle, and an end. It will thus resemble a single and coherent picture of a liv-ing being, and produce the pleasure proper to it. It will differ in structure from historical compositions, which of necessity present not a single action, but a single period, and all that happened within that period to one person or to many, little connected to-gether as the events may be. 2. For as the sea-fight at Salamis and the battle with the Carthaginians in Sicily took place at the same time, but did not tend to any one result, so in the sequence of events, one thing sometimes follows another, and yet no single result is thereby produced. Such is the practice, we may say, of most poets. 3. Here again, then, as has been already observed, the tran-scendent excellence of Homer is manifest. He never attempts to make the whole war of Troy the subject of his poem, though that war had a beginning and an end. It would have been too vast a theme, and not easily embraced in a single view. If, again, he had kept it within moderate limits, it must have been over-complicated by the variety of the incidents. As it is, he detaches a single portion, and admits as episodes many events from the gen-eral story of the war—such as the Catalogue of the ships and others—thus diversifying the poem. All other poets take a single hero, a single period, or an action single indeed, but with a multiplicity of parts. Thus did the author of the Cypria and of the Little Iliad. 4. For this reason the Iliad and the Odyssey each furnish the subject of one tragedy, or, at most, of two; while the Cypria supplies materials for many, and the Little Iliad for eight—the Award of the Arms, the Philoctetes, the Neoptolemus, the Eurypylus, the Mendicant Odysseus, the Laconian Women, the Fall of Ilium, the Departure of the Fleet.

XXIV
[*Epic*]

Again, Epic poetry must have as many kinds as Tragedy: it must be simple, or complex, or "ethical," or "pathetic." The parts also, with the exception of song and scenery, are the same; for it requires Reversals of Intention, Recognitions, and Tragic Incidents. 2. Moreover, the thoughts and the diction must be artistic. In all these respects Homer is our earliest and sufficient model. Indeed each of his poems has a twofold character. The Iliad is at once simple and "pathetic," and the Odyssey complex (for Recognition scenes run through it), and at the same time "ethical." Moreover, in diction and thought he is supreme.

3. Epic poetry differs from Tragedy in the scale on which it is constructed, and in its metre. As regards scale or length, we have already laid down an adequate limit:—the beginning and the end must be capable of being brought within a single view. This condition will be satisfied by poems on a smaller scale than the old epics, and answering in length to the group of tragedies presented at a single sitting.

4. Epic poetry has, however, a great—a special—capacity for enlarging its dimensions, and we can see the reason. In Tragedy we cannot imitate several lines of actions carried on at one and the same time; we must confine ourselves to the action on the stage and the part taken by the players. But in Epic poetry, owing to the narrative form, many events simultaneously transacted can be presented; and these, if relevant to the subject, add mass and dignity to the poem. The Epic has here an advantage, and one

that conduces to grandeur of effect, to diverting the mind of the hearer, and relieving the story with varying episodes. For sameness of incident soon produces satiety, and makes tragedies fail on the stage.

5. As for the metre, the heroic measure has proved its fitness by the test of experience. If a narrative poem in any other metre or in many metres were now composed, it would be found incongruous. For of all measures the heroic is the stateliest and the most massive; and hence it most readily admits rare words and metaphors, which is another point in which the narrative form of imitation stands alone. On the other hand, the iambic and the trochaic tetrameter are stirring measures, the latter being akin to dancing, the former expressive of action. 6. Still more absurd would it be to mix together different metres, as was done by Chaeremon. Hence no one has ever composed a poem on a great scale in any other than heroic verse. Nature herself, as we have said, teaches the choice of the proper measure.

7. Homer, admirable in all respects, has the special merit of being the only poet who rightly appreciates the part he should take himself. The poet should speak as little as possible in his own person, for it is not this that makes him an imitator. Other poets appear themselves upon the scene throughout, and imitate but little and rarely. Homer, after a few prefatory words, at once brings in a man, or woman, or other personage; none of them wanting in characteristic qualities, but each with a character of his own.

8. The element of the wonderful is admitted in Tragedy. The irrational, on which the wonderful depends for its chief effects, has wider scope in Epic poetry, because there the person acting is not seen. Thus, the pursuit of Hector would be ludicrous if placed upon the stage—the Greeks standing still and not joining in the pursuit, and Achilles waving them back. But in the Epic poem the absurdity passes unnoticed. Now the wonderful is pleasing: as may be inferred from the fact that, in telling a story, every one adds something startling of his own, knowing that his hearers like it. 9. It is Homer who has chiefly taught other poets the art of telling lies skilfully. The secret of it lies in a fallacy. For, assuming

that if one thing is or becomes, a second is or becomes, men imagine that, if the second is, the first likewise is or becomes. But this is a false inference. Hence, where the first thing is untrue, it is quite unnecessary, provided the second be true, to add that the first is or has become. For the mind, knowing the second to be true, falsely infers the truth of the first. There is an example of this in the Bath Scene of the Odyssey.

10. Accordingly, the poet should prefer probable impossibilities to improbable possibilities. The tragic plot must not be composed of irrational parts. Everything irrational should, if possible, be excluded; or, at all events, it should lie outside the action of the play (as, in the Oedipus, the hero's ignorance as to the manner of Laius' death); not within the drama,—as in the Electra, the messenger's account of the Pythian games; or as in the Mysians, the man who comes from Tegea to Mysia without speaking. The plea that otherwise the plot would have been ruined, is ridiculous; such a plot should not in the first instance be constructed. But once the irrational has been introduced and an air of likelihood imparted to it, we must accept it in spite of the absurdity. Take even the irrational incidents in the Odyssey, where Odysseus is left upon the shore of Ithaca. How intolerable even these might have been would be apparent if an inferior poet were to treat the subject. As it is, the absurdity is veiled by the poetic charm with which the poet invests it.

11. The diction should be elaborated in the pauses of the action, where there is no expression of character or thought. For, conversely, character and thought are merely obscured by a diction that is over brilliant.

XXV
[*Sources of Critical Objections*]

With respect to critical difficulties and their solutions, the number and nature of the sources from which they may be drawn may be thus exhibited.

The poet being an imitator, like a painter or any other artist, must of necessity imitate one of three objects,—things as they were or are, things as they are said or thought to be, or things as they ought to be. 2. The vehicle of expression is language,—either current terms or, it may be, rare words or metaphors. There are also many modifications of language, which we concede to the poets. 3. Add to this, that the standard of correctness is not the same in poetry and politics, any more than in poetry and any other art. Within the art of poetry itself there are two kinds of faults,—those which touch its essence, and those which are accidental. 4. If a poet has chosen to imitate something, <but has imitated it incorrectly> through want of capacity, the error is inherent in the poetry. But if the failure is due to a wrong choice—if he has represented a horse as throwing out both his off legs at once, or introduced technical inaccuracies in medicine, for example, or in any other art—the error is not essential to the poetry. These are the points of view from which we should consider and answer the objections raised by the critics.

5. First as to matters which concern the poet's own art. If he describes the impossible, he is guilty of an error; but the error may be justified, if the end of the art be thereby attained (the end being that already mentioned),—if, that is, the effect of this or any other part of the poem is thus rendered more striking. A case in point is the pursuit of Hector. If, however, the end might have been as well, or better, attained without violating the special rules of the poetic art, the error is not justified: for every kind of error should, if possible, be avoided.

Again, does the error touch the essentials of the poetic art, or some accident of it? For example,—not to know that a hind has no horns is a less serious matter than to paint it inartistically.

6. Further, if it be objected that the description is not true to fact, the poet may perhaps reply,—"But the objects are as they ought to be": just as Sophocles said that he drew men as they ought to be; Euripides, as they are. 7. In this way the objection may be met. If, however, the representation be of neither kind, the poet may answer,—"This is how men say the thing is." This applies to tales about the gods. It may well be that these stories are not

higher than fact nor yet true to fact: they are, very possibly, what Xenophanes says of them. But anyhow, "this is what is said." Again a description may be no better than the fact: "still, it was the fact"; as in the passage about the arms: "Upright upon their butt-ends stood the spears." This was the custom then, as it now is among the Illyrians.

8. Again, in examining whether what has been said or done by some one is poetically right or not, we must not look merely to the particular act or saying, and ask whether it is poetically good or bad. We must also consider by whom it is said or done, to whom, when, in whose interest, or for what end; whether, for instance, it be to secure a greater good, or avert a greater evil. . . .

17. In general, the impossible must be justified by reference to artistic requirements, or to the higher reality, or to received opinion. With respect to the requirements of art, a probable impossibility is to be preferred to a thing improbable and yet possible. Again, it may be impossible that there should be men such as Zeuxis painted. "Yes," we say, "but the impossible is the higher thing; for the ideal type must surpass the reality." To justify the irrational, we appeal to what is commonly said to be. In addition to which, we urge that the irrational sometimes does not violate reason; just as "it is probable that a thing may happen contrary to probability."

18. Things that sound contradictory should be examined by the same rules as in dialectical refutation—whether the same thing is meant, in the same relation, and in the same sense. We should therefore solve the question by reference to what the poet says himself, or to what is tacitly assumed by a person of intelligence.

19. The element of the irrational, and, similarly, depravity of character, are justly censured when there is no inner necessity for introducing them. Such is the irrational element in the Aegeus of Euripides, and the badness of Menelaus in the Orestes.

20. Thus, there are five sources from which critical objections are drawn. Things are censured either as impossible, or irrational,

or morally hurtful, or contradictory, or contrary to artistic correctness. The answers should be sought under the twelve heads above mentioned.

XXVI
[Comparison of Epic and Tragedy]

The question may be raised whether the Epic or Tragic mode of imitation is the higher. If the more refined art is the higher, and the more refined in every case is that which appeals to the better sort of audience, the art which imitates anything and everything is manifestly most unrefined. The audience is supposed to be too dull to comprehend unless something of their own is thrown in by the performers, who therefore indulge in restless movements. Bad flute-players twist and twirl, if they have to represent "the quoit-throw," or hustle the coryphaeus when they perform the "Scylla." 2. Tragedy, it is said, has this same defect. We may compare the opinion that the older actors entertained of their successors. Mynniscus used to call Callippides "ape" on account of the extravagance of his action, and the same view was held of Pindarus. Tragic art, then, as a whole, stands to Epic in the same relation as the younger to the elder actors. So we are told that Epic poetry is addressed to a cultivated audience, who do not need gesture; Tragedy, to an inferior public. 3. Being then unrefined, it is evidently the lower of the two.

Now, in the first place, this censure attaches not to the poetic but to the histrionic art; for gesticulation may be equally overdone in epic recitation, as by Sosistratus, or in lyrical competition, as by Mnasitheus the Opuntian. Next, all action is not to be condemned —any more than all dancing—but only that of bad performers. Such was the fault found in Callippides, as also in others of our own day, who are censured for representing degraded women. Again, Tragedy like Epic poetry produces its effect even without action; it reveals its power by mere reading. If, then, in all other respects it is superior, this fault, we say, is not inherent in it.

4. And superior it is, because it has all the epic elements—it

may even use the epic metre—with the music and scenic effects as important accessories; and these produce the most vivid of pleasures. Further, it has vividness of impression in reading as well as in representation. 5. Moreover, the art attains its end within narrower limits; for the concentrated effect is more pleasurable than one which is spread over a long time and so diluted. What, for example, would be the effect of the Oedipus of Sophocles, if it were cast into a form as long as the Iliad? 6. Once more, the Epic imitation has less unity; as is shown by this, that any Epic poem will furnish subjects for several tragedies. Thus if the story adopted by the poet has a strict unity, it must either be concisely told and appear truncated; or, if it conform to the Epic canon of length, it must seem weak and watery. <Such length implies some loss of unity,> if, I mean, the poem is constructed out of several actions, like the Iliad and the Odyssey, which have many such parts, each with a certain magnitude of its own. Yet these poems are as perfect as possible in structure; each is, in the highest degree attainable, an imitation of a single action.

7. If, then, Tragedy is superior to Epic poetry in all these respects, and, moreover, fulfils its specific function better as an art—for each art ought to produce, not any chance pleasure, but the pleasure proper to it, as already stated—it plainly follows that Tragedy is the higher art, as attaining its end more perfectly.

8. Thus much may suffice concerning Tragic and Epic poetry in general; their several kinds and parts, with the number of each and their differences; the causes that make a poem good or bad; the objections of the critics and the answers to these objections.

Horace

(65 – 8 B.C.)

ART OF POETRY

The first of a long line of works written by poets on their own art, the *Ars Poetica* (c. 9 B.C.), a title bestowed on Horace's work by the Roman rhetorician Quintilian (who was obviously better at choosing titles), was originally entitled *Epistola ad Pisanos* (*Epistle to the Pisos*). Addressed to the Piso family (one of the two sons was a promising poet), the verse letter follows the conventional three-part structure of Hellenistic treatises on poetry and rhetoric: *poesis* (poetry); *poema* (the poem: techniques, structure); and *poeta* (the poet). Horace, however, takes liberties with the arrangement of the parts.

The translator is John Conington.

SUPPOSE some painter, as a *tour de force,*   **[*Unity*]**
Should couple head of man with neck of horse,
Invest them both with feathers, 'stead of hair,
And tack on limbs picked up from here and there,
So that the figure, when complete, should show
A maid above, a hideous fish below:
Should you be favoured with a private view,
You'd laugh, my friends, I know, and rightly too.
Yet trust me, Pisos, not less strange would look,
To a discerning eye, the foolish book   **10**
Where dream-like forms in sick delirium blend,
And nought is of a piece from end to end.
"Poets and painters (you know the plea)
Have always been allowed their fancy free."
I own it; 'tis a fair excuse to plead;
By turns we claim it, and by turns concede;

But 'twill not screen the unnatural and absurd,
Unions of lamb with tiger, snake with bird.
   When poets would be lofty, they commence
With purple patch of cheap magnificence: 20
Of Dian's altar and her grove we read,
Or rapid streams meandering through the mead;
Or grand descriptions of the river Rhine,
Or watery bow, will take up many a line.
All in their way good things, but not just now:
You're happy at a cypress, we'll allow;
But what of that? you're painting by command
A shipwrecked sailor, striking out for land:
That crockery was a jar when you began;
It ends a pitcher: you an artist, man!   30
Make what you will, in short, so, when 'tis done,
'Tis but consistent, simple, one.
   Ye worthy trio! we poor sons of song
Oft find 'tis fancied right that leads us wrong.
I prove obscure in trying to be terse;
Attempts at ease emasculate my verse;
Who aims at grandeur into bombast falls;
Who fears to stretch his pinions creeps and crawls;
Who hopes by strange variety to please
Puts dolphins among forests, boars in seas.   40
Thus zeal to 'scape from error, if unchecked
By sense of art, creates a new defect.
Fix on some casual sculptor; he shall know
How to give nails their sharpness, hair its flow;
Yet he shall fail, because he lacks the soul
To comprehend and reproduce the whole.
I'd not be he: the blackest hair and eye
Lose all their beauty with the nose awry.
   Good authors, take a brother bard's advice:
Ponder your subject o'er not once nor twice,   50
And oft and oft consider, if the weight
You hope to lift be or be not too great.

Let but our theme be equal to our powers,
Choice language, clear arrangement, both are ours.
Would you be told how best your pearls to thread?
Why, say just now what should just now be said,
But put off other matter for to-day,
To introduce it later by the way.

[Selection and arrangement]

    In words again be cautious and select,
And duly pick out this, and that reject.

60

High praise and honour to the bard is due
Whose dexterous setting makes an old word new.
Nay more, should some recondite subject need
Fresh signs to make it clear to those who read,
A power of issuing terms till now unused,
If claimed with modesty, is ne'er refused.
New words will find acceptance, if they flow
Forth from the Greek, with just a twist or so.
But why should Rome capriciously forbid
Our bards from doing what their fathers did?

70

Or why should Plautus and Caecilius gain
What Virgil or what Varius asks in vain?
Nay, I myself, if with my scanty wit
I coin a word or two, why grudge me it,
When Ennius and old Cato boldly flung
Their terms broadcast, and amplified our tongue?
To utter words stamped current by the mill
Has always been thought right and always will.

    When forests shed their foliage in fall,
The earliest born still drops the first of all:

80

So fades the elder race of words, and so
The younger generations bloom and grow.
Death claims humanity and human things,
Aye, e'en "imperial works and worthy kings":
What though the ocean, girdled by the shore,
Gives shelter to the ships it tossed before?
What though the marsh, once waste and watery, now
Feeds neighbour towns, and groans beneath the plough?

What though the river, late the corn-field's dread,
Rolls fruit and blessing down its altered bed? 90
Man's works must perish: how should words evade
The general doom, and flourish undecayed?
Yes, words long faded may again revive,
And words may fade now blooming and alive,
If usage wills it so, to whom belongs
The rule, the law, the government of tongues.

For metres, Homer shows you how to write [*Meter*]
Heroic deeds and incidents of fight.
Complaint was once the Elegiac's theme;
From thence 'twas used to sing of love's young dream: 100
But who that dainty measure first put out,
Grammarians differ, and 'tis still in doubt.
Archilochus, inspired by fiery rage,
Called forth Iambics: now they tread the stage
In buskin or in sock, conduct discourse,
Lead action on, and awe the mob perforce.
The glorious gods, the gods' heroic seed, [*Decorum*
The conquering boxer, the victorious steed, *in style*]
The joys of wine, the lover's fond desire,
Such themes the Muse appropriates to the lyre. 110
Why hail me poet, if I fail to seize
The shades of style, its fixed proprieties?
Why should false shame compel me to endure
An ignorance which common pains would cure?
A comic subject steadily declines
To be related in high tragic lines.
The Thyestean feast no less disdains
The vulgar vehicle of comic strains.
Each has its place allotted; each is bound
To keep it, nor invade its neighbour's ground. 120
Yet Comedy sometimes will raise her note:
See Chremes, how he swells his angry throat!
And when a tragic hero tells his woes,
The terms he chooses are akin to prose.

Peleus or Telephus, suppose him poor
Or driven to exile, talks in tropes no more;
His yard-long words desert him, when he tries
To draw forth tears from sympathetic eyes.

Mere grace is not enough: a poem should thrill
The hearer's soul, and move it at its will.
Smiles are contagious; so are tears; to see
Another sobbing, brings a sob from me.
No, no, good Peleus; set the example, pray,
And weep yourself; then weep perhaps I may:
But if no sorrow in your speech appear,
I nod or laugh; I cannot squeeze a tear.
Words follow looks: wry faces are expressed
By wailing, scowls by bluster, smiles by jest,
Grave airs by saws, and so of all the rest.
For nature forms our spirits to receive   140
Each bent that outward circumstance can give:
She kindles pleasure, bids resentment glow,
Or bows the soul to earth in hopeless woe;
Then, as the tide of feeling waxes strong,
She vents it through her conduit-pipe, the tongue.

[*Identification of the poet with his characters*]

Unless the speaker's words and fortune suit,
All Rome will join to jeer him, horse and foot.
Gods should not talk like heroes, nor again
Impetuous youth like grave and reverend men;
Lady and nurse a different language crave,   150
Sons of the soil and rovers o'er the wave;
Assyrian, Colchian, Theban, Argive, each
Has his own style, his proper cast of speech.

[*Decorum in characterization*]

In painting characters, follow tradition,
Or in inverting, be consistent,
If great Achilles figure in the scene,
Make him impatient, fiery, ruthless, keen;
All laws, all covenants let him still disown,
And test his quarrel by the sword alone.
Make Medea all revenge and scorn,   160

Ino still sad, Ixion still forsworn,
Io a wanderer still, Orestes still forlorn.
  If you would be original, and seek
To frame some character ne'er seen in Greek,
See it be wrought on one consistent plan,
And end the same creation it began.
'Tis hard, I grant, to treat a subject known
And hackneyed so that it may look one's own;
Far better turn the Iliad to a play
And carve out acts and scenes the readiest way,   170
Than alter facts and characters, and tell
In a strange form the tale men know so well.
But, with some few precautions, you may set
Your private mark on public chattels yet:
Avoid careering and careering still
In the old round, like carthorse in a mill;
Nor, bound too closely to the Grecian Muse,
Translate the words whose soul you should transfuse,
Nor act the copyist's part, and work in chains
Which, once put on by rashness, shame retains.   180
  Don't open like the older epics, with a burst:
"Troy's war and Priam's fate are here rehearsed."
What's coming, pray, that thus he winds his horn?
The mountain labours, and a mouse is born. *[The beginning, middle,*
Far better he who enters at his ease,   *and the end]*
Nor takes your breath with empty flourishes:
"Sing, Muse, the man who, after Troy was burned,
Saw divers cities, and their manners learned."
Not smoke from fire his object is to bring,
But fire from smoke, a very different thing;   190
Yet has he dazzling miracles in store,
Cyclops, and Laestrygons, and fifty more.
He sings not, he, of Diomed's return,
Starting from Meleager's funeral urn,
Nor when he tells the Trojan story, begs
Attention first for Leda and her eggs.

He hurries to the climax, lets you fall
Where facts crowd thick, as though you knew them all,
And what he judges will not turn to gold
Beneath his touch, he passes by untold.   200
And all this glamour, all this glorious dream,
Truth blent with fiction in one motley scheme,
He so contrives, that, when 'tis o'er, you see
Beginning, middle, end alike agree.

    Now listen, dramatists, and I will tell   *[Other rules of*
What I expect, and all the world as well.   *decorum]*
If you would have your auditors to stay
Till curtain-rise and plaudit end the play,
Observe each age's temper, and impart
To each the grace and finish of your art.   210
    Note first the boy who just knows how to talk
And feels his feet beneath him in his walk:
He likes his young companions, loves a game,
Soon vexed, soon soothed, and not two hours the same.

    The beardless youth, at last from tutor freed,
Loves playing-field and tennis, dog and steed:
Pliant as wax to those who lead him wrong,
But all impatience with a faithful tongue;
Imprudent, lavish, hankering for the moon,
He takes things up and lays them down as soon   220
    His nature revolutionized, the man
Makes friends and money when and how he can:
Keen-eyed and cool, though on ambition bent,
He shuns all acts of which he may repent.

    Grey hairs have many evils: without end
The old man gathers what he dares not spend,
While, as for action, do he what he will,
'Tis all half-hearted, spiritless, and chill:
Inert, irresolute, his neck he cranes
Into the future, grumbles, and complains,   230
Extols his own young years with peevish praise,
But rates and censures these degenerate days.

Years, as they come, bring blessings in their train;
Years, as they go, take blessings back again:
Yet haste or chance may blink the obvious truth,
Make youth discourse like age, and age like youth:
Attention fixed on life alone can teach
The traits and adjuncts which pertain to each.
   Sometimes an action on the stage is shown,
Sometimes 'tis done elsewhere, and there made known.   240
A thing when heard, remember, strikes less keen
On the spectator's mind than when 'tis seen.
Yet 'twere not well in public to display
A business best transacted far away,
And much may be secluded from the eye
For well-graced tongues to tell of by and by.
Medea must not shed her children's blood,
Nor savage Atreus cook man's flesh for food,
Nor Philomel turn bird or Cadmus snake,
With people looking on and wide awake.   250
If scenes like these before my eyes be thrust,
They shock belief and generate disgust.
   Would you your play should prosper and endure?
Then let it have five acts, nor more nor fewer.
Bring in no god save as a last resource,
Nor make four speakers join in the discourse.
   An actor's part the chorus should sustain   *[Chorus]*
And do their best to get the plot in train:
And whatsoe'er between the acts they chant
Should all be apt, appropriate, relevant.   260
Still let them give sage counsel, back the good,
Temper wrath, and cool impetuous blood,
Praise the spare meal that pleases but not sates,
Justice, and law, and peace with unbarred gates,
Conceal all secrets, and the gods implore
To crush the proud and elevate the poor.
   Not trumpet-tongued, as now, nor brass-belayed,   *[Music]*
The flute was used to lend the chorus aid:

Simple and slight and moderately loud,
It charmed the ears of not too large a crowd,   270
Which, frugal, rustic, primitive, severe,
Flocked in those early days to see and hear.
    Then, when the city gained increase of land,
And wider walls its waxing greatness spanned,
When the good Genius, frolicsome and gay,
Was soothed at festivals with cups by day,
Change spread to scenic measures: breadth, and ease,
And freedom unrestrained were found in these:
For what (said men) should jovial rustic, placed
At random 'mid his betters, know of taste?   280
    So graceful dance went hand in hand with song,
And robes of kingly splendour trailed along:
So by the side of music words upgrew,
And eloquence came rolling, prompt and new:
Shrewd in things mundane, wise in things divine,
Its voice was like the voice of Delphi's shrine.
    The aspiring bard who served the tragic muse,   *[Satyr plays]*
A paltry goat the summit of his views,
Soon brought in Satyrs from the woods, and tried
If grave and gay could flourish side by side,   290
That the spectator, feasted to his fill,
Noisy and drunk, might ne'ertheless sit still.
    Yet, though loud laugh and frolic jest commend
Your Satyr folk, and mirth and morals blend,
Let not your heroes doff their robes of red
To talk low language in a homely shed,
Nor, in their fear of crawling, mount too high,
Catching at clouds and aiming at the sky.
The Muse, when bidden to be gay,
Like matron dancing on a festal day,   300
Deals not in idle banter, nor consorts
Without reserve with Satyrs and their sports.
    In plays like these I would not deal alone
In words and phrases trite and too well known,

Nor, stooping from the tragic height, drop down
To the low level of buffoon and clown,
As though pert Davus, or the saucy jade
Who sacks the gold and jeers the gull she made,
Were like Silenus, who, though quaint and odd,
Is yet the guide and tutor of a god.   310
A hackneyed subject I would take and treat
So deftly, all should hope to do the feat,
Then, having strained and struggled, should concede
To do the feat were difficult indeed.
So much may order and arrangement do
To make the cheap seem choice, the threadbare new.
   Your rustic Fauns, methinks, should have a care
Lest people deem them bred in city air;
Should shun the cant of exquisites, and shun
Coarse ribaldry no less and blackguard fun.   320
For those who have a father or a horse
Or an estate will take offence of course,
Nor think they're bound in duty to admire
What gratifies the pea and chestnut buyer.
   The Iambic foot is briefly thus defined: [*Versification*]
Two syllables, a short with long behind:
Repeat it six times o'er, so quick its beat,
'Tis trimeter, three measures for six feet:
At first it ran straight on; but, years ago,
Its hearers begged that it would move more slow;   330
On which it took, with a good-natured air,
Stout spondees in, its native rights to share,
Yet so that none should ask it to resign
The sixth, fourth, second places in the line.
But search through Accius' trimeters, or those
Which Ennius took such pleasure to compose,
You'll rarely find it: on the boards they groan,
Laden with spondees, like a cart with stone,
And brand our tragedy with want of skill
Or want of labour, call it which you will.   340

What then? false rhythm few judges can detect,
And Roman bards of course are all correct.
    What shall a poet do? make rules his sport,
And dash through thick and thin, through long and short?
Or pick his steps, endeavour to walk clean,
And fancy every mud-stain will be seen?
What good were that, if though I mind my ways
And shun all blame, I do not merit praise?
My friends, make Greece your model when you write,
And turn her volumes over day and night.   350
    "But Plautus pleased our sires, the good old folks;
They praised his numbers, and they praised his jokes."
They did: 'twas mighty tolerant in them
To praise where wisdom would perhaps condemn;
That is, if you and I and our compeers
Can trust our tastes, our fingers, and our ears,
Know polished wit from horse-play, and can tell
What verses do, and what do not, run well.
    Thespis began the drama: rumour says   *[Origin of tragedy]*
In travelling carts he carried round his plays,   360
Where actors, smeared with lees, before the throng
Performed their parts with gesture and with song.
Then Aechylus brought in the mask and pall,
Put buskins on his men to make them tall,
Turned boards into a platform, not too great,
And taught high monologue and grand debate.
The Old Comedy had next its turn,   *[Suppression of comedy]*
Nor small the glory it contrived to earn:
But freedom passed into unbridled spite,
And law was soon invoked to set things right: 370
Law spoke: the chorus lost the power to sting,
And (shame to say) thenceforth refused to sing.
    Our poets have tried all things; nor do they   *[Roman drama]*
Deserve least praise, who follow their own way,
And tell in comedy or history-piece
Some story of home growth, not drawn from Greece.

Nor would the land we love be now more strong
In warrior's prowess than in poet's song,
Did not her bards with one consent decline
The tedious task, to alter and refine.   380
Dear Pisos! as you prize old Numa's blood,
Set down that work, and that alone, as good,
Which, blurred and blotted, checked and counter-checked,
Has stood all tests, and issued forth correct.

    Because Democritus thinks fit to say,
That wretched art to genius must give way,
Stands at the gate of Helicon, and guards
Its precinct against all but crazy bards,
Our poets keep long nails and untrimmed hair,
Much in solitude, shunning baths.   390
For things are come to this; the merest dunce,
So but he choose, may start up bard at once,
Whose head, too hot for hellebore to cool,
Was ne'er submitted to a barber's tool.
What ails me now, to dose myself each spring?
Else had I been a very swan to sing.
Well, never mind: mine be the whetstone's lot,
Which makes steel sharp, though cut itself will not.
Although no writer, I may yet impart
To writing folk the precepts of their art,   400
Whence come its stores, what trains and forms a bard,
And how a work is made, and how 'tis marred.

    Of writing well, be sure, the secret lies   [*Source of good*
In wisdom: therefore study to be wise.   *writing*]
The page of Plato may suggest the thought,
Which found, the words will come as soon as sought.
The man who once has learned to comprehend
His duty to his country and his friend,
The love that parent, brother, guest may claim,
The judge's, senator's, or general's aim,   410
That man, when need occurs, will soon invent
For every part its proper sentiment.

Look too to life and manners, as they lie
Before you: these will living words supply.
A play, devoid of beauty, strength, and art,
So but the thoughts and morals suit each part,
Will catch men's minds and rivet them when caught
More than the clink of verses without thought.

    To Greece, fair Greece, ambitious but of praise,
The Muse gave ready wit, and rounded phrase.   420
Our Roman youth, by puzzling days and nights,
Bring down a shilling to a hundred mites.
Come, young Albinus, tell us, if you take
A penny from a sixpence, what 'twill make.
Fivepence. Good boy! you'll come to wealth one day.
Now add a penny. Sevenpence, he will say.
O, when this cankering rust, this greed of gain,
Has touched the soul and wrought into its grain,
What hope that poets will produce such lines
As cedar-oil embalms and cypress shrines?   430

    A bard will wish to teach or to please,   *[The poet's aim]*
Or, as a *tertium quid,* do both of these.
Whene'er you lecture, be concise: the soul
Takes in short maxims, and retains them whole:
But pour in water when the vessel's filled,
It simply dribbles over and is spilled.

    Keep near to truth in a fictitious piece,
Nor treat belief as matter of caprice.
If on a child you make a vampire sup,
It must not be alive when she's ripped up.   440
Our elders see an uninstructive strain;
Young lordlings treat grave verse with tall disdain:
But he who, mixing grave and gay, can teach
And yet give pleasure, gains a vote from each:
His works enrich the vendor, cross the sea,
And hand the author down to late posterity.

    Some faults may claim forgiveness: for the lyre
Not always gives the note that we desire;   *[Forgivable faults]*

We ask a flat; a sharp is its reply;
And the best bow will sometimes shoot awry.   450
But when I meet with beauties thickly sown,
A blot or two I readily condone,
Such as may trickle from a careless pen,
Or pass unwatched: for authors are but men.
What then? the copyist who keeps stumbling still
At the same word had best lay down his quill
The harp-player, who forever wounds the ear
With the same discord, makes the audience jeer:
So the poor dolt who's often in the wrong
I rank with Choerilus, the dunce of song,   460
Who, should he ever "deviate into sense,"
Moves but fresh laughter at his own expense:
While e'en good Homer may deserve a tap,
If, as he does, he drop his head and nap.
Yet, when a work is long, 'twere somewhat hard
To blame a drowsy moment in a bard.

Some poems, like some paintings, take the eye
Best at a distance, some when looked at nigh.
One loves the shade; one would be seen in light,
And boldly challenges the keenest sight: 470
One pleases straightway; one, when it has passed
Ten times before the mind, will please at last.

Hope of the Pisos! trained by such a sire,
And wise yourself, small schooling you require;
Yet take this lesson home; some things admit
A moderate point of merit, e'en in wit.
There's yonder counsellor; he cannot reach
Messala's stately altitudes of speech,
He cannot plumb Cascellius' depth of lore,
Yet he's employed, and makes a decent score: 480
But gods, and men, and booksellers agree
To place their ban on middling poetry.
At a great feast an ill-toned instrument,
A sour conserve, or an unfragrant scent

Offends the taste: 'tis reason that it should;
We do without such things, or have them good:
Just so with verse; you seek but to delight;
If by an inch you fail, you fail outright.

   He who knows nought of games abstains from all,
Nor tries his hand at quoit, or hoop, or ball,   490
Lest the thronged circle, witnessing the play,
Should laugh outright, with none to say them nay:
He who knows nought of verses needs must try
To write them ne'ertheless. "Why not?" men cry:
"Free, gently born, unblemished and correct,
His means a knight's, what more can folks expect?"
But you, my friend, at least have sense and grace;
You will not fly in queen Minerva's face
In action or in word. Suppose some day
You should take courage and compose a lay,   500
Entrust it first to Maecius' critical ears,
Your sire's and mine, and keep it back nine years.
What's kept at home you cancel by a stroke:
What's sent abroad you never can revoke.

   Orpheus, the priest and harper, pure and good, *[Power of poetry]*
Weaned savage tribes from deeds and feasts of blood,
Whence he was said to tame the monsters of the wood.
Amphion too, men said, at his desire
Moved massy stones, obedient to the lyre,
And Thebes arose. 'Twas wisdom's province then   510
To judge 'twixt states and subjects, gods and men,
Check vagrant lust, give rules to wedded folk,
Build cities up, engrave a code in oak.
So came great honour and abundant praise,
As to the gods, to poets and their lays.
Then Homer and Tyrtaeus, armed with song,
Made manly spirits for the combat strong:
Verse taught life's duties, showed the future clear,
And won a monarch's favour through his ear:
Verse gave relief from labour, and supplied   520

Light mirth for holiday and festal tide.
Then blush not for the lyre: Apollo sings
In unison with her who sweeps its strings.
    But here occurs a question some men start,
If good verse comes from nature or from art.
For me, I cannot see how native wit   [*Native ability vs. craft*]
Can e'er dispense with art, or art with it.
Set them to pull together, they're agreed,
And each supplies what each is found to need.
    The youth who runs for prizes wisely trains,   530
Bears cold and heat, is patient and abstains:
The flute-player at a festival, before
He plays in public, has to learn his lore.
Not so our bardlings: they come bouncing in—
"I'm your true poet: let them laugh that win:
Plague take the last! although I ne'er was taught,
Is that a cause for owning I know nought?"
    As puffing auctioneers collect a throng,   [*False flattery*]
Rich poets bribe false friends to hear their song:
Who can resist the lord of so much rent,   540
Of so much money at so much per cent.?
He may give a grand regale,
Act as a poor man's counsel or his bail,
Blest though he be, his wealth will cloud his view,
Nor suffer him to know false friends from true.
Don't ask a man whose feelings overflow
For kindness that you've shown or mean to show
To listen to your verse: each line you read,
He'll cry, "Good! bravo! exquisite indeed!"
He'll change his colour, let his eyes run o'er   550
With tears of joy, dance, beat upon the floor.
Hired mourners at a funeral say and do
A little more than they whose grief is true:
'Tis just so here: false flattery displays
More show of sympathy than honest praise.
'Tis said when kings a would-be friend will try,

With wine they rack him and with bumpers ply:
If you write poems, look beyond the skin
Of the smooth fox, and search the heart within.

    Read verses to Quintilius, he would say,   *[Acceptance of*
"I don't like this and that: improve it, pray":   *criticism]*
Tell him you found it hopeless to correct;
You'd tried it twice or thrice without effect
He'd calmly bid you make the three times four,
And take the unlicked cub in hand once more.
But if you chose to vindicate the crime,
Not mend it, he would waste no further time,
But let you live, untroubled by advice,
Sole tenant of your own fool's paradise.

    A wise and faithful counsellor will blame   570
Weak verses, note the rough, condemn the lame,
Retrench luxuriance, make obscureness plain,
Cross-question this, bid that be writ again:
A second Aristarch, he will not ask,
"Why for such trifles take my friend to task?"
Such trifles bring to serious grief ere long
A hapless bard, once flattered and led wrong.

    See the mad poet! another, though sick   *[The mad poet]*
Of itch or jaundice, moon-struck, fanatic,
Was never half so dangerous: men whose mind is sound   580
Avoid him; fools pursue him, children hound.
Suppose, while spluttering verses, head on high,
Like fowler watching blackbirds in the sky,
He falls into a pit; though loud he shout
"Help, neighbours, help!" let no man pull him out:
Should some one seem disposed a rope to fling,
I will strike in with, "Pray do no such thing:
I'll warrant you he meant it," and relate
His brother bard Empedocles's fate,
Who, wishing to be thought a god, poor fool,   590
Leapt down hot Aetna's crater, calm and cool.
"Leave poets free to perish as they will:

Save them by violence, you as good as kill.
'Tis not his first attempt: if saved to-day,
He's sure to die in some outrageous way.
Beside, none knows the reason why this curse
Was sent on him, this love of making verse,
By what offence heaven's anger he incurred,
A grave defiled, a sacred boundary stirred:
So much is plain, he's mad: like bear that beats   600
His prison down and ranges through the streets,
This terrible reciter puts to flight
The learned and unlearned left and right:
Let him catch one, he reads to him till he kills,
As leeches stick till they have sucked their fills."

Longinus

ON THE SUBLIME

Probably dating from the first century A.D., *On the Sublime* is not mentioned in any extant classical or medieval work. It was first published in Basle in 1554; in English in 1652.

The monologue, of which approximately one-third is missing, is a rebuttal to a work on a similar subject by the Sicilian rhetorician and Sophist Caecilius, who lived in Rome. While lacking the dramatic interest of the Platonic dialogue, it has the charm and ease of brilliant conversation, itself a demonstration of the art of achieving the sublime.

The translator is H. L. Havell.

I

[The force of the sublime]

T H E treatise of Caecilius on the Sublime, when, as you remember, my dear Terentian, we examined it together, seemed to us to be beneath the dignity of the whole subject, to fail entirely in seizing the salient points, and to offer little profit (which should be the principal aim of every writer) for the trouble of its perusal. There are two things essential to a technical treatise: the first is to define the subject; the second (I mean second in order, as it is by much the first in importance) to point out how and by what methods we may become masters of it ourselves. And yet Caecilius, while wasting his efforts in a thousand illustrations of the nature of the Sublime, as though here we were quite in the dark, somehow passes by as immaterial the question how we might be able to exalt our own genius to a certain degree of progress in sublimity. However, perhaps it would be fairer to commend this writer's intelligence and zeal in themselves, instead of blaming him for his omissions. And since you have bidden me also to put together, if only for your entertainment, a few notes on the subject of the Sublime, let me see if there is anything in my speculations which promises advantage to men of affairs. In you, dear friend—such is my confidence in your abilities, and such the part which becomes you—I look for a sympathising and discerning critic of the several parts of my treatise. For that was a just remark of his who pronounced that the points in which we resemble the divine nature are benevolence and love of truth.

As I am addressing a person so accomplished in literature, I need only state, without enlarging further on the matter, that the Sublime, wherever it occurs, consists in a certain loftiness and excellence of language, and that it is by this, and this only, that the greatest poets and prose-writers have gained eminence, and won themselves a lasting place in the Temple of Fame. A lofty passage does not convince the reason of the reader, but takes him out of himself. That which is admirable ever confounds our judgment, and eclipses that which is merely reasonable or agreeable. To believe or not is usually in our own power; but the Sublime, acting with an imperious and irresistible force, sways every reader whether he will or no. Skill in invention, lucid arrangement and disposition of facts, are appreciated not by one passage, or by two, but gradually manifest themselves in the general structure of a work; but a sublime thought, if happily timed, illumines an entire subject with the vividness of a lightning-flash, and exhibits the whole power of the orator in a moment of time. Your own experience, I am sure, my dearest Terentian, would enable you to illustrate these and similar points of doctrine.

II
[*The art of achieving the sublime*]

The first question which presents itself for solution is whether there is any art which can teach sublimity or loftiness in writing. For some hold generally that there is mere delusion in attempting to reduce such subjects to technical rules. "The Sublime," they tell us, "is born in a man, and not to be acquired by instruction; genius is the only master who can teach it. The vigorous products of nature" (such is their view) "are weakened and in every respect debased, when robbed of their flesh and blood by frigid technicalities." But I maintain that the truth can be shown to stand otherwise in this matter. Let us look at the case in this way; Nature in her loftier and more passionate moods, while detesting all appearance of restraint, is not wont to show herself utterly wayward and reckless; and though in all cases the vital informing principle is derived from her, yet to determine the right degree and the right moment, and to contribute the precision of practice and experience, is the peculiar province of scientific method. The great passions, when left to their own blind and rash impulses without the control of reason, are in the same danger as a ship let drive at random without ballast. Often they need the spur, but sometimes also the curb. The remark of Demosthenes with regard to human life in general,—that the greatest of all blessings is to be fortunate, but next to that and equal in importance is to be well advised,—for good fortune is utterly ruined by the absence of good counsel,— may be applied to literature, if we substitute genius for fortune, and art for counsel. Then, again (and this is the most important point of all), a writer can only learn from art when he is to abandon himself to the direction of his genius.

These are the considerations which I submit to the unfavourable critic of such useful studies. Perhaps they may induce him to alter his opinion as to the vanity and idleness of our present investigations. [A gap in the manuscript accounts for the abruptness of the next section.]

III

[Bombast, pedantry, and false sentiment]

. . . And let them check the stove's long tongues of fire:
For if I see one tenant of the hearth,
I'll thrust within one curling torrent flame,
And bring that roof in ashes to the ground:
But now not yet is sung my noble lay.

Such phrases cease to be tragic, and become burlesque,—I mean phrases like "curling torrent flames" and "vomiting to heaven," and representing Boreas as a piper, and so on. Such expressions, and such images, produce an effect of confusion and obscurity, not of energy; and if each separately be examined under the light of criticism, what seemed terrible gradually sinks into absurdity. Since then, even in tragedy, where the natural dignity of the subject makes a swelling diction allowable, we cannot pardon a tasteless grandiloquence, how much more incongruous must it seem in sober prose! Hence we laugh at those fine words of Gorgias of Leontini, such as "Xerxes the Persian Zeus" and "vultures, those living tombs," and at certain conceits of Callisthenes which are high-flown rather than sublime, and at some in Cleitarchus more ludicrous still—a writer whose frothy style tempts us to travesty Sophocles and say, "He blows a little pipe, and blows it ill." The same faults may be observed in Amphicrates and Hegesias and Matris, who in their frequent moments (as they think) of inspiration, instead of playing the genius are simply playing the fool.

Speaking generally, it would seem that bombast is one of the hardest things to avoid in writing. For all those writers who are ambitious of a lofty style, through dread of being convicted of feebleness and poverty of language, slide by a natural gradation into the opposite extreme. "Who fails in great endeavour, nobly fails," is their creed. Now bulk, when hollow and affected, is always objectionable, whether in material bodies or in writings, and in danger of producing on us an impression of littleness: "Nothing," it is said, "is drier than a man with the dropsy."

The characteristic, then, of bombast is that it transcends the Sublime: but there is another fault diametrically opposed to grandeur: this is called puerility, and it is the failing of feeble and narrow minds,—indeed, the most ignoble of all vices in writing. By puerility we mean a pedantic habit of mind, which by over-elaboration ends in frigidity. Slips of this sort are made by those who, aiming at brilliancy, polish, and especially attractiveness, are landed in paltriness and silly affectation. Closely associated with this is a third sort of vice, in dealing with the passions, which

Theodorus used to call false sentiment, meaning by that an ill-timed and empty display of emotion, where no emotion is called for, or of greater emotion than the situation warrants. Thus we often see an author hurried by the tumult of his mind into tedious displays of mere personal feeling which has no connection with the subject. Yet how justly ridiculous must an author appear, whose most violent transports leave his readers quite cold! However, I will dismiss this subject, as I intend to devote a separate work to the treatment of the passions in writing.

IV
[Frigidity]

The last of the faults which I mentioned is frequently observed in Timaeus—I mean the fault of frigidity. In other respects he is an able writer, and sometimes not unsuccessful in the loftier style; a man of wide knowledge, and full of ingenuity; a most bitter critic of the failings of others—but unhappily blind to his own. In his eagerness to be always striking out new thoughts he frequently falls into the most childish absurdities. I will only instance one or two passages, as most of them have been pointed out by Caecilius. Wishing to say something very fine about Alexander the Great he speaks of him as a man "who annexed the whole of Asia in fewer years than Isocrates spent in writing his panegyric oration in which he urges the Greeks to make war on Persia." How strange is the comparison of the "great Emathian conqueror" with an Athenian rhetorician! By this mode of reasoning it is plain that the Spartans were very inferior to Isocrates in courage, since it took them thirty years to conquer Messene, while he finished the composition of this harangue in ten. Observe, too, his language on the Athenians taken in Sicily. "They paid the penalty for their impious outrage on Hermes in mutilating his statues; and the chief agent in their destruction was one who was descended on his father's side from the injured deity—Hermocrates, son of Hermon." I wonder, my dearest Terentian, how he omitted to say of the tyrant Dionysius that for his impiety towards Zeus and Herakles he was deprived of his power by Dion and Herakleides. Yet why speak of Timaeus, when even men like Xenophon and Plato— the very demi-gods of literature—though they had sat at the feet of Socrates, sometimes forgot themselves in the pursuit of such paltry conceits. The former, in his account of the Spartan Polity, has these words: "Their voice you would no more hear than if they were of marble, their gaze is as immovable as if they were cast in bronze; you would deem them more modest than the very maidens in their eyes." To speak of the pupils of the eye as "modest maidens" was a piece of absurdity becoming Amphi-crates rather than Xenophon. And then what a strange delusion to suppose that modesty is always without exception expressed in the eye! whereas it is commonly said that there is nothing by which an impudent fellow betrays his character so much as by the expression of his eyes. Thus Achilles addresses Agamemnon in the *Iliad* as "drunkard, with eye of dog." Timaeus, however, with that want of judgment which characterises plagiarists, could not leave to Xeno-phon the possession of even this piece of frigidity. In relating how Agathocles carried off his cousin, who was wedded to another man, from the festival of the unveiling, he asks, "Who could have done such a deed, unless he had harlots instead of maidens in his eyes?" And Plato himself, elsewhere so supreme a master of style, meaning to describe certain recording tablets, says, "They shall write, and deposit in the temples memorials of cypress wood"; and again, "Then concerning walls, Megillus, I give my vote with Sparta that we should let them lie asleep within the ground, and not awaken them." And Herodotus falls pretty much under the same censure, when he speaks of beautiful women as "tor-tures to the eye," though here there is some excuse, as the speakers in this passage are drunken barbarians. Still, even from dramatic motives, such errors in taste should not be permitted to deface the pages of an immortal work.

V
[*Novelty*]

Now all these glaring improprieties of language may be traced to one common root—the pursuit of novelty in thought. It is this that has turned the brain of nearly all the learned world of to-day. Human blessings and human ills commonly flow from the same source: and, to apply this principle to literature, those ornaments of style, those sublime and delightful images, which contribute to success, are the foundation and the origin, not only of excellence, but also of failure. It is thus with the figures called transitions, and hyperboles, and the use of plurals for singulars. I shall show presently the dangers which they seem to involve. Our next task, therefore, must be to propose and to settle the question how we may avoid the faults of style related to sublimity.

VI
[*Judging style*]

Our best hope of doing this will be first of all to grasp some definite theory and criterion of the true Sublime. Nevertheless this is a hard matter; for a just judgment of style is the final fruit of long experience; still, I believe that the way I shall indicate will enable us to distinguish between the true and false Sublime, so far as it can be done by rule.

VII
[*True and false sublime*]

It is proper to observe that in human life nothing is truly great which is despised by all elevated minds. For example, no man of sense can regard wealth, honour, glory, and power, or any of those things which are surrounded by a great external parade of pomp and circumstance, as the highest blessings, seeing that merely to despise such things is a blessing of no common order: certainly those who possess them are admired much less than those who, having the opportunity to acquire them, through greatness of soul neglect it. Now let us apply this principle to the Sublime in poetry or in prose; let us ask in all cases, is it merely a specious sublimity? is this gorgeous exterior a mere false and clumsy pageant, which if laid open will be found to conceal nothing but emptiness? for if so, a noble mind will scorn instead of admire it. It is natural to us to feel our souls lifted up by the true Sublime and conceive a sort of generous exultation to be filled with joy and pride, as though we had ourselves originated the ideas which we read. If then any work, on being repeatedly submitted to the judgment of an acute and cultivated critic, fails to dispose his mind to lofty ideas; if the thoughts which it suggests do not extend beyond what is actually expressed; and if, the longer you read it, the less you think of it,—there can be here no true sublimity, when the effect is not sustained beyond the mere act of perusal. But when a passage is pregnant in suggestion, when it is hard, nay impossible, to distract the attention from it, and when it takes a strong and lasting hold on the memory, then we may be sure that we have lighted on the true Sublime. In general we may regard those words as truly noble and sublime which always please and please all readers. For when the same book always produces the same impression on all who read it, whatever be the difference in their pursuits, their manner of life, their aspirations, their ages, or their language, such a harmony of opposites gives irresistible authority to their favourable verdict.

VIII
[*Sources of the sublime*]

I shall now proceed to enumerate the five principal sources, as we may call them, from which almost all sublimity is derived, assuming, of course, the preliminary gift on which all these five sources depend, namely, command of language. The first and the most important is grandeur of thought, as I have pointed out elsewhere in my work on Xenophon. The second is a vigorous and spirited treatment of the passions. These two conditions of sublimity depend mainly on natural endowments, whereas those which follow derive assistance from Art. The third is a certain artifice in the employment of figures, which are of two kinds, figures of thought and figures of speech. The fourth is dignified expression, which is subdivided into (a) the proper choice of words, and (b) the use of metaphors and other ornaments of diction. The fifth cause of sublimity, which embraces all those preceding, is majesty and elevation of structure. Let us consider what is involved in each of these five forms separately.

I must first, however, remark that some of these five divisions are omitted by Caecilius; for instance, he says nothing about the passions. Now if he made this omission from a belief that the Sublime and the passions are one and the same thing, holding them to be always coexistent and interdependent, he is in error. Some passions are found which, so far from being lofty, are actually low, such as pity, grief, fear; and conversely, sublimity is often not in the least affecting, as we may see (among innumerable other instances) in those bold expressions of our great poet on the sons of Aloëus—

> Highly they raged
> To pile huge Ossa on the Olympian peak,
> And Pelion with all his waving trees
> On Ossa's crest to raise, and climb the sky;

and the yet more tremendous climax—

> And now had they accomplished it.

And in orators, in all passages dealing with panegyric, and in all the more imposing and declamatory places, dignity and sublimity play an indispensable part; but passion is mostly absent. Hence the most emotional orators have usually but little skill in panegyric, and conversely those who are powerful in panegyric generally lack passion. If, on the other hand, Caecilius supposed that passion never contributes to sublimity, and this is why he thought it alien to the subject, he is entirely deceived. For I would confidently pronounce that nothing is so conducive to sublimity as an appropriate display of genuine passion, which bursts out with a kind of "fine madness" and divine inspiration, and falls on our ears like the voice of a god.

IX
[*Loftiness of mind*]

I have already said that of all these five conditions of the Sublime the most important is the first, that is, a certain lofty cast of mind. Therefore, although this is a faculty rather natural than acquired, nevertheless it will be well for us in this instance also to train our souls to sublimity, and make them as it were ever big with noble thoughts. How, it may be asked, is this to be done? I have hinted elsewhere in my writings that sublimity is, so to say, the image of greatness of soul. Hence a thought in its naked simplicity, even though unuttered, is sometimes admirable by the sheer force of its sublimity; for instance, the silence of Ajax in the *Odyssey* is great, and grander than anything he could have said. It is absolutely essential, then, first of all to settle the question whence this grandeur of conception arises; and the answer is that true eloquence can be found only in those whose spirit is generous and aspiring. For those whose whole lives are wasted in paltry and ignoble thoughts and habits cannot possibly produce any work worthy of the lasting reverence of mankind. It is only natural that their words should be full of sublimity whose thoughts are full of majesty. Hence sublime thoughts belong properly to the loftiest minds. . . . And thus the lawgiver of the Jews, no ordinary man, having formed an adequate conception of the Supreme Being, gave it adequate expression in the opening words of his "Laws": "God said"—what?—"let there be light, and there was light: let there be land, and there was."

I trust you will not think me tedious if I quote yet one more passage from our great poet Homer (referring this time to human characters) in illustration of the manner in which he leads us with him to heroic heights. A sudden and baffling darkness as of night has overspread the ranks of his warring Greeks. Then Ajax in sore perplexity cries aloud—

> Almighty Zeus,
> Only from darkness save Achaia's sons;
> No more I ask, but give us back the day;
> Grant but our sight, and slay us, if thou wilt.

The feelings are just what we should look for in Ajax. He does not, you observe, ask for his life—such a request would have been unworthy of his heroic soul—but finding himself paralysed by darkness, and prohibited from employing his valour in any noble action, he chafes because his arms are idle, and prays for a speedy return of light. "At least," he thinks; "I shall find a warrior's grave, even though Zeus himself should fight against me." In such passages the mind of the poet is swept along in the whirlwind of the struggle, and, in his own words, he

> Like the fierce war-god, raves, or wasting fire
> Through the deep thickets on a mountain-side;
> His lips drop foam.

But there is another and a very interesting aspect of Homer's mind. When we turn to the *Odyssey* we find occasion to observe that a great poetical genius in the decline of power which comes with old age naturally leans towards the fabulous. For it is evident that this work was composed after the *Iliad,* in proof of which we may mention, among many other indications, the introduction in the *Odyssey* of the sequel to the story of his heroes' adventures at Troy, as so many additional episodes in the Trojan war, and especially the tribute of sorrow and mourning which is paid in that poem to departed heroes, as if in fulfilment of some previous design. The *Odyssey* is, in fact, a sort of epilogue to the *Iliad*—

> There warrior Ajax lies, Achilles there,
> And there Patroclus, godlike counsellor;
> There lies my own dear son.

And for the same reason, I imagine, whereas in the *Iliad,* which was written when his genius was in its prime, the whole structure of the poem is founded on action and struggle, in the *Odyssey* he generally prefers the narrative style, which is proper to old age. Hence Homer in his *Odyssey* may be compared to the setting sun: he is still as great as ever, but he has lost his fervent heat. The strain is now pitched to a lower key than in the "Tale of Troy divine": we begin to miss that high and equable sublimity which never flags or sinks, that continuous current of moving incidents, those rapid transitions, that force of eloquence, that opulence of imagery which is ever true to Nature. Like the sea when it retires upon itself and leaves its shores waste and bare, henceforth the tide of sublimity begins to ebb, and draws us away into the dim region of myth and legend. In saying this I am not forgetting the fine storm-pieces in the *Odyssey,* the story of the Cyclops, and other striking passages. It is Homer grown old I am discussing, but still it is Homer. Yet in every one of these passages the mythical predominates over the real.

My purpose in making this digression was, as I said, to point out into what trifles the second childhood of genius is too apt to be betrayed; such, I mean, as the bag in which the winds are confined, the tale of Odysseus's comrades being changed by Circe into swine ("whimpering porkers" Zoïlus called them), and how Zeus was fed like a nestling by the doves, and how Odysseus passed ten nights on the shipwreck without food, and the improbable incidents in the slaying of the suitors. When Homer nods like this, we must be content to say that he dreams as Zeus might dream. Another reason for these remarks on the *Odyssey* is that I wished to make you understand that great poets and prose-writers, after they have lost their power of depicting the passions, turn naturally to the delineation of character. Such, for instance, is the lifelike and characteristic picture of the palace of Odysseus, which may be called a comedy of manners.

X
[Selection and arrangement]

Let us now consider whether there is anything further which contributes to the Sublime in writing. It is a law of Nature that in all things there are certain constituent parts, coexistent with their substance. It necessarily follows, therefore, that one cause of sublimity is the choice of the most striking circumstances involved in whatever we are describing, and, further, the power of afterwards combining them into one animate whole. The reader is attracted partly by the selection of the incidents, partly by the skill which has welded them together. For instance, Sappho, in dealing with the passionate manifestations attending on the frenzy of lovers, always chooses her strokes from the signs which she has observed to be actually exhibited in such cases. But her peculiar excellence lies in the felicity with which she chooses and unites together the most striking and powerful features.

> I deem that man divinely blest
> Who sits, and, gazing on thy face,
> Hears thee discourse with eloquent lips,
>   And marks thy lovely smile.
> This, this it is that made my heart
> So wildly flutter in my breast;
> Whene'er I look on thee, my voice
>   Falters, and faints, and fails;
> My tongue's benumbed; a subtle fire
> Through all my body inly steals;
> Mine eyes in darkness reel and swim;
>   Strange murmurs drown my ears;
> With dewy damps my limbs are chilled;
> An icy shiver shakes my frame;
> Paler than ashes grows my cheek;
>   And Death seems nigh at hand.

Is it not wonderful how at the same moment soul, body, ears, tongue, eyes, colour, all fail her, and are lost to her as completely as if they were not her own? Observe too how her sensations contradict one another—she freezes, she burns, she raves, she reasons, and all at the same instant. And this description is designed to show that she is assailed, not by any particular emotion, but by a tumult of different emotions. All these tokens belong to the passion of love; but it is in the choice, as I said, of the most striking features, and in the combination of them into one picture, that the perfection of this Ode of Sappho's lies. . . . [Further examples are cited from Homer.]

XI
[*Amplification*]

Closely associated with the part of our subject we have just treated of is that excellence of writing which is called amplification, when a writer or pleader, whose theme admits of many successive starting-points and pauses, brings on one impressive point after another in a continuous and ascending scale. Now whether this is employed in the treatment of a commonplace, or in the way of exaggeration, whether to place arguments or facts in a strong light, or in the disposition of actions, or of passions—for amplification takes a hundred different shapes—in all cases the orator must be cautioned that none of these methods is complete without the aid of sublimity,—unless, indeed, it be our object to excite pity, or to depreciate an opponent's argument. In all other uses of amplification, if you subtract the element of sublimity you will take as it were the soul from the body. No sooner is the support of sublimity removed than the whole becomes lifeless, nerveless, and dull.

There is a difference, however, between the rules I am now giving and those just mentioned. Then I was speaking of the delineation and co-ordination of the principal circumstances. My next task, therefore, must be briefly to define this difference, and with it the general distinction between amplification and sublimity. Our whole discourse will thus gain in clearness.

XII

[Definition of amplification]

I must first remark that I am not satisfied with the definition of amplification generally given by authorities on rhetoric. They explain it to be a form of language which invests the subject with a certain grandeur. Yes, but this definition may be applied indifferently to sublimity, passion, and the use of figurative language, since all these invest the discourse with some sort of grandeur. The difference seems to me to lie in this, that sublimity gives elevation to a subject, while amplification gives extension as well. Thus the sublime is often conveyed in a single thought, but amplification can only subsist with a certain prolixity and diffusiveness. The most general definition of amplification would explain it to consist in the gathering together of all the constituent parts of topics of a subject, emphasising the argument by repeated insistence, herein differing from proof, that whereas the object of proof is logical demonstration, . . . [A portion of the manuscript is missing.]

Plato, like the sea, pours forth his riches in a copious and expansive flood. Hence the style of the orator, who is the greater master of our emotions, is often, as it were, red-hot and ablaze with passion, whereas Plato, whose strength lay in a sort of weighty and sober magnificence, though never frigid, does not rival the thunders of Demosthenes. And, if a Greek may be allowed to express an opinion on the subject of Latin literature, I think the same difference may be discerned in the grandeur of Cicero as compared with that of his Grecian rival. The sublimity of Demosthenes is generally sudden and abrupt: that of Cicero is equally diffused. Demosthenes is vehement, rapid, vigorous, terrible; he burns and sweeps away all before him; and hence we may liken him to a whirlwind or a thunderbolt: Cicero is like a widespread conflagration, which rolls over and feeds on all around it, whose fire is extensive and burns long, breaking out successively in different places, and finding its fuel now here, now there. Such points, however, I resign to your more competent judgment.

To resume, then, the high-strung sublimity of Demosthenes is appropriate to all cases where it is desired to exaggerate, or to rouse some vehement emotion, and generally when we want to carry away our audience with us. We must employ the diffusive style, on the other hand, when we wish to overpower them with a flood of language. It is suitable, for example, to familiar topics, and to perorations in most cases, and to digressions, and to all descriptive and declamatory passages, and in dealing with history or natural science, and in numerous other cases.

XIII

[*Imitation: a path to the sublime*]

To return, however, to Plato: how grand he can be with all that gentle and noiseless flow of eloquence you will be reminded by this characteristic passage, which you have read in his *Republic:* "They, therefore, who have no knowledge of wisdom and virtue, whose lives are passed in feasting and similar joys, are borne downwards, as is but natural, and in this region they wander all their lives; but they never lifted up their eyes nor were borne upwards to the true world above, nor ever tasted of pleasure abiding and unalloyed; but like beasts they ever look downwards, and their heads are bent to the ground, or rather to the table; they feed full their bellies and their lusts, and longing ever more and more for such things they kick and gore one another with horns and hoofs of iron, and slay one another in their insatiable desires."

We may learn from this author, if we would but observe his example, that there is yet another path besides those mentioned which leads to sublime heights. What path do I mean? The emulous imitation of the great poets and prose-writers of the past. On this mark, dear friend, let us keep our eyes ever steadfastly fixed. Many gather the divine impulse from another's spirit, just as we are told that the Pythian priestess, when she takes her seat on the tripod, where there is said to be a rent in the ground breathing upwards a heavenly emanation, straightway conceives

from that source the godlike gift of prophecy, and utters her inspired oracles; so likewise from the mighty genius of the great
writers of antiquity there is carried into the souls of their rivals, as
from a fount of inspiration, an effluence which breathes upon them
until, even though their natural temper be but cold, they share
the sublime enthusiasm of others. Thus Homer's name is associated with a numerous band of illustrious disciples—not only
Herodotus, but Stesichorus before him, and the great Archilochus,
and above all Plato, who from the great fountain-head of Homer's
genius drew into himself innumerable tributary streams. Perhaps it
would have been necessary to illustrate this point, had not Am-
monius and his school already classified and noted down the various examples. Now what I am speaking of is not plagiarism, but
resembles the process of copying from fair forms or statues or
works of skilled labour. Nor in my opinion would so many fair
flowers of imagery have bloomed among the philosophical dogmas of Plato, nor would he have risen so often to the language
and topics of poetry, had he not engaged heart and soul in a contest for precedence with Homer, like a young champion entering
the lists against a veteran. It may be that he showed too ambitious
a spirit in venturing on such a duel; but nevertheless it was not
without advantage to him: "for strife like this," as Hesiod says,
"is good for men." And where shall we find a more glorious arena
or a nobler crown than here, where even defeat at the hands of
our predecessors is not ignoble?

XIV
[Incentives to great achievement]

Therefore it is good for us also, when we are labouring on some
subject which demands a lofty and majestic style, to imagine to
ourselves how Homer might have expressed this or that, or how
Plato or Demosthenes would have clothed it with sublimity, or, in
history, Thucydides. For by our fixing an eye of rivalry on those
high examples they will become like beacons to guide us, and will
perhaps lift up our souls to the fulness of the stature we conceive.

And it would be still better should we try to realise this further thought, How would Homer, had he been here, or how would Demosthenes, have listened to what I have written, or how would they have been affected by it? For what higher incentive to exertion could a writer have than to imagine such judges or such an audience of his works, and to give an account of his writings with heroes like these to criticise and look on? Yet more inspiring would be the thought, With what feelings will future ages through all time read these my works? If this should awaken a fear in any writer that he will not be intelligible to his contemporaries it will necessarily follow that the conceptions of his mind will be crude, maimed, and abortive, and lacking that ripe perfection which alone can win the applause of ages to come.

XV
[*Images*]

The dignity, grandeur, and energy of a style largely depend on a proper employment of images, a term which I prefer to that usually given. The term *image* in its most general acceptation includes every thought, howsoever presented, which issues in speech. But the term is now generally confined to those cases when he who is speaking, by reason of the rapt and excited state of his feelings, imagines himself to see what he is talking about, and produces a similar illusion in his hearers. Poets and orators both employ images, but with a very different object, as you are well aware. The poetical image is designed to astound; the oratorical image to give vividness. Both, however, seek to work on the emotions.

> Mother, I pray thee, set not thou upon me
> Those maids with bloody face and serpent hair:
> See, see, they come, they're here, they spring upon me!

And again—

> Ah, ah, she'll slay me! whither shall I fly?

The poet when he wrote like this saw the Erinyes with his own eyes, and he almost compels his readers to see them too. Euripides found his chief delight in the labour of giving tragic expression to these two passions of madness and love, showing here a real mastery which I cannot think he exhibited elsewhere . . . [Further examples follow from Euripides, Aeschylus, Sophocles, and Demosthenes.]

XVI
[Figures of speech]

The subject which next claims our attention is that of figures of speech. I have already observed that figures, judiciously employed, play an important part in producing sublimity. It would be a tedious, or rather an endless task, to deal with every detail of this subject here; so in order to establish what I have laid down, I will just run over, without further preface, a few of those figures which are most effective in lending grandeur to language.

Demosthenes is defending his policy; his natural line of argument would have been: "You did not do wrong, men of Athens, to take upon yourselves the struggle for the liberties of Hellas. Of this you have home proofs. *They* did not wrong who fought at Marathon, at Salamis, and Plataea." Instead of this, in a sudden moment of supreme exaltation he bursts out like some inspired prophet with that famous appeal to the mighty dead: "Ye did not, could not have done wrong. I swear it by the men who faced the foe at Marathon!" He employs the figure of adjuration, to which I will here give the name of Apostrophe. And what does he gain by it? He exalts the Athenian ancestors to the rank of divinities, showing that we ought to invoke those who have fallen for their country as gods; he fills the hearts of his judges with the heroic pride of the old warriors of Hellas; forsaking the beaten path of argument he rises to the loftiest altitude of grandeur and passion, and commands assent by the startling novelty of his appeal; he applies the healing charm of eloquence, and thus "ministers to the mind diseased" of his countrymen, until lifted by his brave words above their misfortunes they begin to feel that the disaster of Chaeronea is no less glorious than the victories of Marathon and Salamis. All this he effects by the use of one figure, and so carries his hearers away with him. . . . Demosthenes has so skilfully managed the oath that in addressing his countrymen after the defeat of Chaeronea he takes out of their minds all sense of disaster; and at the same time, while proving that no mistake has been made, he holds up an example, confirms his arguments by an oath, and makes his praise of the dead an incentive to the living. . . .

XVII
[*Figures of speech and the Sublime*]

[This brief section, omitted here, discusses the use of the sublime "to allay the distrust which attaches to the use of figures."]

XVIII
[*Question and interrogation*]

The figures of question and interrogation also possess a specific quality which tends strongly to stir an audience and give energy to the speaker's words. "Or tell me, do you want to run about asking one another, is there any news? what greater news could you have than that a man of Macedon is making himself master of Hellas? Is Philip dead? Not he. However, he is ill. But what is that to you? Even if anything happens to him you will soon raise up another Philip. . . ." Now if this had been put baldly it would have lost greatly in force. As we see it, it is full of the quick alternation of question and answer. The orator replies to himself as though he were meeting another man's objections. And this figure not only raises the tone of his words but makes them more convincing. For an exhibition of feeling has then most effect on an audience when it appears to flow naturally from the occasion, not to have been laboured by the art of the speaker; and this device of questioning and replying to himself reproduces the moment of passion. For as a sudden question addressed to an individual will sometimes startle him into a reply which is an unguarded expression of his genuine sentiments, so the figure of question and interrogation blinds the judgment of an audience, and deceives them into a belief that what is really the result of labour in every detail has been struck out of the speaker by the inspiration of the moment. [A portion of the manuscript is missing here.]

XIX
[Omission of conjunctions]

. . . The removal of connecting particles gives a quick rush and "torrent rapture" to a passage, the writer appearing to be actually almost left behind by his own words. There is an example in Xenophon: "Clashing their shields together they pushed, they fought, they slew, they fell."

XX
[Combining figures of speech]

But nothing is so conducive to energy as a combination of different figures, when two or three uniting their resources mutually contribute to the vigour, the cogency, and the beauty of a speech. So Demosthenes in his speech against Meidias repeats the same words and breaks up his sentences in one lively descriptive passage: "He who receives a blow is hurt in many ways which he could not even describe to another, by gesture, by look, by tone." Then, to vary the movement of his speech, and prevent it from standing still (for stillness produces rest, but passion requires a certain disorder of language, imitating the agitation and commotion of the soul), he at once dashes off in another direction, breaking up his words again, and repeating them in a different form, "by gesture, by look, by tone—when insult, when hatred, is added to violence, when he is struck with the fist, when he is struck as a slave!" By such means the orator imitates the action of Meidias, dealing blow upon blow on the minds of his judges. Immediately after like a hurricane he makes a fresh attack: "When he is struck with the fist, when he is struck in the face; this is what moves, this is what maddens a man, unless he is inured to outrage; no one could describe all this so as to bring home to his hearers its bitterness." You see how he preserves, by continual variation, the intrinsic force of these repetitions and broken clauses, so that his order seems irregular, and conversely his irregularity acquires a certain measure of order.

XXI
[*Adding conjunctions*]

[Effectiveness in style, Longinus maintains, is reduced when connectives are unnecessarily added, for they "smooth away . . . rapidity and rugged abruptness of passion."]

XXII
[*Inversion*]

A hyperbaton belongs to the same class. By hyperbaton we mean a transposition of words or thoughts from their usual order, bearing unmistakably the characteristic stamp of violent mental agitation. In real life we often see a man under the influence of rage, or fear, or indignation, or beside himself with jealousy, or with some other out of the interminable list of human passions, begin a sentence, and then swerve aside into some inconsequent parenthesis, and then again double back to his original statement, being borne with quick turns by his distress, as though by a shifting wind, now this way, now that, and playing a thousand capricious variations on his words, his thoughts, and the natural order of his discourse. Now the figure hyperbaton is the means which is employed by the best writers to imitate these signs of natural emotion. For art is then perfect when it seems to be nature, and nature, again, is most effective when pervaded by the unseen presence of art. An illustration will be found in the speech of Dionysius of Phocaea in Herodotus: "A hair's breadth now decides our destiny, Ionians, whether we shall live as freemen or as slaves—ay, as runaway slaves. Now, therefore, if you choose to endure a little hardship, you will be able at the cost of some present exertion to overcome your enemies." The regular sequence here would have been: "Ionians, now is the time for you to endure a little hardship; for a hair's breadth will now decide our destiny." But the Phocaean transposes the title "Ionians," rushing at once to the subject of alarm, as though in the terror of the moment he had forgotten the usual address to his audience. Moreover, he inverts the logical order of his thoughts, and instead of beginning with the necessity for exertion, which is the point he wishes to urge upon them, he first gives them the reason for that necessity in the words, "a hair's breadth now decides our destiny," so that his words seem unpremeditated, and forced upon him by the crisis. . . . [Demosthenes is mentioned as one who uses inversion "unsparingly."]

XXIII
[Changes in figures of speech]

The juxtaposition of different cases, the enumeration of particulars, and the use of contrast and climax, all, as you know, add much vigour, and give beauty and great elevation and life to a style. The diction also gains greatly in diversity and movement by changes of case, time, person, number, and gender.

With regard to change of number: not only is the style improved by the use of those words which, though singular in form, are found on inspection to be plural in meaning, as in the lines—

A countless host dispersed along the sand
With joyous cries the shoal of tunny hailed,

but it is more worthy of observation that plurals for singulars sometimes fall with a more impressive dignity, rousing the imagination by the mere sense of vast number. Such is the effect of those words of Oedipus in Sophocles—

> Oh fatal, fatal ties!
> Ye gave us birth, and we being born ye sowed
> The self-same seed, and gave the world to view
> Sons, brothers, sires, domestic murder foul,
> Brides, mothers, wives. . . . Ay, ye laid bare
> The blackest, deepest place where Shame can dwell.

Here we have in either case but one person, first Oedipus, then Jocasta; but the expansion of number into the plural gives an impression of multiplied calamity. . . . [Further example from Plato]

XXIV
[*Plurals into singulars*]

On the other hand, the contraction of plurals into singulars sometimes creates an appearance of great dignity; as in that phrase of Demosthenes: "Thereupon all Peloponnesus was divided." There is another in Herodotus: "When Phrynichus brought a drama on the stage entitled *The Taking of Miletus,* the whole theatre fell a weeping"—instead of "all the spectators." This knitting together of a number of scattered particulars into one whole gives them an aspect of corporate life. And the beauty of both uses lies, I think, in their betokening emotion, by giving a sudden change of complexion to the circumstances—whether a word which is strictly singular is unexpectedly changed into a plural,—or whether a number of isolated units are combined by the use of a single sonorous word under one head.

XXV
[*Substitution of tenses*]

When past events are introduced as happening in present time the narrative form is changed into a dramatic action. Such is that description in Xenophon: "A man who has fallen and is being trampled under foot by Cyrus's horse, strikes the belly of the animal with his scimitar; the horse starts aside and unseats Cyrus, and he falls." Similarly in many passages of Thucydides.

XXVI

[Involving the reader]

Equally dramatic is the interchange of persons, often making a reader fancy himself to be moving in the midst of the perils described—

> Unwearied, thou wouldst deem, with toil unspent,
> They met in war; so furiously they fought.

and that line in Aratus—

> Beware that month to tempt the surging sea.

In the same way Herodotus: "Passing from the city of Elephantine you will sail upwards until you reach a level plain. You cross this region, and there entering another ship you will sail on for two days, and so reach a great city, whose name is Meroe." Observe how he takes us, as it were, by the hand, and leads us in spirit through these places, making us no longer readers, but spectators. Such a direct personal address always has the effect of placing the reader in the midst of the scene of action. And by pointing your words to the individual reader, instead of to the readers generally, as in the line

> Thou had'st not known for whom Tydides fought,

and thus exciting him by an appeal to himself, you will rouse interest, and fix attention, and make him a partaker in the action of the book.

XXVII
[*Change in person*]

Sometimes, again, a writer in the midst of a narrative in the third person suddenly steps aside and makes a transition to the first. It is a kind of figure which strikes like a sudden outburst of passion. Thus Hector in the *Iliad:*

> With mighty voice called to the men of Troy
> To storm the ships, and leave the bloody spoils:
> If any I behold with willing foot
> Shunning the ships, and lingering on the plain,
> That hour I will contrive his death.

The poet then takes upon himself the narrative part, as being his proper business; but this abrupt threat he attributes, without a word of warning, to the enraged Trojan chief. To have interposed any such words as "Hector said so and so" would have had a frigid effect. As the lines stand the writer is left behind by his own words, and the transition is effected while he is preparing for it. Accordingly the proper use of this figure is in dealing with some urgent crisis which will not allow the writer to linger, but compels him to make a rapid change from one person to another. So in Hecataeus: "Now Ceyx took this in dudgeon, and straightway bade the children of Heracles to depart. 'Behold, I can give you no help; lest, therefore, ye perish yourselves and bring hurt upon me also, get ye forth into some other land. . . .' " [Further examples discussed from Demosthenes and Homer]

XXVIII
[*Periphrasis*]

None, I suppose, would dispute the fact that periphrasis tends much to sublimity. For, as in music the simple air is rendered more pleasing by the addition of harmony, so in language periphrasis often sounds in concord with a literal expression, adding much to the beauty of its tone,—provided always that it is not inflated and harsh, but agreeably blended. . . . So Xenophon: "Labour you regard as the guide to a pleasant life, and you have laid up in your souls the fairest and most soldier-like of all gifts: in praise is your delight, more than in anything else." By saying, instead of "you are ready to labour," "you regard labour as the guide to a pleasant life," and by similarly expanding the rest of that passage, he gives to his eulogy a much wider and loftier range of sentiment.

XXIX
[Misuse of periphrasis by Plato]

[This brief section omitted here]

XXX
[Use of striking words]

But since the thoughts conveyed by words and the expression of those thoughts are for the most part interwoven with one another, we will now add some considerations which have hitherto been overlooked on the subject of expression. To say that the choice of appropriate and striking words has a marvellous power and an enthralling charm for the reader, that this is the main object of pursuit with all orators and writers, that it is this, and this alone, which causes the works of literature to exhibit the glowing perfections of the finest statues, their grandeur, their beauty, their mellowness, their dignity, their energy, their power, and all their other graces, and that it is this which endows the facts with a vocal soul; to say all this would, I fear, be, to the initiated, an impertinence. Indeed, we may say with strict truth that beautiful words are the very light of thought. I do not mean to say that imposing language is appropriate to every occasion. A trifling subject tricked out in grand and stately words would have the same effect as a huge tragic mask placed on the head of a little child. Only in poetry and . . . [Part of the manuscript is missing here.]

XXXI
[*Ordinary words*]

. . . The most homely language is sometimes far more vivid than
the most ornamental, being recognised at once as the language of
common life, and gaining immediate currency by its familiarity
. . . [Examples of such usage are drawn from Theopompus and
Herodotus.]

XXXII
[*Metaphors*]

Concerning the number of metaphors to be employed together
Caecilius seems to give his vote with those critics who make a law
that not more than two, or at the utmost three, should be combined in the same place. The use, however, must be determined by
the occasion. . . . In the treatment of familiar topics and in descriptive passages, nothing gives such distinctness as a close and
continuous series of metaphors. It is by this means that Xenophon
has so finely delineated the anatomy of the human frame. And there
is a still more brilliant and life-like picture in Plato. The human
head he calls a *citadel;* the neck is an *isthmus* set to divide it from
the chest; to support it beneath are the vertebrae, turning like
hinges; pleasure he describes as a *bait* to tempt men to ill; the
tongue is the *arbiter of tastes*. The heart is at once the *knot* of the
veins and the *source* of the rapidly circulating blood, and is sta-
tioned in the *guard-room* of the body. The ramifying blood-vessels
he calls *alleys*. "And casting about," he says, "for something to
sustain the violent palpitation of the heart when it is alarmed
by the approach of danger or agitated by passion, since at such
times it is overheated, they (the gods) implanted in us the lungs,
which are so fashioned that being soft and bloodless, and having cavities within, they act like a buffer, and when the heart
boils with inward passion by yielding to its throbbing save it from
injury." He compares the seat of the desires to the *women's quar-*

ters, the seat of the passions to the *men's quarters,* in a house. The spleen, again, is the *napkin* of the internal organs, by whose excretions it is saturated from time to time, and swells to a great size with inward impurity. "After this," he continues, "they shrouded the whole with flesh, throwing it forward, like a cushion, as a barrier against injuries from without." The blood he terms the *pasture* of the flesh. "To assist the process of nutrition," he goes on, "they divided the body into ducts, cutting trenches like those in a garden, so that, the body being a system of narrow conduits, the current of the veins might flow as from a perennial fountain-head. And when the end is at hand," he says, "the soul is cast loose from her moorings like a ship, and free to wander whither she will." These, and a hundred similar fancies, follow one another in quick succession. But those which I have pointed out are sufficient to demonstrate how great is the natural power of figurative language, and how largely metaphors conduce to sublimity, and to illustrate the important part which they play in all impassioned and descriptive passages. . . .

XXXIII

[The faults of the great writers]

But supposing now that we assume the existence of a really unblemished and irreproachable writer. Is it not worth while to raise the whole question whether in poetry and prose we should prefer sublimity accompanied by some faults, or a style which never rising above moderate excellence never stumbles and never requires correction? and again, whether the first place in literature is justly to be assigned to the more numerous, or the loftier excellences? For these are questions proper to an inquiry on the Sublime, and urgently asking for settlement.

I know, then, that the largest intellects are far from being the most exact. A mind always intent on correctness is apt to be dissipated in trifles; but in great affluence of thought, as in vast material wealth, there must needs be an occasional neglect of detail. And is it not inevitably so? Is it not by risking nothing, by never

aiming high, that a writer of low or middling powers keeps generally clear of faults and secure of blame? whereas the loftier
walks of literature are by their very loftiness perilous? I am well
aware, again, that there is a law by which in all human productions the weak points catch the eye first, by which their faults remain indelibly stamped on the memory, while their beauties
quickly fade away. Yet, though I have myself noted not a few
faulty passages in Homer and in other authors of the highest rank,
and though I am far from being partial to their failings, nevertheless I would call them not so much wilful blunders as oversights
which were allowed to pass unregarded through that contempt of
little things, that "brave disorder," which is natural to an exalted
genius; and I still think that the greater excellences, though not
everywhere equally sustained, ought always to be voted to the first
place in literature, if for no other reason, for the mere grandeur of
soul they evince. . . .

XXXIV
[*Comparison of Hyperides and Demosthenes*]

[In the course of the discussion, here omitted, Hyperides is judged
as a "far superior" orator to Demosthenes, for he has "a richer
modulation, a greater variety of excellence . . . if the number
and not the loftiness of an author's merits is to be our standard
of success." However, "all the beauties of Hyperides, numerous
as they are, cannot make him sublime. He never exhibits strong
feeling, has little energy, rouses no emotion; certainly he never
kindles terror in the breast of his readers." Despite his failings,
Demosthenes, "by the noble qualities which he does possess, remains supreme above all rivals."]

XXXV
[*Man's aspiring mind*]

. . . What truth, then, was it that was present to those mighty
spirits of the past, who, making whatever is greatest in writing

their aim, thought it beneath them to be exact in every detail? Among many others especially this, that it was not in nature's plan for us her chosen children to be creatures base and ignoble, —no, she brought us into life, and into the whole universe, as into some great field of contest, that we should be at once spectators and ambitious rivals of her mighty deeds, and from the first implanted in our souls an invincible yearning for all that is great, all that is more divine than ourselves. Therefore even the whole world is not wide enough for the soaring range of human thought, but man's mind often overleaps the very bounds of space. When we survey the whole circle of life, and see it abounding everywhere in what is elegant, grand, and beautiful, we learn at once what is the true end of man's being. And this is why nature prompts us to admire, not the clearness and usefulness of a little stream, but the Nile, the Danube, the Rhine, and far beyond all the Ocean; not to turn our wandering eyes from the heavenly fires, though often darkened, to the little flame kindled by human hands, however pure and steady its light; not to think that tiny lamp more wondrous than the caverns of Aetna, from whose raging depths are hurled up stones and whole masses of rock, and torrents sometimes come pouring from earth's centre of pure and living fire.

To sum the whole: whatever is useful or needful lies easily within man's reach; but he admires that which is astounding.

XXXVI
[Those who have achieved the sublime]

How much more do these principles apply to the Sublime in literature, where grandeur is never, as it sometimes is in nature, dissociated from utility and advantage. Therefore, all those who have achieved it, however far from faultless, are still more than mortal. When a writer uses any other resource he shows himself to be a man; but the Sublime lifts him near to the great spirit of the Deity. He who makes no slips must be satisfied with negative approbation, but he who is sublime commands positive reverence.

Why need I add that each one of those great writers often redeems all his errors by one grand and masterly stroke? But the strongest point of all is that, if you were to pick out all the blunders of Homer, Demosthenes, Plato, and all the greatest names in literature, and add them together, they would be found to bear a very small, or rather an infinitesimal proportion to the passages in which these supreme masters have attained absolute perfection. Therefore it is that all posterity, whose judgment envy herself cannot impeach, has brought and bestowed on them the crown of glory, has guarded their fame until this day against all attack, and is likely to preserve it

> As long as lofty trees shall grow,
> And restless waters seaward flow.

It has been urged by one writer that we should not prefer the huge disproportioned Colossus to the Doryphorus of Polycletus. But (to give one out of many possible answers) in art we admire exactness, in the works of nature magnificence; and it is from nature that man derives the faculty of speech. Whereas, then, in statuary we look for close resemblance to humanity, in literature we require something which transcends humanity. Nevertheless (to reiterate the advice which we gave at the beginning of this essay), since that success which consists in avoidance of error is usually the gift of art, while high, though unequal excellence is the attribute of genius, it is proper on all occasions to call in art as an ally to nature. By the combined resources of these two we may hope to achieve perfection.

Such are the conclusions which were forced upon me concerning the points at issue; but every one may consult his own taste.

XXXVII

[This section is missing in the manuscript, hence the abruptness of the following.]

XXXVIII
[*Excess in the use of hyperbole*]

Such absurdities as, "Unless you carry your brains next to the ground in your heels." Hence it is necessary to know where to draw the line; for if ever it is overstepped the effect of the hyperbole is spoilt, being in such cases relaxed by overstraining and producing the very opposite to the effect desired. . . . We may repeat here what we said about figures, and say that the hyperbole is then most effective when it appears in disguise. And this effect is produced when a writer, impelled by strong feeling, speaks in the accents of some tremendous crisis; as Thucydides does in describing the massacre in Sicily. "The Syracusans," he says, "went down after them and slew those especially who were in the river, and the water was at once defiled, yet still they went on drinking it, though mingled with mud and gore, most of them even fighting for it." The drinking of mud and gore, and even the fighting for it, is made credible by the awful horror of the scene described. . . . [A further example from Herodotus]

XXXIX
[*Arrangement of words*]

We have still left, my dear sir, the fifth of those sources which we set down at the outset as contributing to sublimity, that which consists in the mere arrangement of words in a certain order. Having already published two books dealing fully with this subject—so far at least as our investigations had carried us—it will be sufficient for the purpose of our present inquiry to add that harmony is an instrument which has a natural power, not only to win and to delight, but also in a remarkable degree to exalt the soul and sway the heart of man. When we see that a flute kindles certain emotions in its hearers, rendering them almost beside themselves and full of an orgiastic frenzy, and that by starting some kind of rhythmical beat it compels him who listens to move in time and assimilate his gestures to the tune, even though he has no taste whatever for music; when we know that the sounds of a harp, which in themselves have no meaning, by the change of key, by the mutual relation of the notes, and their arrangement in symphony, often lay a wonderful spell on an audience—though these are mere shadows and spurious imitations of persuasion, not, as I have said, genuine manifestations of human nature:—can we doubt that composition (being a kind of harmony of that language which nature has taught us, and which reaches, not our ears only, but our very souls), when it raises changing forms of words, of thoughts, of actions, of beauty, of melody, all of which are engrained in and akin to ourselves, and when by the blending of its manifold tones it brings home to the minds of those who stand by the feelings present to the speaker, and ever disposes the hearer to sympathise with those feelings, adding word to word, until it has raised a majestic and harmonious structure:— can we wonder if all this enchants us, wherever we meet with it, and filling us with the sense of pomp and dignity and sublimity, and whatever else it embraces, gains a complete mastery over our minds? It would be mere folly to dispute truths so universally acknowledged and established by experience.

Now to give an instance: that is doubtless a sublime thought, indeed wonderfully fine, which Demosthenes applies to his decree: "This decree caused the danger which then hung round our city to pass by just as a cloud." But the modulation is as perfect as the sentiment itself is weighty. It is uttered wholly in the dactylic measure, the noblest and most magnificent of all measures, and hence forming the chief constituent in the finest metre we know, the heroic. Supposing we transpose them from their proper place and read, say "This decree just as a cloud caused the danger which then hung over the city to pass by"—nay, let us merely cut off one syllable, reading "caused to pass by as a cloud"—and you will understand how close is the unison between harmony and sublimity. In the passage before us, the words "just as a cloud" move first in a heavy measure, which is metrically equivalent to four short syllables: but on removing one syllable, and reading "as a cloud," the grandeur of movement is at once crippled by the abridgment. So conversely if you lengthen into "caused to pass by just as if a cloud," the meaning is still the same, but it does not strike the ear in the same manner, because by lingering over the final syllables you at once dissipate and relax the abrupt grandeur of the passage.

XL
[*Organic structure*]

There is another method very efficient in exalting a style. As the different members of the body, none of which, if severed from its connection, has any intrinsic excellence, unite by their mutual combination to form a complete and perfect organism, so also the elements of a fine passage, by whose separation from one another its high quality is simultaneously dissipated and evaporates, when joined in one organic whole, and still further compacted by the bond of harmony, by the mere rounding of the period gain power of tone. In fact, a clause may be said to derive its sublimity from the joint contributions of a number of particulars. And further (as we have shown at large elsewhere), many writers in prose and verse, though their natural powers were not high, were perhaps even low, and though the terms they employed were usually common and popular and conveying no impression of refinement, by the mere harmony of their composition have attained dignity and elevation, and avoided the appearance of meanness. Such among many others are Philistus, Aristophanes occasionally, Euripides almost always. Thus when Heracles says, after the murder of his children,

I'm full of woes, I have no room for more,

the words are quite common, but they are made sublime by being cast in a fine mould. . . . [Another example follows from Euripedes.]

XLI
[*Rhythm*]

[Style loses dignity when the rhythm is hurried or uniform. Such "abuse of rhythm," besides producing monotony of tone, distracts the listener's attention from its subject.]

XLII
[*Over-compression*]

Sublimity is further diminished by cramping the diction. Deformity instead of grandeur ensues from over-compression. Here I am not referring to a judicious compactness of phrase, but to a style which is dwarfed, and its force frittered away. To cut your words too short is to prune away their sense, but to be concise is to be direct. On the other hand, we know that a style becomes lifeless by over-extension, I mean by being relaxed to an unseasonable length.

XLIII
[*Vulgarisms*]

The use of undignified words has also a strong tendency to degrade a lofty passage. Thus in that description of the storm in Herodotus the matter is admirable, but some of the words admitted are beneath the dignity of the subject; such, perhaps, as "the seas having *seethed*," because the ill-sounding phrase "having seethed" detracts much from its impressiveness: or when he says "the wind wore away," and "those who clung round the wreck met with an unwelcome end." "Wore away" is ignoble and vulgar, and "unwelcome" inadequate to the extent of the disaster.

Similarly Theopompus, after giving a fine picture of the Persian king's descent against Egypt, has exposed the whole to censure by certain paltry expressions. "There was no city, no people of Asia, which did not send an embassy to the king; no product of the earth, no work of art, whether beautiful or precious, which was not among the gifts brought to him. Many and costly were the hangings and robes, some purple, some embroidered, some white; many the tents, of cloth of gold, furnished with all things useful; many the tapestries and couches of great price. Moreover, there was gold and silver plate richly wrought, goblets and bowls, some of which might be seen studded with gems, and others besides worked in relief with great skill and at vast expense. Besides these there were suits of armour in number past computation, partly Greek, partly foreign, endless trains of baggage animals and fat cattle for slaughter, many bushels of spices, many sacks and sheets of writing-paper; and all other necessaries in the same proportion. And there was salt meat of all kinds of beasts in immense quantity, heaped together to such a height as to show at a distance like mounds and hills thrown up one against another." He runs off from the grander parts of his subject to the meaner, and sinks where he ought to rise. Still worse, by his mixing up *sacks* and *spices* and *bags* with his wonderful recital of that vast and busy scene one would imagine that he was describing a kitchen. Let us suppose that in that show of magnificence some one had taken a set of wretched baskets and bags and placed them in the midst, among vessels of gold, jewelled bowls, silver plate, and tents and goblets of gold; how incongruous would have seemed the effect! Now just in the same way these petty words, introduced out of season, stand out like deformities and blots on the diction. These details might have been given in one or two broad strokes, as when he speaks of mounds being heaped together. So in dealing with the other preparations he might have told us of "waggons and camels and a long train of baggage animals loaded with all kinds of supplies for the luxury and enjoyment of the table," or have mentioned "piles of grain of every species, and of all the choicest delicacies required by the art of the cook or the taste of the epicure," or (if he must needs be so very precise) he might have spoken of "whatever dainties are supplied by those who lay or those who dress the banquet." In our sublimer efforts we should never stoop to what is sordid and despicable, unless very hard pressed by some urgent necessity. If we would write becomingly, our utterance should be worthy of our theme. We should take a lesson from nature, who when she planned the human frame did not set our grosser parts, or the ducts for purging the body, in our face, but as far as she could concealed them, "diverting," as Xenophon says, "those canals as far as possible from our senses," and thus shunning in any part to mar the beauty of the whole creature.

However, it is not incumbent on us to specify and enumerate whatever diminishes a style. We have now pointed out the various means of giving it nobility and loftiness. It is clear, then, that whatever is contrary to these will generally degrade and deform it.

XLIV
[Liberty and literature]

There is still another point which remains to be cleared up, my dear Terentian, and on which I shall not hesitate to add some remarks, to gratify your inquiring spirit. It relates to a question which was recently put to me by a certain philosopher. "To me," he said, "in common, I may say, with many others, it is a matter of wonder that in the present age, which produces many highly skilled in the arts of popular persuasion, many of keen and active powers, many especially rich in every pleasing gift of language, the growth of highly exalted and wide-reaching genius has with a few rare exceptions almost entirely ceased. So universal is the dearth of eloquence which prevails throughout the world. Must we really," he asked, "give credit to that oft-repeated assertion that democracy is the kind nurse of genius, and that high literary excellence has flourished with her prime and faded with her decay? Liberty, it is said, is all-powerful to feed the aspirations of high intellects, to hold out hope, and keep alive the flame of mutual rivalry and ambitious struggle for the highest place. Moreover, the prizes which are offered in every free state keep the spirits of her foremost orators whetted by perpetual exercise; they are, as it were, ignited by friction, and naturally blaze forth freely because they are surrounded by freedom. But we of to-day," he continued, "seem to have learnt in our childhood the lessons of a benignant despotism, to have been cradled in her habits and customs from the time when our minds were still tender, and never to have tasted the fairest and most fruitful fountain of eloquence, I mean liberty. Hence we develop nothing but a fine genius for flattery. This is the reason why, though all other faculties are consistent with the servile condition, no slave ever became an orator; because in him there is a dumb spirit which will not be kept down: his soul is chained: he is like one who has learnt to be ever expecting a blow. For, as Homer says—

> The day of slavery
> Takes half our manly worth away.

As, then (if what I have heard is credible), the cages in which those pigmies commonly called dwarfs are reared not only stop the growth of the imprisoned creature, but absolutely make him smaller by compressing every part of his body, so all despotism, however equitable, may be defined as a cage of the soul and a general prison."

My answer was as follows: "My dear friend, it is so easy, and so characteristic of human nature, always to find fault with the present. Consider, now, whether the corruption of genius is to be attributed, not to a world-wide peace, but rather to the war within us which knows no limit, which engages all our desires, yes, and still further to the bad passions which lay siege to us to-day, and make utter havoc and spoil of our lives. Are we not enslaved, nay, are not our careers completely shipwrecked, by love of gain, that fever which rages unappeased in us all, and love of pleasure?— one the most debasing, the other the most ignoble of the mind's diseases. When I consider it I can find no means by which we, who hold in such high honour, or, to speak more correctly, who idolise boundless riches, can close the door of our souls against those evil spirits which grow up with them. For Wealth unmeasured and unbridled is dogged by Extravagance: she sticks close to him, and treads in his footsteps: and as soon as he opens the gates of cities or of houses she enters with him and makes her abode with him.

And after a time they build their nests (to use a wise man's words) in that corner of life, and speedily set about breeding, and beget Boastfulness, and Vanity, and Wantonness, no base-born children, but their very own. And if these also, the offspring of Wealth, be allowed to come to their prime, quickly they engender in the soul those pitiless tyrants, Violence, and Lawlessness, and Shamelessness. Whenever a man takes to worshipping what is mortal and irrational in him, and neglects to cherish what is immortal, these are the inevitable results. He never looks up again; he has lost all care for good report; by slow degrees the ruin of his life goes on, until it is consummated all round; all that is great in his soul fades, withers away, and is despised.

"If a judge who passes sentence for a bribe can never more give a free and sound decision on a point of justice or honour (for to him who takes a bribe honour and justice must be measured by his own interests), how can we of to-day expect, when the whole life of each one of us is controlled by bribery, while we live in wait for other men's death and plan how to get a place in their wills, when we buy gain, from whatever source, each one of us, with our very souls in our slavish greed, how, I say, can we expect, in the midst of such a moral pestilence, that there is still left even one liberal and impartial critic, whose verdict will not be biassed by avarice in judging of those great works which live on through all time? Alas! I fear that for such men as we are it is better to serve than to be free. If our appetites were let loose altogether against our neighbours, they would be like wild beasts uncaged, and bring a deluge of calamity on the whole civilised world."

I ended by remarking generally that the genius of the present age is wasted by that indifference which with a few exceptions runs through the whole of life. If we ever shake off our apathy and apply ourselves to work, it is always with a view to pleasure or applause, not for that solid advantage which is worthy to be striven for and held in honour.

We had better then leave this generation to its fate, and turn to what follows, which is the subject of the passions, to which we promised early in this treatise to devote a separate work. They play an important part in literature generally, and especially in relation to the Sublime. . . . [The rest of the manuscript is missing.]

II

THE RENAISSANCE &
THE 18TH CENTURY:
THE CLASSICAL
REVIVAL

Preface

I

Throughout the Middle Ages, poetry, studied as a branch of grammar, logic, or rhetoric, was generally defined as didactic allegory. As "handmaid," or perhaps the workhorse, of theology and philosophy, it consequently justified its existence by presenting truths in pleasing fictions. As we have seen, the allegorical assumption was made as early as the sixth century B.C. by Anaxagoras, who attempted to rescue Homer from the charge of lying about the gods, and later in the Alexandrian period (300-146 B.C.) by Zeno in his *Homeric Problems,* which made allegory hunting fashionable.

Inherited from classical antiquity and deeply rooted in early Christianity, allegory continued as the primary stuff of literature for such later writers as Petrarch and Boccaccio, despite their strong humanistic interests, and for Dante, who, in a famous letter to his patron, presents his *Divine Comedy* as a structure involving four levels of meaning—one literal and three allegorical. In short, the value of poetry lay in its capacity to reveal truth in vivid, pleasing images. The Middle Ages believed this to be the formula expressed by Horace—to please and instruct. (In point of fact, however, his *Art of Poetry* states that poetry should please *or* instruct *or* do both.)

II

During the fourteenth and fifteenth centuries, poetry attained new prestige in the hands of the Italian humanists, for now the literature of classical antiquity was being gathered with greater intensity, dusted off, commented on, and used for purposes of education. Rational inquiry into all areas of knowledge, including literature, was replacing reliance on dogmatic authority as established by scholastic philosophy and theology. In literature, new authority was to replace old, in its own way just as dogmatic. Oratory, perfected by Quintilian and Cicero, the humanists believed, became a central study along with classical Latin. In time, the humanistic studies were regarded as the essential embodiments of a culture, an idea that Matthew Arnold was later to rephrase as "the best that is known and thought in the world."

But before they could devote serious study to imaginative literature, the humanists had to overcome strong, traditional distrust, a distrust engendered by Plato and for centuries tenaciously held to by the Church Fathers. Study of pagan literature, embodying doctrines and attitudes fundamentally different from those of Christian teaching, had been sanctioned by the Church, in the past, so long as allegorical interpretation revealed truths compatible with Christian doctrine. But humanistic inquiry into purely aesthetic matters and use of such literature for education were morally questionable and spiritually dangerous. The situation was awkward, for many humanists, devoutly religious, were reluctant to undertake such study without proper moral sanction, for protest had been raised in some quarters. The Dominican friar Savonarola (1452-1498), for example, denounced Renaissance "paganism" in Italy, accusing the ancients of arousing passion rather than quieting it.

In 1498, however, there appeared a Latin translation by Giorgio Valla of Aristotle's *Poetics,* long neglected in the Middle Ages. The humanists were now provided with arguments to numerous objections. In its contention that poetry was concerned with truth rather than with fact (hence, more philosophical than history), that the poet should portray not what is but what ought to be, that tragedy purges strong emotions, the *Poetics* was used to nullify protests first raised by Plato.

Paradoxically, as Aristotle's authority in philosophy and science declined in the sixteenth century, his *Poetics* achieved pre-eminence unknown by any other ancient work, except perhaps for Horace's *Art of Poetry*. An extraordinary number of commentaries and treatises, based on Aristotle and Horace—the latter now grown in stature—appeared through the century, the most notable of which were by Vida (1527), Daniello (1536), Scaliger (1561), and Castelvetro (1570). The new doctrines in the epic and in tragedy, later systematized by the French into what was to be called "neo-classicism," involved new dogmas to replace old.

III

In England, the effects of the new learning were felt early in the sixteenth century. Like the Italian humanists, their English counterparts now regarded the literature of the ancients as an instrumental force in education; poetry, freed from its medieval subservience as a branch of logic or grammar, acquired new importance in the training of skills and the formation of character. In *The Book Named the Governor* (1531), for example, a work concerned with the preparation of boys for careers in public service, Sir Thomas Elyot defended the educational value of ancient poetry in a statement of his intention:

> . . . to show what profit may be taken by the diligent reading of ancient poets, contrary to the false opinion, that now reigneth, of them that suppose that in the works of poets is contained nothing but bawdry (such is their foul word of reproach) and unprofitable leasings.

However, liberation of criticism from medieval theory was slow and difficult. Such notable works in the Tudor period as Thomas Wilson's *Art of Rhetoric* (1553) and Roger Ascham's *The School-*

master (1570), despite their reverence for the ancients, indicate the persistence, even at these late dates, of the medieval conception of poetry as didactic allegory. The lack of originality and rational inquiry in these works may possibly be the result of a decline in the study of Greek at Oxford and Cambridge during the reign of Henry VIII. In literature, the strength of the medieval tradition continued to influence poets through the sixteenth and seventeenth centuries, notable instances being Spenser's *Faerie Queene* (1590-96), a multi-leveled allegory reminiscent of Dante's structure in the *Divine Comedy;* and Bunyan's *Pilgrim's Progress* (1678), a prose narrative in which landscapes and characters represent moral abstractions.

IV

With the increasing intensity of Puritan attacks on poetry and drama, there arose during this time a body of criticism whose primary intention was to defend the moral function of imaginative literature. The earliest of these Elizabethan works, Richard Willis' *De re poetica disputio* (1573), a short treatise in Latin, contends that poetry inculcates virtue, not vice. The Platonic theory concerning "imitations" of reality, hence false, is not, however, discussed, though the doctrine provided the Puritans with the weapon for attack.

The most famous of the Puritan tracts, a pamphlet by Stephen Gosson, appeared in 1579 with the mocking dedication "To the right noble Gentleman, Master Philip Sidney, Esquire." Its breathless title all but eliminates the necessity of proceeding further:

> *School of Abuse: Containing a pleasant invective against Poets, Pipers, Players, Jesters, and such like Caterpillars of a Commonwealth: Setting up the Flag of Defiance to their mischievous exercise, and overthrowing their Bulwarks, by Prophane Writers, Natural Reason, and common experience: A Discourse as Pleasant for them that favor learning, as profitable for all that will follow virtue.*

No "caterpillar" of the commonwealth, Sir Philip, the English embodiment of the courtly ideal as expounded in Castiglione's

The Courtier (1528), replied to Gosson's charges with an essay which established him as the first important critic in English letters. An astonishing synthesis of Renaissance and classical learning, his *Apology for Poetry* attacks the notion that poets tell lies, debilitate morality, and lead one to vice—charges endlessly repeated by the Puritans—by insisting that Plato had not vilified poetry but its abuses. Maintaining that good poetry, in transcending common experience, creates an ideal world, produces a beneficial moral effect, and results in virtuous action, the *Apology* concludes that the real world is "brazen," the poet's "golden."

V

As a restatement of classical theory, Sidney's essay extended approval to neo-classical doctrines then being systematized in France. In the early seventeenth century, Malherbe was hailed as the lawgiver of French neo-classical theory, though, in fact, he made extensive use of sixteenth-century Italian commentaries. Rationalistic in his approach, Malherbe insisted on correctness in language, decorum in character and action, strict adherence to rules governing each genre, and imitation of the ancients. Later in the century, Boileau, in his *L'Art poétique* (1674), Le Bossu, and Rapin were instrumental in disseminating neo-classical theory on the continent, though not without resistance from such critics as La Bruyère, Saint-Évremond, and even Corneille.

Mistakenly, Scaliger was hailed as the formulator of the unities of time, place, and action, as the lawgiver of *les unités scaligeriennes,* whereas he had insisted only on verisimilitude in drama, but with sufficient authority to prompt Castelvetro, in his *Poetics* (1570), to invent the rule of the three unities, believing that it would achieve the verisimilitude which Scaliger had demanded. (Aristotle, universally referred to as the "source" of the unities, had, in fact, discussed the unity of action but had only observed that most tragedies present their action within the revolution of the sun; of the unity of place, he says nothing.)

VI

By the middle of the seventeenth century, neo-classical doctrine passed into English hands through a series of influences brought about by political events. Early contact with French intellectuals occurred in 1625 through the marriage of Charles I to Henrietta Maria, who was herself a patron of the arts. Later, during the Civil War between the Puritans and Royalists (1642-48), Thomas Hobbes, Sir William Davenant, Abraham Cowley, and other Royalists fled to France. With the restoration of the monarchy in 1660, French influences, not only in literature but also in dress, manners, and morals, began to permeate English intellectual life.

Transplanted to English soil, French neo-classicism never took complete hold, for the individualism of the British temperament and the memory of a great literary tradition resisted the dogmatism and rigid restrictions of the French theorists, a viewpoint wittily expressed by Alexander Pope in his *Essay on Criticism* (1711):

> . . . critic learning flourished most in France:
> The rules, a nation born to serve, obeys;
> And Boileau still in right of Horace sways.
> But we, brave Britons, foreign laws despised,
> And kept unconquered, and uncivilized;
> Fierce for the liberties of wit, and bold,
> We still defied the Romans, as of old.

Moreover, with the recovery of Longinus' treatise *On the Sublime* (Boileau's translation in 1674 received greatest attention), which emphasized individual genius rather than strict adherence to rules, emotional "transport" rather than universally recognized truth as the standard of value, the neo-classical insistence on correctness was seriously questioned.

Even before Dryden was acquainted with Longinus' extraordinarily influential work, he was reluctant to accept any dogmatism, as his defense of English drama in the *Essay of Dramatic Poesy* (1668) demonstrates. Though he later acknowledged that "Aris-

totle with his interpreters, and Horace, and Longinus are the authors to whom I owe my lights," he could not, as a sensible Englishman, condemn Chaucer and Shakespeare as rude and barbaric.
Accepting the neo-classical belief that verisimilitude could be
achieved by strict adherence to the unities, Dryden, in the "Prologue" to his comedy *Secret Love* (1668) reveals his attempt to
fuse French neo-classical theory with his own native tradition:

> He who writ this, not without pains and
>   thought,
> From French and English theatres has brought
> The exactest rules, by which a play is wrought.
>
> The Unities of Action, Place, and Time;
> The scenes unbroken; and a mingled chime
> Of Jonson's humour, with Corneille's rhyme.

By Pope's time, many neo-classical doctrines, though nominally
accepted, were seriously questioned and frequently ignored. The
increasing hesitation on the part of Dryden (whom Dr. Johnson
called "the father of English criticism"), in his later essays, to
embrace the doctrines of the French served as a guide to the
eighteenth century. With Dr. Johnson's rejection of the rigidity
and irrationality of the system and with the rise of an expressive
theory of art, the brief neo-classical interlude in England was to
end, not, however, without having had brilliant achievements. Its
major successes were not in epic or tragedy but in parody and
satire, successes unparalleled in French neo-classicism or, indeed,
perhaps, in classical antiquity.

Sir Philip Sidney

(1554–1586)

AN APOLOGY FOR POETRY

Written in the 1580's before Sidney was thirty, the *Apology* was not published until after his death, though it had circulated in manuscript, a practice customary in Renaissance literary circles. In 1595, two different versions appeared: the one printed here, published by Henry Olney; and *The Defense of Poesie,* by William Ponsonby. The former is generally regarded as the better text. The spelling is, of course, modernized.

As used by Sidney, the term *apology* indicates a defense, not an excuse. According to Kenneth O. Myrick, the essay, in seven parts, is structured after the classical oration, from the exordium to the peroration.

Perceptive and graceful, the *Apology*—which Sidney calls "this ink-wasting toy of mine"—marks the beginning of a tradition of great English poet-critics.

WHEN the right virtuous Edward Wotton and I were at the Emperor's Court together, we gave ourselves to learn horsemanship of John Pietro Pugliano, one that with great commendation had the place of an esquire in his stable. And he, according to the fertileness of the Italian wit, did not only afford us the demonstration of his practice, but sought to enrich our minds with the contemplations therein which he thought most precious. But with none I remember mine ears were at any time more loaden, than when (either angered with slow payment, or moved with our learnerlike admiration) he exercised his speech in the praise of his faculty. He said, soldiers were the noblest estate of mankind, and horsemen the noblest of soldiers. He said they were the masters of war and ornaments of peace; speedy goers and strong abiders; triumphers both in camps and courts. Nay, to so unbelieved a point he proceeded, as that no earthly thing bred such wonder to a prince as to be a good horseman. Skill of government was but a *pedanteria* ["pedantry"] in comparison. Then would he add certain praises, by telling what a peerless beast a horse was, the only serviceable courtier without flattery, the beast of most beauty, faithfulness, courage, and such more, that, if I had not been a piece of a logician before I came to him, I think he would have persuaded me to have wished myself a horse. But thus much at least with his no few words he drove into me, that self-love is better than any gilding to make that seem gorgeous wherein ourselves are parties. Wherein, if Pugliano's strong affection and weak arguments will not satisfy you, I will give you a nearer example of myself, who (I know not by what mischance) in these my not old years and idlest times having slipped into the title of a poet, am provoked to say something unto you in the defence of that my unelected vocation, which if I handle with more good will than good reasons, bear with me, since the scholar is to be pardoned that followeth the steps of his master. And yet I must say that, as I have just cause to make a pitiful defence of poor Poetry, which from almost the highest estimation of learning is fallen to be the laughing-stock of children, so have I need to bring some more available proofs, since the former is by no man barred of his deserved credit, the silly latter hath had even the names of philosophers used to the defacing of it, with great danger of civil war among the Muses.

And first, truly, to all them that professing learning inveigh against Poetry may justly be objected, that they go very near to ungratefulness, to seek to deface that which, in the noblest nations and languages that are known, hath been the first light-giver to ignorance, and first nurse, whose milk by little and little enabled them to feed afterwards of tougher knowledges. And will they now play the hedgehog that, being received into the den, drove out his host, or rather the vipers, that with their birth kill their parents? Let learned Greece in any of her manifold sciences be able to show me one book before Musaeus, Homer, and Hesiod, all three nothing else but poets. Nay, let any history be brought that can say any writers were there before them, if they were not men of the same skill, as Orpheus, Linus, and some other are named, who, having been the first of that country that made pens deliverers of their knowledge to their posterity, may justly challenge to be called their fathers in learning, for not only in time they had this priority (although in itself antiquity be venerable) but went before them, as causes to draw with their charming sweetness the wild untamed wits to an admiration of knowledge, so, as Amphion was said to move stones with his poetry to build Thebes, and Orpheus to be listened to by beasts—indeed stony and beastly people. So among the Romans were Livius Andronicus, and Ennius. So in the Italian language the first that made it aspire to be a treasure-house of Science were the poets Dante, Boccaccio, and Petrarch. So in our English were Gower and Chaucer.

After whom, encouraged and delighted with their excellent fore-going, others have followed, to beautify our mother tongue, as well in the same kind as in other arts. This did so notably show itself, that the philosophers of Greece durst not a long time appear to the world but under the masks of poets. So Thales, Empedocles, and Parmenides sang their natural philosophy in verses; so did Pythagoras and Phocylides their moral counsels; so did Tyrtaeus in war matters, and Solon in matters of policy: or rather, they, being poets, did exercise their delightful vein in those points of highest knowledge, which before them lay hid to the world. For that wise Solon was directly a poet it is manifest, having written in verse the notable fable of the Atlantic Island, which was continued by Plato.

And truly, even Plato, whosoever well considereth shall find that in the body of his work, though the inside and strength were Philosophy, the skin as it were and beauty depended most of Poetry: for all standeth upon dialogues, wherein he feigneth many honest burgesses of Athens to speak of such matters, that, if they had been set on the rack, they would never have confessed them, besides his poetical describing the circumstances of their meetings, as the well ordering of a banquet, the delicacy of a walk, with inter-

lacing mere tales, as Gyges' Ring, and others, which who knoweth not to be flowers of poetry did never walk into Apollo's garden. . . .

Among the Romans a poet was called *Vates,* which is as much
as a diviner, foreseer, or prophet, as by his conjoined words
vaticinium and *vaticinari* is manifest: so heavenly a title did that
excellent people bestow upon this heart-ravishing knowledge. And
so far were they carried into the admiration thereof, that they
thought in the chanceable hitting upon any such verses great fore-
tokens of their following fortunes were placed. Whereupon grew
the word of *Sortes Virgilianae,* when, by sudden opening Virgil's
book, they lighted upon any verse of his making: whereof the histories of the emperors' lives are full, as of Albinus, the governor
of our island, who in his childhood met with this verse,

Arma amens capio nec sat rationis in armis;
["In my frenzy I seize arms, but there is insufficient reason for
arms." *Aeneid,* II, 314.]

and in his age performed it: which, although it were a very vain
and godless superstition, as also it was to think that spirits were
commanded by such verses—whereupon this word charms, derived of *carmina,* cometh—so yet serveth it to show the great
reverence those wits were held in. And altogether not without
ground, since both the Oracles of Delphos and Sibylla's prophecies
were wholly delivered in verses. For that same exquisite observing
of number and measure in words, and that high flying liberty of
conceit proper to the poet, did seem to have some divine force in it.

And may not I presume a little further, to show the reasonable-
ness of this word *Vates,* and say that the holy David's Psalms are a
divine poem? If I do, I shall not do it without the testimony of
great learned men, both ancient and modern. But even the name
Psalms will speak for me, which, being interpreted, is nothing but
Songs; then that it is fully written in metre, as all learned Hebri-
cians agree, although the rules be not yet fully found; lastly and
principally, his handling his prophecy, which is merely poetical.
For what else is the awaking his musical instruments, the often

and free changing of persons, his notable prosopopeias [personifications], when he maketh you, as it were, see God coming in His majesty, his telling of the beasts' joyfulness, and hills' leaping, but a heavenly poesy, wherein almost he showeth himself a passionate lover of that unspeakable and everlasting beauty to be seen by the eyes of the mind, only cleared by faith? But truly now having named him, I fear me I seem to profane that holy name, applying it to Poetry, which is among us thrown down to so ridiculous an estimation. But they that with quiet judgements will look a little deeper into it, shall find the end and working of it such, as, being rightly applied, deserveth not to be scourged out of the Church of God.

But now, let us see how the Greeks named it, and how they deemed of it. The Greeks called him "a poet," which name hath, as the most excellent, gone through other languages. It cometh of this word *Poiein,* which is "to make": wherein, I know not whether by luck or wisdom, we Englishmen have met with the Greeks in calling him "a maker": which name, how high and incomparable a title it is, I had rather were known by marking the scope of other sciences than by my partial allegation.

There is no art delivered to mankind that hath not the works of Nature for his principal object, without which they could not consist, and on which they so depend, as they become actors and players, as it were, of what Nature will have set forth. So doth the astronomer look upon the stars, and, by that he seeth, setteth down what order Nature hath taken therein. So do the geometrician and arithmetician in their diverse sorts of quantities. So doth the musician in times tell you which by nature agree, which not. The natural philosopher thereon hath his name, and the moral philosopher standeth upon the natural virtues, vices, and passions of man; and "follow Nature" (saith he) "therein, and thou shalt not err." The lawyer saith what men have determined; the historian what men have done. The grammarian speaketh only of the rules of speech; and the rhetorician and logician, considering what in Nature will soonest prove and persuade, thereon give artificial rules, which still are compassed within the circle of a question according to the proposed matter. The physician weigheth the nature of a man's body, and the nature of things helpful or hurtful unto it. And the metaphysic, though it be in the second and abstract notions, and therefore be counted supernatural, yet doth he indeed build upon the depth of Nature. Only the poet, disdaining to be tied to any such subjection, lifted up with the vigour of his own invention, doth grow in effect another nature, in making things either better than Nature bringeth forth, or, quite anew, forms such as never were in Nature, as the Heroes, Demigods, Cyclopes, Chimeras, Furies, and such like: so as he goeth hand in hand with Nature, not enclosed within the narrow warrant of her gifts, but freely ranging only within the zodiac of his own wit.

Nature never set forth the earth in so rich tapestry as divers poets have done—neither with pleasant rivers, fruitful trees, sweet-smelling flowers, nor whatsoever else may make the too much loved earth more lovely. Her world is brazen, the poets only deliver a golden. . . .

Poesy therefore is an art of imitation, for so Aristotle termeth it in his word *Mimesis,* that is to say, a representing, counterfeiting, or figuring forth—to speak metaphorically, a speaking picture; with this end, to teach and delight. Of this have been three several kinds. The chief, both in antiquity and excellency, were they that did imitate the inconceivable excellencies of God. Such were David in his Psalms; Solomon in his Song of Songs, in his Ecclesiastes, and Proverbs; Moses and Deborah in their Hymns; and the writer of Job, which, beside other, the learned Emanuel Tremellius and Franciscus Junius do entitle the poetical part of the Scripture. Against these none will speak that hath the Holy Ghost in due holy reverence.

In this kind, though in a full wrong divinity, were Orpheus, Amphion, Homer in his Hymns, and many other, both Greeks and Romans, and this poesy must be used by whosoever will follow St. James's counsel in singing psalms when they are merry, and I know is used with the fruit of comfort by some, when, in sorrowful pangs of their death-bringing sins, they find the consolation of the never-leaving goodness.

The second kind is of them that deal with matters philosophical: either moral, as Tyrtaeus, Phocylides, and Cato; or natural, as Lucretius and Virgil's Georgics; or astronomical, as Manilius and Pontanus; or historical, as Lucan; which who mislike, the fault is in their judgements quite out of taste, and not in the sweet food of sweetly uttered knowledge. But because this second sort is wrapped within the fold of the proposed subject, and takes not the course of his own invention, whether they properly be poets or no let grammarians dispute; and go to the third, indeed right poets, of whom chiefly this question ariseth, betwixt whom and these second is such a kind of difference as betwixt the meaner sort of painters, who counterfeit only such faces as are set before them, and the more excellent, who, having no law but wit, bestow that in colours upon you which is fittest for the eye to see, as the constant though lamenting look of Lucretia, when she punished in herself another's fault.

Wherein he painteth not Lucretia whom he never saw, but painteth the outward beauty of such a virtue. For these third be they which most properly do imitate to teach and delight, and to imitate borrow nothing of what is, hath been, or shall be; but range, only reined with learned discretion, into the divine consideration of what may be, and should be. These be they that, as the first and most noble sort may justly be termed *Vates,* so there are waited on in the excellentest languages and best understandings, with the foredescribed name of Poets; for these indeed do merely make to imitate, and imitate both to delight and teach, and delight to move men to take that goodness in hand, which without delight they would fly as from a stranger, and teach, to make them know that goodness whereunto they are moved: which being the noblest scope to which ever any learning was directed, yet want there not idle tongues to bark at them. These be subdivided into sundry more special denominations. The most notable be the Heroic, Lyric, Tragic, Comic, Satiric, Iambic, Elegiac, Pastoral, and certain others, some of these being termed according to the matter they deal with, some by the sorts of verses they liked best to write in; for indeed the greatest part of poets have apparelled their poetical inventions in that numbrous kind of writing which is called verse—indeed but apparelled, verse being but an ornament and no cause to Poetry, since there have been many most excellent poets that never versified, and now swarm many versifiers that need never answer to the name of poets. For Xenophon, who did imitate so excellently as to give us *effigiem iusti imperii,* "the portraiture of a just Empire," under name of Cyrus (as Cicero saith of him), made therein an absolute heroical poem.

So did Heliodorus in his sugared invention of that picture of love in Theagenes and Chariclea; and yet both these writ in prose: which I speak to show that it is not rhyming and versing that maketh a poet—no more than a long gown maketh an advocate, who though he pleaded in armour should be an advocate and no soldier. But it is that feigning notable images of virtues, vices, or what else, with that delightful teaching, which must be the right describing note to know a poet by, although indeed the Senate of Poets hath chosen verse as their fittest raiment, meaning, as in matter they passed all in all, so in manner to go beyond them—not speaking (table talk fashion or like men in a dream) words as they chanceably fall from the mouth, but peizing each syllable of each word by just proportion according to the dignity of the subject.

Now therefore it shall not be amiss first to weigh this latter sort of Poetry by his works, and then by his parts, and, if in neither of these anatomies he be condemnable, I hope we shall obtain a more favourable sentence. This purifying of wit, this enriching of memory, enabling of judgement, and enlarging of conceit, which commonly we call learning, under what name soever it come forth, or to what immediate end soever it be directed, the final end is to lead and draw us to as high a perfection as our degenerate souls, made worse by their clayey lodgings, can be capable of. This, according to the inclination of the man, bred many formed impressions. For some that thought this felicity principally to be gotten by knowledge and no knowledge to be so high and heavenly as acquaintance with the stars, gave themselves to Astronomy; others, persuading themselves to be demigods if they knew the causes of things, became natural and supernatural philosophers; some an admirable delight drew to Music; and some the certainty of demonstration to the Mathematics. But all, one and other, having this scope—to know, and by knowledge to lift up the mind from the dungeon of the body to the enjoying his own divine essence. But when by the balance of experience it was found that the astronomer looking to the stars might fall into a ditch, that the inquiring philosopher might be blind in himself, and the mathematician might draw forth a straight line with a crooked heart, then, lo, did proof, the overruler of opinions, make manifest that all these are but serving sciences, which, as they have each a private end in themselves, so yet are they all directed to the highest end of the mistress-knowledge, by the Greeks called *Architectonike,* which stands (as I think) in the knowledge of a man's self, in the ethic and politic consideration, with the end of well doing and not of well knowing only: even as the saddler's next end is to make a good saddle, but his farther end to serve a nobler faculty, which is horsemanship; so the horseman's to soldiery, and the soldier not only to have the skill, but to perform the practice of a soldier. So that, the ending end of all earthly learning being virtuous action, those skills, that most serve to bring forth that, have a most just title to be princes over all the rest. Wherein we can show the poet's nobleness, by setting him before his other competitors, among whom as principal challengers step forth the moral philosophers, whom, me thinketh, I see coming towards me with a sullen gravity, as though they could not abide vice by daylight, rudely clothed for to witness outwardly their contempt of outward things, with books in their hands against glory, whereto they set their names, sophistically speaking against sublety, and angry with any man in whom they see the foul fault of anger. These men casting largesse as they go of definitions, divisions, and distinctions, with a scornful interrogative do soberly ask whether it be possible to find any path so ready to lead a man to virtue as that which teacheth what virtue is—and teacheth it not only by delivering forth his very being, his causes, and effects, but also by making known his enemy, Vice (which must be destroyed), and his cumbersome servant, Passion (which must be mastered), by showing the generalities that containeth it, and the specialities that are derived from it; lastly, by plain setting down, how it extendeth itself out of the limits of a man's own little world to the government of families, and maintaining of public societies.

The historian scarcely giveth leisure to the moralist to say so much, but that he, laden with old mouse-eaten records, authorizing himself (for the most part) upon other histories, whose greatest authorities are built upon the notable foundation of hearsay; having much ado to accord differing writers and to pick truth out of partiality; better acquainted with a thousand years ago than with the present age, and yet better knowing how this world goeth than how his own wit runneth; curious for antiquities and inquisitive of novelties; a wonder to young folks and a tyrant in table talk, denieth, in a great chafe, that any man for teaching of virtue, and virtuous actions, is comparable to him. "I am *Lux vitae, Temporum magistra, Vita memoriae, Nuncia vetustatis"* ["the light of life, the master of the ages, the life of memory, the messenger of antiquity." Cicero, *On the Orator,* II, 9, 36].

The philosopher (saith he) "teacheth a disputative virtue, but I do an active. His virtue is excellent in the dangerless Academy of Plato, but mine showeth forth her honourable face in the battles of Marathon, Pharsalia, Poitiers, and Agincourt. He teacheth virtue by certain abstract considerations, but I only bid you follow the footing of them that have gone before you. Old-aged experience goeth beyond the fine-witted philosopher, but I give the experience of many ages. Lastly, if he make the song-book, I put the learner's hand to the lute; and if he be the guide, I am the light."

Then would he allege you innumerable examples, conferring story by story, how much the wisest senators and princes have been directed by the credit of history, as Brutus, Alphonsus of Aragon, and who not, if need be? At length the long line of their disputation maketh a point in this, that the one giveth the precept, and the other the example.

Now, whom shall we find (since the question standeth for the highest form in the School of Learning) to be Moderator? Truly, as me seemeth, the poet; and if not a Moderator, even the man that ought to carry the title from them both, and much more from all other serving sciences. Therefore compare we the poet with the historian, and with the moral philosopher; and, if he go beyond them both, no other human skill can match him. . . .

The philosopher therefore and the historian are they which would win the goal, the one by precept, the other by example. But both, not having both, do both halt. For the philosopher, setting down with thorny argument the bare rule, is so hard of utterance, and so misty to be conceived, that one that hath no other guide but him shall wade in him till he be old before he shall find sufficient cause to be honest. For his knowledge standeth so upon the abstract and general, that happy is that man who may understand him, and more happy that can apply what he doth understand.

On the other side, the historian, wanting the precept, is so tied, not to what should be but to what is, to the particular truth of things and not to the general reason of things, that his example draweth no necessary consequence, and therefore a less fruitful doctrine.

Now doth the peerless poet perform both: for whatsoever the philosopher saith should be done, he giveth a perfect picture of it in some one by whom he presupposeth it was done; so as he coupleth the general notion with the particular example. A perfect picture I say, for he yieldeth to the powers of the mind an image of that whereof the philosopher bestoweth but a wordish description: which doth neither strike, pierce, nor possess the sight of the soul so much as that other doth.

For as in outward things, to a man that had never seen an elephant or a rhinoceros, who should tell him most exquisitely all their shapes, colour, bigness, and particular marks, or of a gorgeous palace the architecture, with declaring the full beauties might well make the hearer able to repeat, as it were by rote, all he had heard, yet should never satisfy his inward conceits with being witness to itself of a true lively knowledge: but the same man, as soon as he might see those beasts well painted, or the house well in model, should straightways grow, without need of any description, to a judicial comprehending of them: so no doubt the philosopher with his learned definition—be it of virtue, vices, matters of public policy or private government—replenisheth the memory with many infallible grounds of wisdom, which, notwithstanding, lie dark before the imaginative and judging power, if they be not illuminated or figured forth by the speaking picture of Poesy. . . .

But now may it be alleged that, if this imagining of matters be so fit for the imagination, then must the historian needs surpass, who bringeth you images of true matters, such as indeed were done, and not such as fantastically or falsely may be suggested to have been done. Truly, Aristotle himself, in his discourse of Poesy, plainly determineth this question, saying that Poetry is *Philosophoteron* and *Spoudaioteron,* that is to say, it is more philosophical and more studiously serious than history. His reason is, because Poesy dealeth with *Katholou,* that is to say, with the universal consideration, and the history with *Kathekaston,* the particular: "now," saith he, "the universal weighs what is fit to be said or done, either in likelihood or necessity (which the Poesy considereth in his imposed names), and the particular only marks whether Alcibiades did, or suffered, this or that." Thus far Aristotle: which reason of his (as all his) is most full of reason. For indeed, if the question were whether it were better to have a particular act truly or falsely set down, there is no doubt which is to be chosen, no more than whether you had rather have Vespasian's picture right as he was, or at the painter's pleasure nothing resembling. But if the question be for your own use and learning, whether it be better to have it set down as it should be, or as it was, then certainly is more doctrinable the feigned Cyrus in Xenophon than the true Cyrus in Justin, and the feigned Aeneas in Virgil than the right Aeneas in Dares Phrygius. . . .

Now, to that which commonly is attributed to the praise of histories, in respect of the notable learning is gotten by marking the success, as though therein a man should see virtue exalted and vice punished—truly that commendation is peculiar to Poetry, and far off from History. For indeed Poetry ever setteth virtue so out in her best colours, making Fortune her well-waiting handmaid, that one must needs be enamoured of her. Well may you see Ulysses in a storm, and in other hard plights; but they are but exercises of patience and magnanimity, to make them shine the more in the near-following prosperity. And of the contrary part, if evil men come to the stage, they ever go out (as the tragedy writer answered to one that misliked the show of such persons) so manacled as they little animate folks to follow them. But the historian, being captived to the truth of a foolish world, is many times a terror from well doing, and an encouragement to unbridled wickedness.

. . . I conclude, therefore, that he [the poet] excelleth History, not only in furnishing the mind with knowledge, but in setting it forward to that which deserveth to be called and accounted good: which setting forward, and moving to well doing, indeed setteth the laurel crown upon the poet as victorious, not only of the historian, but over the philosopher, howsoever in teaching it may be questionable.

For suppose it be granted (that which I suppose with great reason may be denied) that the philosopher, in respect of his methodical proceeding, doth teach more perfectly than the poet, yet do I think that no man is so much *Philophilosophos* ["a lover of the philosopher"] as to compare the philosopher, in moving, with the poet.

And that moving is of a higher degree than teaching, it may by this appear, that it is well-nigh the cause and the effect of teaching. For who will be taught, if he be not moved with desire to be taught, and what so much good doth that teaching bring forth (I speak still of moral doctrine) as that it moveth one to do that which it doth teach? For, as Aristotle saith, it is not *Gnosis* but *Praxis* ["not abstract knowledge, but action"] must be the fruit. And how *Praxis* cannot be, without being moved to practise, it is no hard matter to consider.

The philosopher showeth you the way, he informeth you of the particularities, as well of the tediousness of the way, as of the pleasant lodging you shall have when your journey is ended, as of the many by-turnings that may divert you from your way. But this is to no man but to him that will read him, and read him with attentive studious painfulness; which constant desire whosoever hath in him, hath already passed half the hardness of the way, and therefore is beholding to the philosopher but for the other half. Nay truly, learned men have learnedly thought that where once reason hath so much overmastered passion as that the mind hath a free desire to do well, the inward light each mind hath in itself is as good as a philosopher's book; seeing in nature we know it is well to do well, and what is well and what is evil, although not in the words of art which philosophers bestow upon us. For out of natural conceit the philosophers drew it; but to be moved to do that which we know, or to be moved with desire to know.

Now therein of all sciences (I speak still of human, and according to the humane conceits) is our poet the monarch. For he doth not only show the way, but giveth so sweet a prospect into the way, as will entice any man to enter into it. Nay, he doth, as if your journey should lie through a fair vineyard, at the first give you a cluster of grapes, that, full of that taste, you may long to pass further. He beginneth not with obscure definitions, which must blur the margent [margins of the page] with interpretations, and load the memory with doubtfulness; but he cometh to you with words set in delightful proportion, either accompanied with, or prepared for, the well enchanting skill of music; and with a tale forsooth he cometh unto you, with a tale which holdeth children from play, and old men from the chimney corner. And, pretending no more, doth intend the winning of the mind from wickedness to virtue: even as the child is often brought to take most wholesome things by hiding them in such other as have a pleasant taste: which, if one should begin to tell them the nature of aloes or rhubarb they should receive, would sooner take their physic at their ears than at their mouth. So is it in men (most of which are childish in the best things, till they be cradled in their graves): glad they will be to hear the tales of Hercules, Achilles, Cyrus, and Aeneas; and, hearing them, must needs hear the right description of wisdom, valour, and justice; which, if they had been barely, that is to say philosophically, set out, they would swear they be brought to school again.

That imitation whereof Poetry is, hath the most conveniency to Nature of all other, insomuch that, as Aristotle saith, those things which in themselves are horrible, as cruel battles, unnatural monsters, are made in poetical imitation delightful. Truly, I have known men, that even with reading *Amadis de Gaule* (which God knoweth wanteth much of a perfect poesy) have found their hearts moved to the exercise of courtesy, liberality, and especially courage.

Who readeth Aeneas carrying old Anchises on his back, that wisheth not it were his fortune to perform so excellent an act? . . .

By these, therefore, examples and reasons, I think it may be manifest that the Poet, with that same hand of delight, doth draw the mind more effectually than any other art doth: and so a conclusion not unfitly ensueth, that, as Virtue is the most excellent resting place for all worldly learning to make his end of, so Poetry, being the most familiar to teach it, and most princely to move towards it, in the most excellent work is the most excellent workman. But I am content not only to decipher him by his works (although works in commendation or dispraise must ever hold an high authority), but more narrowly will examine his parts: so that, as in a man, though all together may carry a presence full of majesty and beauty, perchance in some one defectious piece we may find a blemish. Now in his parts, kinds, or species (as you list to term them), it is to be noted that some poesies have coupled together two or three kinds, as tragical and comical, whereupon is risen the tragi-comical. Some, in the like manner, have mingled prose and verse, as Sannazzaro and Boethius. Some have mingled matters heroical and pastoral. But that cometh all to one in this question, for, if severed they be good, the conjunction cannot be hurtful. Therefore, perchance forgetting some, and leaving some as needless to be remembered, it shall not be amiss in a word to cite the special kinds, to see what faults may be found in the right use of them.

. . . [If] anything be already said in the defence of sweet Poetry, all concurreth to the maintaining the Heroical [epic], which is not only a kind, but the best and most accomplished kind of Poetry. For as the image of each action stirreth and instructeth the mind, so the lofty image of such worthies most inflameth the mind with desire to be worthy, and informs with counsel how to be worthy. Only let Aeneas be worn in the tablet of your memory, how he governeth himself in the ruin of his country, in the preserving his old father, and carrying away his religious ceremonies, in obeying the god's commandment to leave Dido, though not only all passionate kindness, but even the human consideration of virtuous gratefulness, would have craved other of him; how in storms, how in sports, how in war, how in peace, how a fugitive, how victorious, how besieged, how besieging, how to strangers, how to allies, how to enemies, how to his own; lastly, how in his inward self, and how in his outward government, and I think, in a mind not prejudiced with a prejudicating humour, he will be found in excellency fruitful.

But truly I imagine it falleth out with these poet-whippers, as with some good women, who often are sick, but in faith they cannot tell where. So the name of Poetry is odious to them, but neither his cause nor effects, neither the sum that contains him nor the particularities descending from him, give any fast handle to their carping dispraise.

Since then Poetry is of all human learning the most ancient and of most fatherly antiquity, as from whence other learnings have taken their beginnings; since it is so universal that no learned nation doth despise it, nor no barbarous nation is without it; since both Roman and Greek gave divine names unto it, the one of "prophesying," the other of "making," and that indeed that name of "making" is fit for him, considering that whereas other Arts retain themselves within their subject, and receive, as it were, their being from it, the poet only bringeth his own stuff, and doth not learn a conceit out of a matter, but maketh matter for a conceit; since neither his description nor his end containeth any evil, the thing described cannot be evil; since his effects be so good as to reach goodness and to delight the learners; since therein (namely in moral doctrine, the chief of all knowledges) he doth not only far pass the historian, but, for instructing, is wellnigh comparable to the philosopher, and, for moving, leaves him behind him; since the Holy Scripture (wherein there is no uncleanness) hath whole parts in it poetical, and that even our Saviour Christ vouchsafed to use the flowers of it; since all his kinds are not only in their united forms but in their severed dissections fully commendable; I think (and think I think rightly) the laurel crown appointed for triumphing captains doth worthily (of all other learnings) honour the poet's triumph. But because we have ears as well as tongues, and that the lightest reasons that may be will seem to weigh greatly, if nothing be put in the counterbalance, let us hear, and, as well as we can, ponder, what objections may be made against this art, which may be worthy either of yielding or answering.

First, truly I note not only in these *Mysomousoi,* poet-haters, but in all that kind of people who seek a praise by dispraising others, that they do prodigally spend a great many wandering words in quips and scoffs, carping and taunting at each thing, which, by stirring the spleen, may stay the brain from a thorough beholding the worthiness of the subject.

. . . Marry, these other pleasant faultfinders, who will correct the verb before they understand the noun, and confute others' knowledge before they confirm their own, I would have them only remember that scoffing cometh not of wisdom; so as the best title in true English they get with their merriments is to be called good fools, for so have our grave forefathers ever termed that humorous kind of jesters. But that which giveth greatest scope to their scorning humours is rhyming and versing. It is already said (and, as I think, truly said) it is not rhyming and versing that maketh Poesy. One may be a poet without versing, and a versifier without poetry. But yet presuppose it were inseparable (as indeed it seemeth Scaliger judgeth) truly it were an inseparable commendation. For if *Oratio* next to *Ratio,* Speech next to Reason, be the greatest gift bestowed upon mortality, that cannot be praiseless which doth most polish that blessing of speech; which considers each word, not only (as a man may say) by his forcible quality, but by his best measured quantity, carrying even in themselves a harmony (without, perchance, number, measure, order, proportion be in our time grown odious). But lay aside the just praise it hath, by being the only fit speech for Music (Music, I say, the most divine striker of the senses), thus much is undoubtedly true, that if reading be foolish without remembering, memory being the only treasurer of knowledge, those words which are fittest for memory are likewise most convenient for knowledge.

Now, that verse far exceedeth prose in the knitting up of the memory, the reason is manifest,—the words (besides their delight, which hath a great affinity to memory) being so set as one word cannot be lost but the whole work fails; which accuseth itself, call-eth the remembrance back to itself, and so most strongly confirm-eth it. Besides, one word so, as it were, begetting another, as, be it in rhyme or measured verse, by the former a man shall have a near guess to the follower: lastly, even they that have taught the art of memory have showed nothing so apt for it as a certain room divided into many places well and thoroughly known. Now, that hath the verse in effect perfectly, every word having his natural seat, which seat must needs make the words remembered. But what needeth more in a thing so known to all men? Who is it that ever was a scholar that doth not carry away some verses of Virgil, Horace, or Cato, which in his youth he learned, and even to his old age serve him for hourly lessons? But the fitness it hath for memory is notably proved by all delivery of Arts: wherein for the most part, from Grammar to Logic, Mathematic, Physic, and the rest, the rules chiefly necessary to be borne away are compiled in verses. So that, verse being in itself sweet and orderly, and being best for memory, the only handle of knowledge, it must be in jest that any man can speak against it. Now then go we to the most important imputations laid to the poor poets. For aught I can yet learn, they are these. First, that there being many other more fruitful knowledges, a man might better spend his time in them than in this. Secondly, that it is the mother of lies. Thirdly, that it is the nurse of abuse, infecting us with many pestilent desires, with a siren's sweetness drawing the mind to the serpent's tale of sinful fancy,—and herein, especially, comedies give the largest field to ear (as Chaucer saith),—how both in other nations and in ours, before poets did soften us, we were full of courage, given to martial exercises, the pillars of man-like liberty, and not lulled asleep in shady idleness with poets' pas-times. And lastly, and chiefly, they cry out with an open mouth, as if they outshot Robin Hood, that Plato banished them out of his Commonwealth. Truly, this is much, if there be much truth in it. First, to the first, that a man might better spend his time is a reason indeed: but it doth (as they say) but *petere principium* ["beg the question"]: for if it be, as I affirm, that no learning is so good as that which teacheth and moveth to virtue, and that none can both teach and move thereto so much as Poetry, then is the conclusion manifest that ink and paper cannot be to a more profitable purpose employed. And certainly, though a man should grant their first assumption, it should follow (methinks) very unwillingly, that good is not good because better is better. But I still and utterly deny that there is sprung out of earth a more fruitful knowledge. To the second therefore, that they should be the principal liars, I answer paradoxically, but truly, I think truly, that of all writers under the sun the poet is the least liar, and, though he would, as a poet can scarcely be a liar. The astronomer, with his cousin the geometrician, can hardly escape, when they take upon them to measure the height of the stars.

How often, think you, do the physicians lie, when they aver things good for sicknesses, which afterwards send Charon a great number of souls drowned in a potion before they come to his ferry? And no less of the rest, which take upon them to affirm. Now, for the poet, he nothing affirms, and therefore never lieth. For, as I take it, to lie is to affirm that to be true which is false; so as the other artist, and especially the historian, affirming many things, can, in the cloudy knowledge of mankind, hardly escape from many lies. But the poet (as I said before) never affirmeth. The poet never maketh any circles about your imagination, to conjure you to believe for true what he writes. He citeth not authorities of other histories, but even for his entry calleth the sweet Muses to inspire into him a good invention; in truth, not labouring to tell you what is, or is not, but what should or should not be. And therefore, though he recount things not true, yet because he telleth them not for true, he lieth not,—without we will say that Nathan lied in his speech, before alleged, to David; which as a wicked man durst scarce say, so think I none so simple would say that Aesop lied in the tales of his beasts: for who thinks that Aesop writ it for actually true were well worthy to have his name chronicled among the beasts he writeth of.

What child is there that, coming to a play, and seeing *Thebes* written in great letters upon an old door, doth believe that it is Thebes? If then a man can arrive, at that child's age, to know that the poets' persons and doings are but pictures what should be, and not stories what have been, they will never give the lie to things not affirmatively but allegorically and figuratively written. And therefore, as in History, looking for truth, they go away full fraught with falsehood, so in Poesy, looking for fiction, they shall use the narration but as an imaginative ground-plot of a profitable invention.

But hereto is replied, that the poets give names to men they write of, which argueth a conceit of an actual truth, and so, not being true, proves a falsehood. And doth the lawyer lie then, when under the names of "John a Stile" and "John a Noakes" he puts his case? But that is easily answered. Their naming of men is but to make their picture the more lively, and not to build any history; painting men, they cannot leave men nameless. We see we cannot play at chess but that we must give names to our chessmen; and yet, methinks, he were a very partial champion of truth that would say we lied for giving a piece of wood the reverend title of a bishop. The poet nameth Cyrus or Aeneas no other way than to show what men of their fames, fortunes, and estates should do.

Their third is, how much it abuseth men's wit, training it to wanton sinfulness and lustful love: for indeed that is the principal, if not the only, abuse I can hear alleged. They say the Comedies rather teach than reprehend amorous conceits. They say the Lyric is larded with passionate sonnets, the Elegiac weeps the want of his mistress, and that even to the Heroical Cupid hath ambitiously climbed. Alas, Love, I would thou couldst as well defend thyself as thou canst offend others. I would those on whom thou dost attend could either put thee away, or yield good reason why they keep thee. But grant love of beauty to be a beastly fault (although it be very hard, since only man, and no beast, hath that gift to discern beauty); grant that lovely name of Love to deserve all hateful reproaches (although even some of my masters the philosophers spent a good deal of their lamp-oil in setting forth the excellency of it); grant, I say, whatsoever they will have granted; that not only love, but lust, but vanity, but (if they list) scurrility, possesseth many leaves of the poets' books: yet think I, when this is granted, they will find their sentence may with good manners put the last words foremost, and not say that Poetry abuseth man's wit, but that man's wit abuseth Poetry.

For I will not deny but that man's wit may make Poesy, which should be *Eikastike,* which some learned have defined, "figuring forth good things," to be *Phantastike,* which doth, contrariwise, infect the fancy with unworthy objects, as the painter, that should give to the eye either some excellent perspective, or some fine picture, fit for building or fortification, or containing in it some notable example, as Abraham sacrificing his son Isaac, Judith killing Holofernes, David fighting with Goliath, may leave those, and please an ill-pleased eye with wanton shows of better hidden matters. But what, shall the abuse of a thing make the right use odious? Nay truly, though I yield that Poesy may not only be abused, but that being abused, by the reason of his sweet charming force, it can do more hurt than any other army of words, yet shall it be so far from concluding that the abuse should give reproach to the abused, that contrariwise it is a good reason, that whatsoever, being abused, doth most harm, being rightly used (and upon the right use each thing conceiveth his title), doth most good.

Do we not see the skill of Physic (the best rampire to our often-assaulted bodies), being abused, teach poison, the most violent destroyer? Doth not knowledge of Law, whose end is to even and right all things, being abused, grow the crooked fosterer of horrible injuries? Doth not (to go to the highest) God's word abused breed heresy, and His Name abused become blasphemy? Truly, a needle cannot do much hurt, and as truly (with leave of ladies be it spoken) it cannot do much good. With a sword thou mayest kill thy father, and with a sword thou mayest defend thy prince and country. So that, as in their calling poets the fathers of lies they say nothing, so in this their argument of abuse they prove the commendation.

They allege herewith, that before poets began to be in price our nation hath set their heart's delight upon action, and not upon imagination, rather doing things worthy to be written, than writing things fit to be done. What that beforetime was, I think scarcely Sphinx can tell, since no memory is so ancient that hath the precedence of Poetry. And certain it is that, in our plainest homeliness, yet never was the Albion nation without Poetry. Marry, this argument, though it be levelled against Poetry, yet is it indeed a chainshot against all learning, or bookishness, as they commonly term it. Of such mind were certain Goths, of whom it is written that, having in the spoil of a famous city taken a fair library, one hangman, belike, fit to execute the fruits of their wits, who had murdered a great number of bodies, would have set fire on it. "No," said another very gravely, "take heed what you do, for while they are busy about these toys, we shall with more leisure conquer their countries."

This indeed is the ordinary doctrine of ignorance, and many words sometimes I have heard spent in it: but because this reason is generally against all learning, as well as Poetry, or rather, all learning but Poetry; because it were too large a digression to handle, or at least too superfluous (since it is manifest that all government of action is to be gotten by knowledge, and knowledge best by gathering many knowledges, which is reading), I only, with Horace, to him that is of that opinion,

Iubeo stultum esse libenter;
["I bid him to be as much of a fool as he wishes," *Satires,* I, I, 63.]

for as for Poetry itself, it is the freest from this objection. For Poetry is the companion of the camps.

. . . But now indeed my burden is great; now Plato's name is laid upon me, whom, I must confess, of all philosophers I have ever esteemed most worthy of reverence, and with great reason, since of all philosophers he is the most poetical. Yet if he will defile the fountain out of which his flowing streams have proceeded, let us boldly examine with what reasons he did it. First truly, a man might maliciously object that Plato, being a philosopher, was a natural enemy of poets. For indeed, after the philosophers had picked out of the

sweet mysteries of Poetry the right discerning true points of knowledge, they forthwith, putting it in method, and making a school art
of that which the poets did only teach by a divine delightfulness,
beginning to spurn at their guides, like ungrateful prentices, were
not content to set up shops for themselves, but sought by all means
to discredit their masters; which by the force of delight being barred
them, the less they could overthrow them, the more they hated
them. For indeed, they found for Homer seven cities strove who
should have him for their citizen; where many cities banished philosophers as not fit members to live among them. For only repeating certain of Euripides' verses, many Athenians had their lives
saved of the Syracusians, when the Athenians themselves thought
many philosophers unworthy to live.

Certain poets, as Simonides and Pindarus, had so prevailed with
Hiero the First, that of a tyrant they made him a just king; where
Plato could do so little with Dionysius, that he himself of a philosopher was made a slave. But who should do thus, I confess, should
requite the objections made against poets with like cavillation
against philosophers; as likewise one should do that should bid one
read Phaedrus or Symposium in Plato, or the discourse of love in
Plutarch, and see whether any poet do authorize abominable filthi-
ness, as they do. Again, a man might ask out of what Commonwealth Plato did banish them. In sooth, thence where he himself
alloweth community of women. So as belike this banishment grew
not for effeminate wantonness, since little should poetical sonnets
be hurtful when a man might have what woman he listed. But I
honour philosophical instructions, and bless the wits which bred
them: so as they be not abused, which is likewise stretched to
Poetry.

St. Paul himself, who yet, for the credit of poets, allegeth twice
two poets, and one of them by the name of a prophet, setteth a
watchword upon Philosophy,—indeed upon the abuse. So doth
Plato upon the abuse, not upon Poetry. Plato found fault that the
poets of his time filled the world with wrong opinions of the gods,
making light tales of that unspotted essence, and therefore would
not have the youth depraved with such opinions. Herein may

much be said; let this suffice: the poets did not induce such opinions, but did imitate those opinions already induced. For all the Greek stories can well testify that the very religion of that time stood upon many and many-fashioned gods, not taught so by the poets, but followed according to their nature of imitation. Who list may read in Plutarch the discourses of Isis and Osiris, of the cause why oracles ceased, of the divine providence, and see whether the theology of that nation stood not upon such dreams which the poets indeed superstitiously observed, and truly (since they had not the light of Christ) did much better in it than the philosophers, who, shaking off superstition, brought in atheism. Plato therefore (whose authority I had much rather justly construe than unjustly resist) meant not in general of poets, in those words of which Julius Scaliger saith, *Qua authoritate barbari quidam atque hispidi abuti velint ad poetas e republica exigendos* ["Which authority some crude and insensible men would abuse to drive poets from the republic"]; but only meant to drive out those wrong opinions of the Deity (whereof now, without further law, Christianity hath taken away all the hurtful belief), perchance (as he thought) nourished by the then esteemed poets. And a man need go no further than to Plato himself to know his meaning: who, in his Dialogue called *Ion*, giveth high and rightly divine commendation to Poetry. So as Plato, banishing the abuse, not the thing, not banishing it, but giving due honour unto it, shall be our patron and not our adversary. For indeed I had much rather (since truly I may do it) show their mistaking of Plato (under whose lion's skin they would make an asslike braying against Poesy) than go about to overthrow his authority; whom, the wiser a man is, the more just cause he shall find to have in admiration; especially since he attributeth unto Poesy more than myself do, namely, to be a very inspiring of a divine force, far above man's wit, as in the afore-named Dialogue is apparent.

Of the other side, who would show the honours have been by the best sort of judgements granted them, a whole sea of examples would present themselves: Alexanders, Caesars, Scipios, all favourers of poets; Laelius, called the Roman Socrates, himself a poet, so as part of *Heautontimorumenos* in Terence was supposed to be made by him, and even the Greek Socrates, whom Apollo confirmed to be the only wise man, is said to have spent part of his old time in putting Aesop's fables into verses. And therefore, full evil should it become his scholar Plato to put such words in his master's mouth against poets. But what need more? Aristotle writes the Art of Poesy: and why, if it should not be written? Plutarch teacheth the use to be gathered of them, and how, if they should not be read? And who reads Plutarch's either history or philosophy, shall find he trimmeth both their garments with guards of Poesy. But I list not to defend Poesy with the help of her underling Historiography. Let it suffice that it is a fit soil for praise to well upon; and what dispraise may set upon it, is either easily overcome, or transformed into just commendation. So that, since the excellencies of it may be so easily and so justly confirmed, and the low-creeping objections so soon trodden down; it not being an art of lies, but oft true doctrine; not of effeminateness, but of notable stirring of courage; not of abusing man's wit, but of strengthening man's wit; not banished, but honoured by Plato; let us rather plant more laurels for to engarland our poets' heads (which honour of being laureate, as besides them only triumphant captains wear, is a sufficient authority to show the price they ought to be had in) than suffer the ill-favouring breath of such wrong-speakers once to blow upon the clear springs of Poesy.

But since I have run so long a career in this matter, methinks, before I give my pen a full stop, it shall be but a little more lost time to inquire why England (the mother of excellent minds) should be grown so hard a stepmother to poets, who certainly in wit ought to pass all other, since all only proceedeth from their wit, being indeed makers of themselves, not takers of others. . . . ["Base men," Sidney writes, "with servile wits undertake it, who think it enough if they can be rewarded by the printer."] I that, before ever I durst aspire unto the dignity, am admitted into the company of the paper-blurrers, do find the very true cause of our wanting estimation is want of desert, taking upon us to be poets in despite of Pallas. Now, wherein we want desert were a thankworthy labour to express: but if I knew, I should have mended myself. But I, as I never desired the title, so have I neglected the means to come by it. Only, overmastered by some thoughts, I yielded an inky tribute unto them. Marry, they that delight in Poesy itself should seek to know what they do, and how they do, and, especially, look themselves in an unflattering glass of reason, if they be inclinable unto it. For Poesy must not be drawn by the ears; it must be gently led, or rather it must lead; which was partly the cause that made the ancient-learned affirm it was a divine gift, and no human skill; since all other knowledges lie ready for any that hath strength of wit; a poet no industry can make, if his own genius be not carried unto it; and therefore is it an old proverb, *Orator fit, Poeta nascitur* ["The orator is made; the poet is born."]. Yet confess I always that as the fertilest ground must be manured, so must the highest-flying wit have a Daedalus to guide him. That Daedalus, they say, both in this and in other, hath three wings to bear itself up into the air of due commendation: that is, Art, Imitation, and Exercise. But these, neither artificial rules nor imitative patterns, we much cumber ourselves withal. Exercise indeed we do, but that very fore-backwardly: for where we should exercise to know, we exercise as having known: and so is our brain delivered of much matter which never was begotten by knowledge. For, there being two principal parts—matter to be expressed by words and words to express the matter—in neither we use Art or Imitation rightly. . . .

Chaucer, undoubtedly, did excellently in his *Troilus and Cressida;* of whom, truly, I know not whether to marvel more, either that he in that misty time could see so clearly, or that we in this clear age walk so stumblingly after him. Yet had he great wants, fit to be forgiven in so reverent antiquity. I account the *Mirrour of Magistrates* meetly furnished of beautiful parts, and in the Earl of Surrey's *Lyrics* many things tasting of a noble birth, and worthy of a noble mind. The *Shepheard's Calendar* hath much poetry in his Eclogues, indeed worthy the reading, if I be not deceived. That same framing of his style to an old rustic language I dare not allow, since neither Theocritus in Greek, Virgil in Latin, nor Sannazzaro in Italian did affect it. Besides these, do I not remember to have seen but few (to speak boldly) printed, that have poetical sinews in them: for proof whereof, let but most of the verses be put in prose, and then ask the meaning; and it will be found that one verse did but beget another, without ordering at the first what should be at the last; which becomes a confused mass of words with a tingling sound of rhyme, barely accompanied with reason.

Our Tragedies and Comedies (not without cause cried out against), observing rules neither of honest civility nor of skilful Poetry, excepting *Gorboduc* (again, I say, of those that I have seen), which notwithstanding, as it is full of stately speeches and well-sounding phrases, climbing to the height of Seneca's style, and as full of notable morality, which it doth most delightfully teach, and so obtain the very end of Poesy, yet in truth it is very defectious in the circumstances, which grieveth me, because it might not remain as an exact model of all Tragedies. For it is faulty both in place and time, the two necessary companions of all corporal actions. For where the stage should always represent but one place, and the uttermost time presupposed in it should be, both by Aristotle's precept and common reason, but one day, there is both many days, and many places, inartificially imagined. But if it be so in *Gorboduc,* how much more in all the rest, where you shall have Asia of the one side, and Afric of the other, and so many other under-kingdoms, that the player, when he cometh in, must ever begin with telling where he is, or else the tale will not be conceived? Now ye shall have three ladies walk to gather flowers and then we must believe the stage to be a garden. By and by we hear news of shipwreck in the same place, and then we are to blame if we accept it not for a rock.

Upon the back of that comes out a hideous monster, with fire and smoke, and then the miserable beholders are bound to take it for a cave. While in the meantime two armies fly in, represented with four swords and bucklers, and then what hard heart will not receive it for a pitched field? Now, of time they are much more liberal, for ordinary it is that two young princes fall in love. After many traverses, she is got with child, delivered of a fair boy; he is lost, groweth a man, falls in love, and is ready to get another child; and all this in two hours' space: which, how absurd it is in sense, even sense may imagine, and Art hath taught, and all ancient examples justified, and, at this day, the ordinary players in Italy will not err in. Yet will some bring in an example of Eunuchus in Terence, that containeth matter of two days, yet far short of twenty years. True it is, and so was it to be played in two days, and so fitted to the time it set forth. And though Plautus hath in one place done amiss, let us hit with him, and not miss with him. But they will say, How then shall we set forth a story, which containeth both many places and many times? And do they not know that a Tragedy is tied to the laws of Poesy, and not of History; not bound to follow the story, but, having liberty, either to feign a quite new matter, or to frame the history to the most tragical conveniency? Again, many things may be told which cannot be showed, if they know the difference betwixt reporting and representing. As, for example, I may speak (though I am here) of Peru, and in speech digress from that to the description of Calicut; but in action I cannot represent it without Pacolet's horse. And so was the manner the ancients took, by some Nuncius [messenger] to recount things done in former time or other place. Lastly, if they will represent an history, they must not (as Horace saith) begin *ab ovo* ["from the egg," i.e., at the beginning], but they must come to the principal point of that one action which they will represent. By example this will be best expressed. I have a story of young Polydorus, delivered for safety's sake, with great riches, by his father Priam to Polymnestor, king of Thrace, in the Trojan war time. He, after some years, hearing the overthrow of Priam, for to make the treasure his own, murdereth the child. The body of the child is taken up by Hecuba. She, the same day, findeth a slight to be revenged most cruelly of the tyrant. Where now would one of our tragedy writers begin, but with the delivery of the child? Then should he sail over into Thrace, and so spend I know not how many years, and travel numbers of places. But where doth Euripides? Even with the finding of the body, leaving the rest to be told by the spirit of Polydorus. This need no further to be enlarged; the dullest wit may conceive it. But besides these gross absurdities, how all their plays be neither right tragedies, nor right comedies, mingling kings and clowns, not because the matter so carrieth it, but thrust in clowns by head and shoulders, to play a part in majestical matters, with neither decency [decorum] nor discretion, so as neither the admiration and commiseration, nor the right sportfulness, is by their mongrel tragi-comedy obtained. I know Apuleius did somewhat so, but that is a thing recounted with space of time, not represented in one moment: and I know the ancients have one or two examples of tragi-comedies, as Plautus hath *Amphitrio*. But, if we mark them well, we shall find, that they never, or very daintily, match hornpipes and funerals. So falleth it out that, having indeed no right comedy, in that comical part of our tragedy we have nothing but scurrility, unworthy of any chaste ears, or some extreme show of doltishness, indeed fit to lift up a loud laughter, and nothing else: where the whole tract of a comedy should be full of delight, as the tragedy should be still maintained in a well-raised admiration. But our comedians think there is no delight without laughter; which is very wrong, for though laughter may come with delight, yet cometh it not of delight, as though delight should be the cause of laughter; but well may one thing breed both together. Nay, rather in themselves they have, as it were, a kind of contrariety: for delight we scarcely do but in things that have a conveniency to ourselves or to the general nature: laughter almost ever cometh of things most disproportioned to ourselves and nature. Delight hath a joy in it, either permanent or present. Laughter hath only a scornful tickling.

For example, we are ravished with delight to see a fair woman, and yet are far from being moved to laughter. We laugh at deformed creatures, wherein certainly we cannot delight. We delight in good chances, we laugh at mischances; we delight to hear the happiness of our friends, or country, at which he were worthy to be laughed at that would laugh. We shall, contrarily, laugh sometimes to find a matter quite mistaken and go down the hill against the bias, in the mouth of some such men, as for the respect of them one shall be heartily sorry, yet he cannot choose but laugh; and so is rather pained than delighted with laughter. Yet deny I not but that they may go well together. For as in Alexander's picture well set out we delight without laughter, and in twenty mad antics we laugh without delight, so in Hercules, painted with his great beard and furious countenance, in woman's attire, spinning at Omphale's commandment, it breedeth both delight and laughter. For the representing of so strange a power in love procureth delight: and the scornfulness of the action stirreth laughter. But I speak to this purpose, that all the end of the comical part be not upon such scornful matters as stirreth laughter only, but, mixed with it, that delightful teaching which is the end of Poesy. And the great fault even in that point of laughter, and forbidden plainly by Aristotle, is that they stir laughter in sinful things, which are rather execrable than ridiculous; or in miserable, which are rather to be pitied than scorned. For what is it to make folks gape at a wretched beggar, or a beggarly clown; or, against law of hospitality, to jest at strangers, because they speak not English so well as we do? . . . But I have lavished out too many words of this play matter. I do it because, as they are excelling parts of Poesy, so is there none so much used in England, and none can be more pitifully abused; which, like an unmannerly daughter showing a bad education, causeth her mother Poesy's honesty to be called in question. Other sorts of Poetry almost have we none, but that lyrical kind of songs and sonnets: which, Lord, if He gave us so good minds, how well it might be employed, and with how heavenly fruit, both private and public, in singing the praises of the immortal beauty, the immortal goodness of that God who giveth us hands to write and wits to conceive; of which we might well want words, but never matter; of which we could turn our eyes to nothing, but we should ever have new budding occasions. But truly many of such writings as come under the banner of unresistible love, if I were a mistress, would never persuade me they were in love; so coldly they apply fiery speeches, as men that had rather read lovers' writings, and so caught up certain swelling phrases (which hang together like a man which once told me the wind was at north-west, and by south, because he would be sure to name winds enough), than that in truth they feel those passions, which easily (as I think) may be betrayed by that same forcibleness or *Energia* (as the Greeks call it) of the writer. But let this be a sufficient though short note, that we miss the right use of the material point of Poesy. . . .

Undoubtedly (at least to my opinion undoubtedly) I have found in divers small-learned courtiers a more sound style than in some professors of learning: of which I can guess no other cause, but that the courtier, following that which by practice he findeth fittest to nature, therein (though he know it not) doth according to Art, though not by Art: where the other, using Art to show Art, and not to hide Art (as in these cases he should do), flieth from nature, and indeed abuseth Art.

But what? Methinks I deserve to be pounded for straying from Poetry to Oratory: but both have such an affinity in this wordish consideration, that I think this digression will make my meaning receive the fuller understanding—which is not to take upon me to teach poets how they should do, but only, finding myself sick among the rest, to show some one or two spots of the common infection grown among the most part of writers: that, acknowledging ourselves somewhat awry, we may bend to the right use both of matter and manner; whereto our language giveth us great occasion, being capable of any excellent exercising of it. I know some will say it is a mingled language. And why not so much the better, taking the best of both the other? Another will say it wanteth grammar. Nay truly, it hath that praise, that it wanteth grammar: for grammar it might have, but it needs it not; being so easy of itself, and so void of those cumbersome differences of cases, genders, moods, and tenses, which I think was a piece of the Tower of Babylon's curse, that a man should be put to school to learn his mothertongue. But for the uttering sweetly and properly the conceits of the mind, which is the end of speech, that hath it equally with any other tongue in the world: and is particularly happy in compositions of two or three words together, near the Greek, far beyond the Latin: which is one of the greatest beauties can be in a language.

Now, of versifying there are two sorts, the one ancient, the other modern: the ancient marked the quantity of each syllable, and according to that framed his verse; the modern observing only number (with some regard of the accent), the chief life of it standeth in that like sounding of the words, which we call rhyme. Whether of these be the most excellent, would bear many speeches. The ancient (no doubt) more fit for music, both words and tune observing quantity, and more fit lively to express divers passions, by the low and lofty sound of the well-weighed syllable. The latter likewise, with his rhyme, striketh a certain music to the ear: and, in fine, since it doth delight, though by another way, it obtains the same purpose: there being in either sweetness, and wanting in neither majesty. Truly the English, before any other vulgar language I know, is fit for both sorts: for, for the ancient, the Italian is so full of vowels that it must ever be cumbered with elisions; the Dutch so, of the other side, with consonants, that they cannot yield the sweet sliding fit for a verse; the French, in his whole language, hath not one word that hath his accent in the last syllable saving two, called *Antepenultima;* and little more hath the Spanish: and, therefore, very gracelessly may they use dactyls. The English is subject to none of these defects.

Now, for the rhyme, though we do not observe quantity, yet we observe the accent very precisely: which other languages either cannot do, or will not do so absolutely. That *caesura,* or breathing place in the midst of the verse, neither Italian nor Spanish have, the French, and we, never almost fail of. Lastly, even the very rhyme itself the Italian cannot put in the last syllable, by the French named the "masculine rhyme," but still in the next to the last, which the French call the "female," or the next before that, which the Italians term *sdrucciola.* The example of the former is *buono : suono,* of the *sdrucciola, femina : semina.* The French, of the other side, hath both the male, as *bon : son,* and the female, as *plaise : taise,* but the *sdrucciola* he hath not: where the English hath all three, as *due : true, father : rather, motion : potion,* with much more which might be said, but that I find already the triflingness of this discourse is much too much enlarged. So that since the ever-praiseworthy Poesy is full of virtue-breeding delightfulness, and void of no gift that ought to be in the noble name of learning; since the blames laid against it are either false or feeble; since the cause why it is not esteemed in England is the fault of poet-apes, not poets; since, lastly, our tongue is most fit to honour Poesy, and to be honoured by Poesy; I conjure you all that have had the evil luck to read this ink-wasting toy of mine, even in the name of the Nine Muses, no more to scorn the sacred mysteries of Poesy, no more to laugh at the name of "poets," as though they were next inheritors to fools, no more to jest at the reverent title of a "rhymer"; but to believe, with Aristotle, that they were the ancient treasurers of the Grecians' Divinity; to believe, with Bembus, that they were first bringers-in of all civility; to believe, with Scaliger, that no philosopher's precepts can sooner make you an honest man than the reading of Virgil; to believe, with Clauserus, the translator of Cornutus, that it pleased the heavenly Deity, by Hesiod and Homer, under the veil of fables, to give us all knowledge, Logic, Rhetoric, Philosophy, natural and moral, and *Quid non?* ["What not?"]; to believe, with me, that there are many mysteries contained in Poetry, which of purpose were written darkly, lest by profane wits it should be abused; to believe, with Landino, that they are so beloved of the gods that whatsoever they write proceeds of a divine fury; lastly, to believe themselves, when they tell you they will make you immortal by their verses.

Thus doing, your name shall flourish in the printers' shops; thus doing, you, shall be of kin to many a poetical preface; thus doing, you shall be most fair, most rich, most wise, most all; you shall dwell upon superlatives. . . . Thus doing, your soul shall be placed with Dante's Beatrix, or Virgil's Anchises. But if (fie of such a but) you be born so near the dullmaking cataract of Nilus that you cannot hear the planet-like music of Poetry, if you have so earth-creeping a mind that it cannot lift itself up to look to the sky of Poetry, or rather, by a certain rustical disdain, will become such a Mome as to be a Momus of Poetry; then, though I will not wish unto you the ass's ears of Midas, nor to be driven by a poet's verses (as Bubonax was) to hang himself, nor to be rhymed to death, as is said to be done in Ireland; yet thus much curse I must send you, in the behalf of all poets, that while you live, you live in love, and never get favour for lacking skill of a Sonnet, and, when you die, your memory die from the earth for want of an Epitaph.

John Dryden

(1631–1700)

AN ESSAY OF DRAMATIC POESY

In 1665, Dryden fled the London plague, settled in the country residence of his father-in-law, and wrote his *Essay* with the intention of defending English drama in the face of rigid neo-classical prejudices.

The dialogue, suitable to the exploration of ideas, attempts not to dogmatize but to weigh arguments. Traditionally the discussants have been identified as follows; Crites—Sir Robert Howard, Dryden's brother-in-law and collaborator on *The Indian Queen* (1664); Lisideus—Sir Charles Sedley, the poet; Eugenius—Lord Buckhurst, Dryden's friend and patron, to whom the essay was dedicated (On the day of the imaginary dialogue, June 3, 1665, he was in the fleet engaged in battling the Dutch.); Neander—Dryden himself. However, since there is no certainty that identified speakers actually held such opinions, the various critical positions stated in the *Essay* may be regarded as Dryden's device for clarifying his own point of view.

First published in 1668, the *Essay* was slightly revised in 1684, the version used here. The spelling has been modernized.

———————————◆———————————

IT WAS that memorable day, in the first summer of the late war, when our navy engaged the Dutch; a day wherein the two most mighty and best appointed fleets which any age had ever seen, disputed the command of the greater half of the globe, the commerce of nations, and the riches of the universe: while these vast floating bodies, on either side, moved against each other in parallel lines, and our countrymen, under the happy conduct of his Royal Highness, went breaking, by little and little, into the line of the enemies; the noise of the cannon from both navies reached our ears about the City, so that all men being alarmed with it, and in a dreadful suspense of the event, which they knew was then deciding, every one went following the sound as his fancy led him; and leaving the town almost empty, some took towards the park, some cross the river, others down it; all seeking the noise in the depth of silence.

Among the rest, it was the fortune of Eugenius, Crites, Lisideius, and Neander, to be in company together; three of them persons whom their wit and quality have made known to all the town; and whom I have chose to hide under these borrowed names, that they may not suffer by so ill a relation as I am going to make of their discourse.

Taking then a barge, which a servant of Lisideius had provided for them, they made haste to shoot the bridge, and left behind them that great fall of waters which hindered them from hearing what they desired: after which, having disengaged themselves from many vessels which rode at anchor in the Thames, and almost blocked up the passage towards Greenwich, they ordered the watermen to let fall their oars more gently; and then, everyone favouring his own curiosity with a strict silence, it was not long ere they perceived the air to break about them like the noise of distant thunder, or of swallows in a chimney: those little undulations of sound, though almost vanishing before they reached them, yet still seeming to retain somewhat of their first horror, which they had betwixt the fleets. After they had attentively listened till such time as the sound by little and little went from them, Eugenius, lifting up his head, and taking notice of it, was the first who congratulated to the rest that happy omen of our Nation's victory: adding, that we had but this to desire in confirmation of it, that we might hear no more of that noise, which was now leaving the English coast. When the rest had concurred in the same opinion, Crites, a person of a sharp judgment, and somewhat too delicate a taste in wit, which the world have mistaken in him for ill-nature, said, smiling to us, that if the concernment of this battle had not been so exceeding great, he could scarce have wished the victory at the price he knew he must pay for it, in being subject to the reading and hearing of so many ill verses as he was sure would be made on that subject. Adding, that no argument could scape some of those eternal rhymers, who watch a battle with more diligence than the ravens and birds of prey; and the worst of them surest to be first in upon the quarry: while the better able, either out of modesty writ not at all, or set that due value upon their poems, as to let them be often desired and long expected. "There are some of those impertinent people of whom you speak," answered Lisideius, "who to my knowledge are already so provided, either way, that they can produce not only a Panegyric upon the victory, but, if need be, a Funeral Elegy on the Duke; wherein, after they have crowned his valour with many laurels, they will at last deplore the odds under which he fell, concluding that his courage deserved a better destiny." All the company smiled at the conceipt of Lisideius; but Crites, more eager than before, began to make particular exceptions against some writers, and said, the public magistrate ought to send betimes to forbid them; and that it concerned the peace and quiet of all honest people, that ill poets should be as well silenced as seditious preachers. "In my opinion," replied Eugenius, "you pursue your point too far; for as to my own particular, I am so great a lover of poesy, that I could wish them all rewarded who attempt but to do well; . . . "There are so few who write well in this age," says Crites, "that methinks any praises should be welcome; they neither rise to the dignity of the last age, nor to any of the Ancients: and we may cry out of the writers of this time, with more reason than Petronius of his, *Pace vestrâ liceat dixisse, primi omnium eloquentiam perdidistis* ["If I may, permit me to say that you were the first to lose that eloquence which all before you had"]: you have debauched the true old poetry so far, that Nature, which is the soul of it, is not in any of your writings."

"If your quarrel," said Eugenius, "to those who now write, be grounded only on your reverence to antiquity, there is no man more ready to adore those great Greeks and Romans than I am: but on the other side, I cannot think so contemptibly of the age in which I live, or so dishonourably of my own country, as not to judge we equal the Ancients in most kinds of poesy, and in some surpass them; neither know I any reason why I may not be as zealous for the reputation of our age as we find the Ancients themselves were in reference to those who lived before them. . . .

"But I see I am engaging in a wide dispute, where the arguments are not like to reach close on either side; for Poesy is of so large an extent, and so many both of the Ancients and Moderns have done well in all kinds of it, that in citing one against the other, we shall take up more time this evening than each man's occasions will allow him: therefore I would ask Crites to what part of Poesy he would confine his arguments, and whether he would defend the general cause of the Ancients against the Moderns, or oppose any age of the Moderns against this of ours?"

Crites, a little while considering upon this demand, told Eugenius, that if he pleased, he would limit their dispute to Dramatic Poesy; in which he thought it not difficult to prove, either that the Ancients were superior to the Moderns, or the last age of this of ours.

Eugenius was somewhat surprised, when he heard Crites make choice of that subject. "For aught I see," said he, "I have undertaken a harder province than I imagined; for though I never judged the plays of the Greek or Roman poets comparable to ours, yet, on the other side, those we now see acted come short of many which were written in the last age: but my comfort is, if we are overcome, it will be only by our own countrymen: and if we yield to them in this one part of poesy, we more surpass them in all the other: for in the epic or lyric way, it will be hard for them to show us one such amongst them, as we have many now living, or who lately were: they can produce nothing so courtly writ, or which expresses so much the conversation of a gentleman, as Sir John Suckling; nothing so even, sweet, and flowing as Mr. Waller; nothing so majestic, so correct, as Sir John Denham; nothing so elevated, so copious, and full of spirit as Mr. Cowley; as for the Italian, French, and Spanish plays, I can make it evident, that those who now write surpass them; and that the Drama is wholly ours."

All of them were thus far of Eugenius his opinion, that the sweetness of English verse was never understood or practised by our fathers; even Crites himself did not much oppose it; and every one was willing to acknowledge how much our poesy is improved by the happiness of some writers yet living; who first taught us to mould our thoughts into easy and significant words,—to retrench the superfluities of expression,—and to make our rhyme so properly a part of the verse, that it should never mislead the sense, but itself be led and governed by it.

Eugenius was going to continue this discourse, when Lisideius told him that it was necessary, before they proceeded further, to take a standing measure of their controversy; for how was it possible to be decided who writ the best plays, before we know what a play should be? But, this once agreed on by both parties, each might have recourse to it, either to prove his own advantages, or to discover the failings of his adversary.

He had no sooner said this, but all desired the favour of him to give the definition of a play; and they were the more importunate, because neither Aristotle, nor Horace, nor any other, who had writ of that subject, had ever done it.

Lisideius, after some modest denials, at last confessed he had a rude notion of it; indeed, rather a description than a definition; but which served to guide him in his private thoughts, when he was to make a judgment of what others writ: that he conceived a play ought to be, *A just and lively image of human nature, representing its passions and humours, and the changes of fortune to which it is subject, for the delight and instruction of mankind.*

This definition, though Crites raised a logical objection against it—that it was only a *genere et fine* ["by general classification and purpose"], and so not altogether perfect, was yet well received by the rest; and after they had given order to the watermen to turn their barge, and row softly, that they might take the cool of the evening in their return, Crites, being desired by the company to begin, spoke on behalf of the Ancients, in this manner:—

"If confidence presage a victory, Eugenius, in his own opinion, has already triumphed over the Ancients: nothing seems more easy to him, than to overcome those whom it is our greatest praise to have imitated well; for we do not only build upon their foundations, but by their models. Dramatic Poesy had time enough, reckoning from Thespis (who first invented it) to Aristophanes, to be born, to grow up, and to flourish in maturity. It has been observed of arts and sciences, that in one and the same century they have arrived to great perfection; and no wonder, since every age has a kind of universal genius, which inclines those that live in it to some particular studies: the work then, being pushed on by many hands, must of necessity go forward.

"Is it not evident, in these last hundred years, (when the study of philosophy has been the business of all the Virtuosi in Christendom), that almost a new nature has been revealed to us? That more errors of the school have been detected, more useful experiments in philosophy have been made, more noble secrets in optics, medicine, anatomy, astronomy, discovered, than in all those credulous and doting ages from Aristotle to us?—so true it is, that nothing spreads more fast than science, when rightly and generally cultivated.

"Add to this, the more than common emulation that was in those times of writing well; which though it be found in all ages and all persons that pretend to the same reputation, yet Poesy, being then in more esteem than now it is, had greater honours decreed to the professors of it, and consequently the rivalship was more high between them; they had judges ordained to decide their merit, and prizes to reward it. . . . Emulation is the spur of wit; and sometimes envy, sometimes admiration, quickens our endeavours.

"But now, since the rewards of honour are taken away, that virtuous emulation is turned into direct malice; yet so slothful, that it contents itself to condemn and cry down others, without attempting to do better: it is a reputation too unprofitable, to take the necessary pains for it; yet, wishing they had it, that desire is incitement enough to hinder others from it. And this, in short, Eugenius, is the reason why you have now so few good poets, and so many severe judges. Certainly, to imitate the Ancients well, much labour and long study is required; which pains, I have already shown, our poets would want encouragement to take, if yet they had ability to go through the work. Those Ancients have been faithful imitators and wise observers of that Nature which is so torn and ill represented in our plays; they have handed down to us a

perfect resemblance of her; which we, like ill copiers, neglecting
to look on, have rendered monstrous, and disfigured. But, that you
may know how much you are indebted to those your masters, and
be ashamed to have so ill requited them, I must remember you,
that all the rules by which we practise the Drama at this day
(either such as relate to the justness and symmetry of the plot,
or the episodical ornaments, such as descriptions, narrations, and
other beauties, which are not essential to the play,) were delivered
to us from the observations which Aristotle made, of those poets,
who either lived before him, or were his contemporaries: we have
added nothing of our own, except we have the confidence to say
our wit is better; of which, none boast in this our age, but such
as understand not theirs. Of that book [*Poetics*] which Aristotle
has left us Horace his *Art of Poetry* is an excellent comment, and,
I believe, restores to us that Second Book of his concerning
Comedy, which is wanting in him.

"Out of these two have been extracted the famous Rules, which
the French call *Des Trois Unitez,* or, The Three Unities, which
ought to be observed in every regular play; namely, of Time, Place,
and Action.

"The Unity of Time they comprehend in twenty-four hours, the
compass of a natural day, or as near as it can be contrived; and
the reason of it is obvious to every one,—that the time of the feigned
action, or fable of the play, should be proportioned as near as can
be to the duration of that time in which it is represented: since,
therefore, all plays are acted on the theatre in the space of time
much within the compass of twenty-four hours, that play is to be
thought the nearest imitation of nature, whose plot or action is confined within that time; and, by the same rule which concludes this
general proportion of time, it follows, that all the parts of it are (as
near as may be) to be equally subdivided; namely, that one act take
not up the supposed time of half a day, which is out of proportion
to the rest; since the other four are then to be straitened within the
compass of the remaining half: for it is unnatural that one act,
which being spoke or written is not longer than the rest, should be
supposed longer by the audience; it is therefore the poet's duty,

to take care that no act should be imagined to exceed the time in which it is represented on the stage; and that the intervals and inequalities of time be supposed to fall out between the acts.

"This rule of time, how well it has been observed by the Ancients, most of their plays will witness: you see them in their tragedies (wherein to follow this rule is certainly most difficult), from the very beginning of their plays, falling close into that part of the story which they intend for the action or principal object of it, leaving the former part to be delivered by narration: so that they set the audience, as it were, at the post where the race is to be concluded; and, saving them the tedious expectation of seeing the poet set out and ride the beginning of the course, they suffer you not to behold him, till he is in sight of the goal, and just upon you.

"For the second Unity, which is that of Place, the Ancients meant by it, that the scene ought to be continued through the play, in the same place where it was laid in the beginning: for, the stage on which it is represented being but one and the same place, it is unnatural to conceive it many,—and those far distant from one another. I will not deny but, by the variation of painted scenes, the fancy, which in these cases will contribute to its own deceit, may sometimes imagine it several places, with some appearance of probability; yet it still carries the greater likelihood of truth if those places be supposed so near each other as in the same town or city; which may all be comprehended under the larger denomination of one place; for a greater distance will bear no proportion to the shortness of time which is allotted, in the acting, to pass from one of them to another; for the observation of this, next to the ancients, the French are to be most commended. They tie themselves so strictly to the Unity of Place that you never see in any of their plays a scene changed in the middle of an act: if the act begins in a garden, a street, or chamber, 'tis ended in the same place; and that you may know it to be the same, the stage is so supplied with persons, that it is never empty all the time: he who enters second, has business with him who was on before; and before the second quits the stage, a third appears who has business with him. This Corneille calls *la liaison des scenes,* the continuity or joining of the scenes; and 'tis a good mark of a well-contrived play, when all the persons are known to each other, and every one of them has some affairs with all the rest.

"As for the third Unity, which is that of Action, the Ancients meant no other by it than what the logicians do by their *finis,* the end or scope of any action; that which is the first in intention, and last in execution: now the poet is to aim at one great and complete action, to the carrying on of which all things in his play, even the very obstacles, are to be subservient; and the reason of this is as evident as any of the former. For two actions, equally laboured and driven on by the writer, would destroy the unity of the poem; it would be no longer one play, but two: not but that there may be many actions in a play, as Ben Jonson has observed in his *Discoveries;* but they must be all subservient to the great one, which our language happily expresses in the name of *under-plots:* such as in Terence's *Eunuch* is the difference and reconcilement of Thais and Phaedria, which is not the chief business of the play, but promotes the marriage of Chaerea and Chremes's sister, principally intended by the poet. There ought to be but one action, says Corneille, that is, one complete action, which leaves the mind of the audience in a full repose; but this cannot be brought to pass but by many other imperfect actions, which conduce to it, and hold the audience in a delightful suspense of what will be.

"If by these rules (to omit many other drawn from the precepts and practice of the Ancients) we should judge our modern plays, 'tis probable that few of them would endure the trial: that which should be the business of a day, takes up in some of them an age; instead of one action, they are the epitomes of a man's life; and for one spot of ground, which the stage should represent, we are sometimes in more countries than the map can show us.

"But if we allow the Ancients to have contrived well, we must acknowledge them to have written better. Questionless we are deprived of a great stock of wit in the loss of Menander among the Greek poets, and of Caecilius, Afranius, and Barius, among the Romans; we may guess at Menander's excellency by the plays of Terence, who translated some of his; and yet wanted so much of him, that he was called by C. Caesar the half-Menander; and may judge by Varius, by the testimonies of Horace, Martial, and Velleius Paterculus. 'Tis probable that these, could they be recovered, would decide the controversy; but so long as Aristophanes and Plautus are extant, while the tragedies of Euripides, Sophocles, and Seneca, are in our hands, I can never see one of those plays which are now written but it increases my admiration of the Ancients. And yet I must acknowledge further, that to admire them as we ought, we should understand them better than we do. Doubtless many things appear flat to us, the wit of which depended on some custom or story, which never came to our knowledge; or perhaps on some criticism in their language, which being so long dead, and only remaining in their books, 'tis not possible they should make us understand perfectly. . . . Since I have a great veneration for [Jonson], and you, Eugenius, prefer him above all other poets, I will use no farther argument to you than his example: I will produce before you Father Ben, dressed in all the ornaments and colours of the Ancients; you will need no other guide to our party, if you follow him; and whether you consider the bad plays of our age, or regard the good plays of the last, both the best and worst of the modern poets will equally instruct you to admire the Ancients."

Crites had no sooner left speaking, but Eugenius, who had waited with some impatience for it, thus began:

"I have observed in your speech, that the former part of it is convincing as to what the Moderns have profited by the rules of the Ancients; but in the latter you are careful to conceal how much they have excelled them; we own all the helps we have from them, and want neither veneration nor gratitude, while we acknowledge that, to overcome them, we must make use of the advantages we have received from them: but to these assistances we have joined our own industry; for, had we sat down with a dull imitation of them, we might then have lost somewhat of the old perfection, but never acquired any that was new. We draw not therefore after their lines, but those of Nature; and having the life before us, besides the experience of all they knew, it is no wonder if we hit some airs and features which they have missed. I deny not what you urge of arts and sciences, that they have flourished in some ages more than others; but your instance in philosophy makes for me: for if natural causes be more known now than in the time of Aristotle, because more studied, it follows that poesy and other arts may, with the same pains, arrive still nearer to perfection; and, that granted, it will rest for you to prove that they wrought more perfect images of human life than we; which seeing in your discourse you have avoided to make good, it shall now be my task to show you some part of their defects, and some few excellencies of the Moderns. And I think there is none among us can imagine I do it enviously, or with purpose to detract from them; for what interest of fame or profit can the living lose by the reputation of the dead? . . .

"Be pleased then in the first place to take notice that the Greek poesy, which Crites has affirmed to have arrived to perfection in the reign of the Old Comedy, was so far from it that the distinction of it into acts was not known to them; or if it were, it is yet so darkly delivered to us that we cannot make it out. . . .

"Next, for the plot, which Aristotle called τὸ μῦθος, and often τῶν πραγμάτων σύνθεσις, ["the putting together of actions"] and from him the Romans *Fabula;* it has already been judiciously observed by a late writer, that in their tragedies it was only some tale derived from Thebes or Troy, or at least something that happened in those two ages; which was worn so threadbare by the pens of all the epic poets, and even by tradition, itself of the talkative Greeklings (as Ben Jonson calls them), that before it came upon the stage it was already known to all the audience: and the people, so soon as ever they heard the name of Oedipus, knew as well as the poet, that he had killed his father by a mistake, and committed incest with his mother, before the play; that they were now to hear of a great plague, an oracle, and the ghost of Laius: so that they sat with a yawning kind of expectation, till he was to come with his eyes pulled out, and speak a hundred or more verses in a tragic tone, in complaint of his misfortunes. But one Oedipus, Hercules, or Medea, had been tolerable: poor people, they escaped not so good cheap, they had still the *Chapon bouille* [boiled capon, i.e., luxurious dishes] set before them, till their appetites were cloyed with the same dish, and, the novelty being gone, the pleasure vanished; so that one main end of Dramatic Poesy in its definition, which was to cause delight, was of consequence destroyed.

"In their comedies, the Romans generally borrowed their plots from the Greek poets; and theirs was commonly a little girl stolen or wandered from her parents, brought back unknown to the city, there [falling into the hands of] some young fellow, who, by the help of his servant, cheats his father; and when her time comes, to cry,—*Juno Lucina fer opem* ["Juno Lucina, goddess of childbirth, help me!"]—one or other sees a little box or cabinet which was carried away with her, and so discovers her to her friends, if some god do not prevent it, by coming down in a machine, and taking the thanks of it to himself. . . .

"These are plots built after the Italian mode of houses, you see through them all at once: the characters are indeed the imitation of Nature, but so narrow, as if they had imitated only an eye or an hand, and did not dare to venture on the lines of a face, or the proportion of a body.

"But in how strait a compass soever they have bounded their plots and characters, we will pass it by, if they have regularly pursued them, and perfectly observed those three Unities of Time, Place, and Action; the knowledge of which you say is derived to us from them. But in the first place give me leave to tell you, that the Unity of Place, however it might be practised by them, was never any of their rules: we neither find it in Aristotle, Horace, or any who have written of it, till in our age the French poets first made it a precept of the stage. The Unity of Time, even Terence himself, who was the best and most regular of them, has neglected: his *Heautontimorumenos,* or Self-Punisher, takes up visibly two days, says Scaliger; the two first acts concluding the first day, the three last the day ensuing; and Euripides, in tying himself to one day, has committed an absurdity never to be forgiven him; for in one of his tragedies he has made Theseus go from Athens to Thebes, which was about forty English miles, under the walls of it to give battle, and appear victorious in the next act; and yet, from the time of his departure to the return of the Nuntius, who gives the relation of his victory, Æthra and the Chorus have but thirty-six verses; which is not for every mile a verse. . . .

"It is true, they have kept the continuity, or, as you called it, *liaison des scenes,* somewhat better: two do not perpetually come in together, talk, and go out together; and other two succeed them, and do the same throughout the act, which the English call by the name of single scenes; but the reason is, because they have seldom above two or three scenes, properly so called, in every act; for it is to be accounted a new scene, not only every time the stage is empty; but every person who enters, though to others, makes it so; because he introduces a new business. Now the plots of their plays being narrow, and the persons few, one of their acts was written in a less compass than one of our well-wrought scenes; and yet they are often deficient even in this. . . .

"But as they have failed both in laying of their plots, and in the management, swerving from the rules of their own art by mis-representing Nature to us, in which they have ill satisfied one intention of a play, which was delight; so in the instructive part they have erred worse: instead of punishing vice and rewarding virtue, they have often shewn a prosperous wickedness, and an unhappy piety: they have set before us a bloody image of revenge in Medea, and given her dragons to convey her safe from punishment; a Priam and Astyanax murdered, and Cassandra ravished, and the lust and murder ending in the victory of him who acted them: in short, there is no indecorum in any of our modern plays, which if I would excuse, I could not shadow with some authority from the Ancients.

"And one farther note of them let me leave you: tragedies and comedies were not writ then as they are now, promiscuously, by the same person; but he who found his genius bending to the one, never attempted the other way. This is so plain, that I need not instance to you, that Aristophanes, Plautus, Terence, never any of them writ a tragedy; Æschylus, Euripides, Sophocles, and Seneca, never meddled with comedy: the sock and buskin were not worn by the same poet. Having then so much care to excel in one kind, very little is to be pardoned them, if they miscarried in it; and this would lead me to the consideration of their wit, had not Crites given me sufficient warning not to be too bold in my judgment of it; because, the languages being dead, and many of the customs and little accidents on which it depended lost to us, we are not competent judges of it. But though I grant that here and there we may miss the application of a proverb or a custom, yet a thing well said will be wit in all languages; and though it may lose something in the translation, yet to him who reads it in the original, 'tis still the same: he has an idea of its excellency, though it cannot pass from his mind into any other expression or words than those in which he finds it. . . .

"But, to return from whence I have digressed, to the consideration of the Ancients' writing, and their wit (of which by this time you will grant us in some measure to be fit judges). Though I see many excellent thoughts in Seneca, yet he of them who had a genius most proper for the stage, was Ovid; he had a way of writing so fit to stir up a pleasing admiration and concernment, which are the objects of a tragedy, and to show the various movements of a soul combating betwixt two different passions, that, had he lived in our age, or in his own could have writ with our advantages, no man but must have yielded to him. . . .

The masterpiece of Seneca I hold to be that scene in the *Troades*, where Ulysses is seeking for Astyanax to kill him: there you see the tenderness of a mother so represented in Andromache, that it raises compassion to a high degree in the reader, and bears the nearest resemblance of anything in the tragedies of the ancients to the excellent scenes of passion in Shakespeare, or in Fletcher: for love-scenes, you will find few among them; their tragic poets dealt not with that soft passion, but with lust, cruelty, revenge, ambition, and those bloody actions they produced; which were more capable of raising horror than compassion in an audience: leaving love untouched, whose gentleness would have tempered them; which is the most frequent of all the passions, and which, being the private concernment of every person, is soothed by viewing its own image in a public entertainment.

"Among their comedies, we find a scene or two of tenderness, and that where you would least expect it, in Plautus; but to speak generally, their lovers say little, when they see each other, but *anima mea, vita mea* ["my soul, my life"] as the women in Juvenal's time used to cry out in the fury of their kindness. Any sudden gust of passion (as an ecstasy of love in an unexpected meeting) cannot better be expressed than in a word and a sigh, breaking one another. Nature is dumb on such occasions; and to make her speak would be to represent her unlike herself. But there are a thousand other concernments of lovers, as jealousies, complaints, contrivances, and the like, where not to open their minds at large to each other, were to be wanting to their own love, and to the expectation of the audience; who watch the movements of their minds, as much as the changes of their fortunes. For the imagining of the first is properly the work of a poet; the latter he borrows from the historian."

Eugenius was proceeding in that part of his discourse, when Crites interrupted him. "I see," said he, "Eugenius and I are never like to have this question decided betwixt us; for he maintains, the Moderns have acquired a new perfection in writing; I can only grant they have altered the mode of it. . . . So in their love-scenes, of which Eugenius spoke last, the ancients were more hearty, were more talkative: they writ love as it was then the mode to make it; and I will grant thus much to Eugenius, that perhaps one of their poets had he lived in our age, he had altered many things; not that they were not natural before, but that he might accommodate himself to the age in which he lived. Yet in the meantime, we are not to conclude anything rashly against those great men, but preserve to them the dignity of masters, and give that honour to their memories, part of which we expect may be paid to us in future times."

This moderation of Crites, as it was pleasing to all the company, so it put an end to that dispute; which Eugenius, who seemed to have the better of the argument, would urge no farther: but Lisideius, after he had acknowledged himself of Eugenius his opinion concerning the Ancients, yet told him, he had forborne, till his discourse were ended, to ask him why he preferred the English plays above those of other nations? and whether we ought not to submit our stage to the exactness of our next neighbours?

"Though," said Eugenius, "I am at all times ready to defend the honour of my country against the French, and to maintain, we are as well able to vanquish them with our pens, as our ancestors have been with their swords; yet, if you please," added he, looking upon Neander, "I will commit this cause to my friend's management; his opinion of our plays is the same with mine, and besides, there is no reason, that Crites and I, who have now left the stage, should re-enter so suddenly upon it; which is against the laws of comedy."

"If the question had been stated," replied Lisideius, "who had writ best, the French or English, forty years ago, I should have been of your opinion, and adjudged the honour to our own nation; but since that time" (said he, turning towards Neander), "we have been so long together bad Englishmen that we had not leisure to be good poets. Beaumont, Fletcher, and Jonson (who were only capable of bringing us to that degree of perfection which we have), were just then leaving the world; as if in an age of so much horror, wit, and those milder studies of humanity, had no farther business among us. But the Muses, who ever follow peace, went to plant in another country: it was then that the great Cardinal Richelieu began to take them into his protection; and that, by this encouragement, Corneille and some other Frenchmen, reformed their theatre (which before was as much below ours, as it now surpasses it and the rest of Europe). But because Crites in his discourse for the Ancients has prevented me, by observing many rules of the stage which the Moderns have borrowed from them, I shall only, in short, demand of you, whether you are not convinced that of all nations the French have best observed them? In the Unity of Time you find them so scrupulous that it yet remains a dispute among their poets, whether the artificial day of twelve hours, more or less, be not meant by Aristotle, rather than the natural one of twenty-four; and consequently, whether all plays ought not to be reduced into that compass. This I can testify, that in all their dramas writ within these last twenty years and upwards, I have not observed any that have extended the time to thirty hours: in the Unity of Place they are full as scrupulous; for many of their critics limit it to that very spot of ground where the play is supposed to begin; none of them exceed the compass of the same town or city. The Unity of Action in all plays is yet more conspicuous; for they do not burden them with under-plots, as the English do: which is the reason why many scenes of our tragi-comedians carry on a design that is nothing of kin to the main plot; and that we see two distinct webs in a play, like those in ill-wrought stuffs; and two actions, that is, two plays, carried on together, to the confounding of the audience; who, before they are warm in their concernments for one part, are diverted to another; and by that means espouse the interest of neither. From hence likewise it arises that the one half of our actors are not known to the other. They keep their distances, as if they were Montagues and Capulets, and seldom begin an acquaintance till the last scene of the fifth act, when they are all to meet upon the stage. There is no theatre in the world has anything so absurd as the English tragi-comedy; 'tis a drama of our own invention, and the fashion of it is enough to proclaim it so; here a course of mirth, there another of sadness and passion, and a third of honour and a duel: thus, in two hours and a half, we run through all the fits of Bedlam. The French affords you as much variety on the same day, but they do it not so unseasonably, or *mal à propos,* as we: our poets present you the play and the farce together. . . . The end of tragedies or serious plays, says Aristotle, is to beget admiration, compassion, or concernment; but are not mirth and compassion things incompatible? and is it not evident that the poet must of necessity destroy the former by intermingling of the latter? that is, he must ruin the sole end and object of his tragedy, to introduce somewhat that is forced into it, and is not of the body of it. Would you not think that physician mad, who, having prescribed a purge, should immediately order you to take restringents?

"But to leave our plays, and return to theirs. I have noted one great advantage they have had in the plotting of their tragedies;

that is, they are always grounded upon some known history. . . . and in that they have so imitated the Ancients that they have surpassed them. For the Ancients, as was observed before, took for the foundation of their plays some poetical fiction, such as under that consideration could move but little concernment in the audience, because they already knew the event of it. But the French goes farther. . . . He so interweaves truth with probable fiction that he puts a pleasing fallacy upon us; mends the intrigues of fate, and dispenses with the severity of history, to reward that virtue which has been rendered to us there unfortunate. Sometimes the story has left the success so doubtful that the writer is free, by the privilege of a poet, to take that which of two or more relations will best suit with his design: as for example, in the death of Cyrus, whom Justin and some others report to have perished in the Scythian war, but Xenophon affirms to have died in his bed of extreme old age. Nay more, when the event is past dispute, even then we are willing to be deceived, and the poet, if he contrives it with appearance of truth, has all the audience of his party; at least during the time his play is acting: so naturally we are kind to virtue, when our own interest is not in question, that we take it up as the general concernment of mankind. On the other side, if you consider the historical plays of Shakespeare, they are rather so many chronicles of kings, or the business many times of thirty or forty years, cramped into a representation of two hours and a half; which is not to imitate or paint Nature, but rather to draw her in miniature, to take her in little; to look upon her through the wrong end of a perspective, and receive her images not only much less, but infinitely more imperfect than the life: this, instead of making a play delightful, renders it ridiculous. . . . For the spirit of man cannot be satisfied but with truth, or at least verisimility; and a poem is to contain, if not τὰ ἔτυμα ["true things"], yet ἐτύμοισιν ὁμοῖα ["things like the truth"], as one of the Greek poets has expressed it.

"Another thing in which the French differ from us and from the Spaniards, is that they do not embarrass, or cumber themselves with too much plot; they only represent so much of a story as will constitute one whole and great action sufficient for a play; we, who undertake more, do but multiply adventures which, not being produced from one another, as effects from causes, but rarely following, constitute many actions in the drama, and consequently make it many plays.

"But by pursuing closely one argument, which is not cloyed with many turns, the French have gained more liberty for verse, in which they write; they have leisure to dwell on a subject which deserves it; and to represent the passions (which we have acknowledged to be the poet's work), without being hurried from one thing to another, as we are in the plays of Calderon, which we have seen lately upon our theatres under the name of Spanish plots. . . .

"But I return again to the French writers, who, as I have said, do not burden themselves too much with plot, which has been reproached to them by an *ingenious person* of our nation as a fault; for, he says, they commonly make but one person considerable in a play; they dwell on him, and his concernments, while the rest of the persons are only subservient to set him off. If he intends this by it,—that there is one person in the play who is of greater dignity than the rest, he must tax, not only theirs, but those of the Ancients, and which he would be loth to do, the best of ours; for it is impossible but that one person must be more conspicuous in it than any other, and consequently the greatest share in the action must devolve on him. We see it so in the management of all affairs; even in the most equal aristocracy, the balance cannot be so justly poised but some one will be superior to the rest, either in parts, fortune, interest, or the consideration of some glorious exploit; which will reduce the greatest part of business into his hands.

"But, if he would have us to imagine, that in exalting one character the rest of them are neglected, and that all of them have not some share or other in the action of the play, I desire him to produce any of Corneille's tragedies, wherein every person, like so many servants in a well-governed family, has not some employment, and who is not necessary to the carrying on of the plot, or at least to your understanding it.

"There are indeed some protatic [introductory] persons in the

Ancients, whom they make use of in their plays, either to hear or give the relation: but the French avoid this with great address, making their narrations only to, or by such, who are some way interested in the main design. And now I am speaking of relations, I cannot take a fitter opportunity to add this in favour of the French, that they often use them with better judgment and more *à propos* than the English do. Not that I commend narrations in general,—but there are two sorts of them. One, of those things which are antecedent to the play, and are related to make the conduct of it more clear to us. But 'tis a fault to choose such subjects for the stage as will force us on that rock because we see they are seldom listened to by the audience and that is many times the ruin of the play; for, being once let pass without attention, the audience can never recover themselves to understand the plot: and indeed it is somewhat unreasonable that they should be put to so much trouble, as that, to comprehend what passes in their sight, they must have recourse to what was done, perhaps, ten or twenty years ago.

"But there is another sort of relations, that is, of things happening in the action of the play, and supposed to be done behind the scenes; and this is many times both convenient and beautiful; for by it the French avoid the tumult to which we are subject in England, by representing duels, battles, and the like; which renders our stage too like the theatres where they fight prizes. For what is more ridiculous than to represent an army with a drum and five men behind it; all which the hero of the other side is to drive in before him; or to see a duel fought, and one slain with two or three thrusts of the foils, which we know are so blunted that we might give a man an hour to kill another in good earnest with them.

"I have observed that in all our tragedies, the audience cannot forbear laughing when the actors are to die; it is the most comic part of the whole play. All *passions* may be lively represented on the stage, if to the well-writing of them the actor supplies a good commanded voice, and limbs that move easily, and without stiffness; but there are many *actions* which can never be imitated to a just height: dying especially is a thing which none but a Roman gladiator could naturally perform on the stage, when he did not imitate or represent, but do it; and therefore it is better to omit the representation of it.

"The words of a good writer, which describe it lively, will make a deeper impression of belief in us than all the actor can insinuate into us, when he seems to fall dead before us; as a poet in the description of a beautiful garden, or a meadow, will please our imagination more than the place itself can please our sight. When we see death represented, we are convinced it is but fiction; but when we hear it related, our eyes, the strongest witnesses, are wanting, which might have undeceived us; and we are all willing to favour the sleight, when the poet does not too grossly impose on us. They therefore who imagine these relations would make no concernment in the audience, are deceived, by confounding them with the other, which are of things antecedent to the play: those are made often in cold blood, as I may say, to the audience; but these are warmed with our concernments, which were before awakened in the play. What the philosophers say of motion, that, when it is once begun, it continues of itself, and will do so to eternity, without some stop put to it, is clearly true on this occasion: the soul being already moved with the characters and fortunes of those imaginary persons, continues going of its own accord; and we are no more weary to hear what becomes of them when they are not on the stage, than we are to listen to the news of an absent mistress. But it is objected, that if one part of the play may be related, then why not all? I answer, some parts of the action are more fit to be represented, some to be related. Corneille says judiciously that the poet is not obliged to expose to view all particular actions which conduce to the principal: he ought to select such of them to be seen, which will appear with the greatest beauty, either by the magnificence of the show, or the vehemence of passions which they produce, or some other charm which they have in them; and let the rest arrive to the audience by narration. 'Tis a great mistake in us to believe the French present no part of the action on the stage; every alteration or crossing of a design, every new-sprung passion, and turn of it, is a part of the action, and much the noblest, except we conceive nothing to be action till the players come to blows; as if the painting of the hero's mind were not more properly the poet's work than the strength of his body. . . . Those actions which by reason of their cruelty, will cause aversion in us, or by reason of their impossibility, unbelief, ought either wholly to be avoided by a poet, or only delivered by narration. To which we may have leave to add, such as, to avoid tumult (as was before hinted), or to reduce the plot into a more reasonable compass of time, or for defect of beauty in them, are rather to be related than presented to the eye. Examples of all these kinds are frequent, not only among all the Ancients, but in the best received of our English poets. . . .

"But I find I have been too long in this discourse, since the French have many other excellencies not common to us; as that you never see any of their plays end with a conversion, or simple change of will, which is the ordinary way which our poets use to end theirs. It shows little art in the conclusion of a dramatic poem, when they who have hindered the felicity during the four acts, desist from it in the fifth, without some powerful cause to take them off their design; and though I deny not but such reasons may be found, yet it is a path that is cautiously to be trod, and the poet is to be sure he convinces the audience that the motive is strong enough. As for example, the conversion of the Usurer in *The Scornful Lady* seems to me a little forced; for, being an Usurer, which implies a lover of money to the highest degree of covetousness,—and such the poet has represented him,—the account he gives for the sudden change is, that he has been duped by the wild young fellow; which in reason might render him more wary another time, and make him punish himself with harder fare and coarser clothes, to get up again what he had lost: but that he should look on it as a judgment, and so repent, we may expect to hear in a sermon, but I should never endure it in a play.

"I pass by this; neither will I insist on the care they take that no person after his first entrance shall ever appear, but the business which brings him upon the stage shall be evident; which rule, if observed, must needs render all the events in the play more natural;

for there you see the probability of every accident, in the cause that produced it; and that which appears chance in the play, will seem so reasonable to you, that you will there find it almost necessary: so that in the exit of the actor you have a clear account of his purpose and design in the next entrance (though, if the scene be well wrought, the event will commonly deceive you); for there is nothing so absurd, says Corneille, as for an actor to leave the stage only because he has no more to say.

"I should now speak of the beauty of their rhyme, and the just reason I have to prefer that way of writing in tragedies before ours in blank verse; but because it is partly received by us, and therefore not altogether peculiar to them, I will say no more of it in relation to their plays. For our own, I doubt not but it will exceedingly beautify them; and I can see but one reason why it should not generally obtain, that is, because our poets write so ill in it. This indeed may prove a more prevailing argument than all others which are used to destroy it, and therefore I am only troubled when great and judicious poets, and those who are acknowledged such, have writ or spoke against it. . . .

Lisideius concluded in this manner; and Neander, after a little pause, thus answered him:

"I shall grant Lisideius, without much dispute, a great part of what he has urged against us; for I acknowledge that the French contrive their plots more regularly, and observe the laws of comedy, and decorum of the stage (to speak generally), with more exactness than the English. Farther, I deny not but he has taxed us justly in some irregularities of ours, which he has mentioned; yet, after all, I am of opinion that neither our faults nor their virtues are considerable enough to place them above us.

"For the lively imitation of Nature being in the definition of a play, those which best fulfil that law ought to be esteemed superior to the others. 'Tis true, those beauties of the French poesy are such as will raise perfection higher where it is, but are not sufficient to give it where it is not: they are indeed the beauties of a statue, but not of a man, because not animated with the soul of Poesy, which is imitation of humour and passions: and this Lisideius himself, or any other, however biassed to their party, cannot but acknowledge, if he will either compare the humours of our comedies, or the characters of our serious plays, with theirs. He who will look upon theirs which have been written till these last ten years, or thereabouts, will find it a hard matter to pick out two or three passable humours amongst them. Corneille himself, their arch-poet, what has he produced except *The Liar,* and you know how it was cried up in France; but when it came upon the English stage, though well translated, and that part of Dorant acted to so much advantage as I am confident it never received in its own country, the most favourable to it would not put it in competition with many of Fletcher's or Ben Jonson's. In the rest of Corneille's comedies you have little humour; he tells you himself, his way is, first to show two lovers in good intelligence with each other; in the working up of the play to embroil them by some mistake, and in the latter end to clear it, and reconcile them.

"But of late years Molière, the younger Corneille, Quinault, and some others, have been imitating afar off the quick turns and graces of the English stage. They have mixed their serious plays with mirth, like our tragi-comedies, since the death of Cardinal Richelieu. . . . But their humours, if I may grace them with that name, are so thin-sown, that never above one of them comes up in any play. I dare take upon me to find more variety of them in some one play of Ben Jonson's than in all theirs together; as he who has seen *The Alchemist, The Silent Woman,* or *Bartholomew-Fair,* cannot but acknowledge with me.

"I grant the French have performed what was possible on the ground-work of the Spanish plays; what was pleasant before, they have made regular: but there is not above one good play to be writ on all those plots; they are too much alike to please often; which we need not the experience of our own stage to justify. As for their new way of mingling mirth with serious plot, I do not, with Lisideius, condemn the thing, though I cannot approve their manner of doing it. He tells us, we cannot so speedily recollect ourselves after a scene of great passion and concernment, as to pass to another of mirth and humour, and to enjoy it with any relish: but why should he imagine the soul of man more heavy than his senses? Does not the eye pass from an unpleasant object to a pleasant in a much shorter time than is required to this? and does not the unpleasantness of the first commend the beauty of the latter? The old rule of logic might have convinced him, that contraries, when placed near, set off each other. A continued gravity keeps the spirit too much bent; we must refresh it sometimes, as we bait in a journey that we may go on with greater ease. A scene of mirth, mixed with tragedy, has the same effect upon us which our music has betwixt the acts; which we find a relief to us from the best plots and language of the stage, if the discourses have been long. I must therefore have stronger arguments, ere I am convinced that compassion and mirth in the same subject destroy each other; and in the meantime cannot but conclude, to the honour of our nation, that we have invented, increased, and perfected a more pleasant way of writing for the stage, than was ever known to the ancients or moderns of any nation, which is tragi-comedy.

"And this leads me to wonder why Lisideius and many others should cry up the barrenness of the French plots above the variety and copiousness of the English. Their plots are single; they carry on one design, which is pushed forward by all the actors, every scene in the play contributing and moving towards it. Our plays, besides the main design, have under-plots or by-concernments, of less considerable persons and intrigues, which are carried on with the motion of the main plot: as they say the orb of the fixed stars, and those of the planets, though they have motions of their own, are whirled about by the motion of the *primum mobile,* in which they are contained. That similitude expresses much of the English stage; for if contrary motions may be found in nature to agree; if a planet can go east and west at the same time;—one way by virtue of his own motion, the other by the force of the First Mover;—it will not be difficult to imagine how the under-plot, which is only different, not contrary to the great design, may naturally be conducted along with it.

"Eugenius has already shown us, from the confession of the French poets, that the Unity of Action is sufficiently preserved, if all the imperfect actions of the play are conducing to the main design; but when those petty intrigues of a play are so ill ordered, that they have no coherence with the other, I must grant that Lisideius has reason to tax that want of due connection; for coordination in a play is as dangerous and unnatural as in a state. In the meantime he must acknowledge, our variety, if well ordered, will afford a greater pleasure to the audience.

"As for his other argument, that by pursuing one single theme they gain an advantage to express and work up the passions, I wish any example he could bring from them would make it good; for I confess their verses are to me the coldest I have ever read. Neither, indeed, is it possible for them, in the way they take, so to express passion, as that the effects of it should appear in the concernment of an audience, their speeches being so many declamations, which tire us with the length; so that instead of persuading us to grieve for their imaginary heroes, we are concerned for our own trouble, as we are in tedious visits of bad company; we are in pain till they are gone. When the French stage came to be reformed by Cardinal Richelieu, those long harangues were introduced to comply with the gravity of a churchman. . . . Since that time it is grown into a custom, and their actors speak by the hour-glass, like our parsons; nay, they account it the grace of their parts, and think themselves disparaged by the poet, if they may not twice or thrice in a play entertain the audience with a speech of an hundred lines. I deny not but this may suit well enough with the French; for as we, who are a more sullen people, come to be diverted at our plays, so they, who are of an airy and gay temper, come thither to make themselves more serious: and this I conceive to be one reason why comedies are more pleasing to us, and tragedies to them. But to speak generally: it cannot be denied that short speeches and replies are more apt to move the passions and beget concernment in us, than the other; for it is unnatural for any one in a gust of passion to speak long together, or for another in the same condition to suffer him, without interruption. Grief and passion are like floods raised in little brooks by a sudden rain; they are quickly up; and

if the concernment be poured unexpectedly in upon us, it over-
flows us: but a long sober shower gives them leisure to run out as
they came in, without troubling the ordinary current. As for Comedy, repartee is one of its chiefest graces; the greatest pleasure of
the audience is a chase of wit, kept up on both sides, and swiftly
managed. And this our forefathers, if not we, have had in Fletcher's
plays, to a much higher degree of perfection than the French poets
can reasonably hope to reach.

"There is another part of Lisideius his discourse, in which he
rather excused our neighbours than commended them; that is, for
aiming only to make one person considerable in their plays. 'Tis
very true what he has urged, that one character in all plays, even
without the poet's care, will have advantage of all the others; and
that the design of the whole drama will chiefly depend on it. But
this hinders not that there may be more shining characters in the
play: many persons of a second magnitude, nay, some so very
near, so almost equal to the first, that greatness may be opposed
to greatness, and all the persons be made considerable, not only by
their quality, but their action. 'Tis evident that the more the persons are, the greater will be the variety of the plot. If then the parts
are managed so regularly, that the beauty of the whole be kept entire, and that the variety become not a perplexed and confused
mass of accidents, you will find it infinitely pleasing to be led in a
labyrinth of design, where you see some of your way before you,
yet discern not the end till you arrive at it. And that all this is
practicable, I can produce for examples many of our English plays:
as *The Maid's Tragedy, The Alchemist, The Silent Woman:* I was
going to have named *The Fox,* but that the unity of design seems
not exactly observed in it; for there appear two actions in the
play; the first naturally ending with the fourth act; the second
forced from it in the fifth; which yet is the less to be condemned
in him, because the disguise of Volpone, though it suited not with
his character as a crafty or covetous person, agreed well enough
with that of a voluptuary; and by it the poet gained the end at
which he aimed, the punishment of vice, and the reward of virtue,

both which that disguise produced. So that to judge equally of it, it was an excellent fifth act, but not so naturally proceeding from the former.

"But to leave this, and pass to the latter part of Lisideius his discourse, which concerns relations: I must acknowledge with him, that the French have reason to hide that part of the action which would occasion too much tumult on the stage, and to choose rather to have it made known by narration to the audience. Farther, I think it very convenient, for the reasons he has given, that all incredible actions were removed; but whether custom has so insinuated itself into our countrymen, or nature has so formed them to fierceness, I know not; but they will scarcely suffer combats and other objects of horror to be taken from them. And indeed, the indecency of tumults is all which can be objected against fighting: for why may not our imagination as well suffer itself to be deluded with the probability of it, as with any other thing in the play? For my part, I can with as great ease persuade myself that the blows are given in good earnest, as I can that they who strike them are kings or princes, or those persons which they represent. . . . To conclude on this subject of relations; if we are to be blamed for showing too much of the action, the French are as faulty for discovering too little of it: a mean betwixt both should be observed by every judicious writer, so as the audience may neither be left unsatisfied by not seeing what is beautiful, or shocked by beholding what is either incredible or undecent.

"I hope I have already proved in this discourse, that though we are not altogether so punctual as the French in observing the laws of Comedy, yet our errors are so few, and little, and those things wherein we excel them so considerable, that we ought of right to be preferred before them. But what will Lisideius say, if they themselves acknowledge they are too strictly bounded by those laws, for breaking which he has blamed the English? I will allege Corneille's words, as I find them in the end of his Discourse of the Three Unities: *Il est facile aux spéculatifs d'estre sévères, etc.* ' 'Tis easy for speculative persons to judge severely; but if they would produce to public view ten or twelve pieces of this nature, they would perhaps give more latitude to the rules than I have done, when by experience they had known how much we are limited and constrained by them, and how many beauties of the stage they banished from it.' To illustrate a little what he has said: By their servile observations of the Unities of Time and Place, and integrity of scenes, they have brought on themselves that death of plot, and narrowness of imagination, which may be observed in all their plays. How many beautiful accidents might naturally happen in two or three days, which cannot arrive with any probability in the compass of twenty-four hours? There is time to be allowed also for maturity of design, which, amongst great and prudent persons, such as are often represented in Tragedy, cannot, with any likelihood of truth, be brought to pass at so short a warning. Farther; by tying themselves strictly to the Unity of Place, and unbroken scenes, they are forced many times to omit some beauties which cannot be shown where the act began; but might, if the scene were interrupted, and the stage cleared for the persons to enter in another place; and therefore the French poets are often forced upon absurdities; for if the act begins in a chamber, all the persons in the play must have some business or other to come thither, or else they are not to be shown that act; and sometimes their characters are very unfitting to appear there: as, suppose it were the king's bed-chamber; yet the meanest man in the tragedy must come and dispatch his business there, rather than in the lobby or courtyard (which is fitter for him), for fear the stage should be cleared, and the scenes broken. Many times they fall by it in a greater inconvenience; for they keep their scenes unbroken, and yet change the place; as in one of their newest plays, where the act begins in the street. There a gentleman is to meet his friend; he sees him with his man, coming out from his father's house; they talk together, and the first goes out: the second, who is a lover, has made an appointment with his mistress; she appears at the window, and then we are to imagine the scene lies under it. This gentleman is called away, and leaves his servant with his mistress; presently her father is heard from within; the young lady is afraid the serving-man should be discovered, and thrusts him into a place of safety, which is supposed to be her closet. After this, the father enters to the daughter, and now the scene is in a house; for he is seeking from one room to another for this poor Philipin, or French Diego, who is heard from within, drolling and breaking many a miserable conceit on the subject of his sad condition. In this ridiculous manner the play goes forward, the stage being never empty all the while: so that the street, the window, the houses, and the closet, are made to walk about, and the persons to stand still. Now what, I beseech you, is more easy than to write a regular French play, or more difficult than to write an irregular English one, like those of Fletcher, or of Shakespeare?

"If they content themselves, as Corneille did, with some flat design, which, like an ill riddle, is found out ere it be half proposed, such plots we can make every way regular, as easily as they; but whenever they endeavour to rise to any quick turns and counterturns of plot, as some of them have attempted, since Corneille's plays have been less in vogue, you see they write as irregularly as we, though they cover it more speciously. Hence the reason is perspicuous why no French plays, when translated, have, or ever can succeed on the English stage. For, if you consider the plots, our own are fuller of variety; if the writing, ours are more quick and fuller of spirit; and therefore 'tis a strange mistake in those who decry the way of writing plays in verse, as if the English therein imitated the French. We have borrowed nothing from them; our plots are weaved in English looms: we endeavour therein to follow the variety and greatness of characters which are derived to us from Shakespeare and Fletcher; the copiousness and well-knitting of the intrigues we have from Jonson; and for the verse itself we have English precedents of elder date than any of Corneille's plays. Not to name our old comedies before Shakespeare, which were all writ in verse of six feet, or Alexandrines, such as the French now use,—I can show in Shakespeare many scenes of rhyme together, and the like in Ben Jonson's tragedies: in *Catiline* and *Sejanus* sometimes thirty or forty lines,—I mean besides the Chorus, or the monologues; which, by the way, showed Ben no enemy to this way of writing, especially if you read his *Sad Shep-*

herd, which goes sometimes on rhyme, sometimes on blank verse, like an horse who eases himself on trot and amble. You find him likewise commending Fletcher's pastoral of *The Faithful Shepherdess,* which is for the most part rhyme, though not refined to that purity to which it hath since been brought. And these examples are enough to clear us from a servile imitation of the French.

"But to return whence I have digressed: I dare boldly affirm these two things of the English drama;—First, that we have many plays of ours as regular as any of theirs, and which, besides, have more variety of plot and characters; and secondly, that in most of the irregular plays of Shakespeare or Fletcher (for Ben Jonson's are for the most part regular), there is a more masculine fancy and greater spirit in the writing than there is in any of the French. I could produce, even in Shakespeare's and Fletcher's works, some plays which are almost exactly formed; as *The Merry Wives of Windsor,* and *The Scornful Lady:* but because (generally speaking) Shakespeare, who writ first, did not perfectly observe the laws of comedy, and Fletcher, who came nearer to perfection, yet through carelessness made many faults; I will take the pattern of a perfect play from Ben Jonson, who was a careful and learned observer of the dramatic laws, and from all his comedies I shall select *The Silent Woman:* of which I will make a short examen, according to those rules which the French observe."

As Neander was beginning to examine *The Silent Woman,* Eugenius, earnestly regarding him; "I beseech you, Neander," said he, "gratify the company, and me in particular, so far, as before you speak of the play, to give us a character of the author; and tell us frankly your opinion, whether you do not think all writers, both French and English, ought to give place to him."

"I fear," replied Neander, "that in obeying your commands I shall draw some envy on myself. Besides, in performing them, it will be first necessary to speak somewhat of Shakespeare and Fletcher, his rivals in poesy; and one of them, in my opinion, at least his equal, perhaps his superior.

"To begin, then, with Shakespeare. He was the man who of all modern, and perhaps ancient poets, had the largest and most comprehensive soul. All the images of Nature were still present to him, and he drew them, not laboriously, but luckily; when he describes anything, you more than see it, you feel it too. Those who accuse him to have wanted learning, give him the greater commendation: he was naturally learned; he needed not the spectacles of books to read Nature; he looked inwards, and found her there. I cannot say he is everywhere alike; were he so, I should do him injury to compare him with the greatest of mankind. He is many times flat, insipid; his comic wit degenerating into clenches [puns], his serious swelling into bombast. But he is always great, when some great occasion is presented to him; no man can say he ever had a fit subject for his wit, and did not then raise himself as high above the rest of poets. . . . The consideration of this made Mr. Hales of Eaton say, that there was no subject of which any poet ever writ, but he would produce it much better done in Shakespeare; and however others are now generally preferred before him, yet the age wherein he lived, which had contemporaries with him Fletcher and Jonson, never equalled them to him in their esteem: and in the last King's court, when Ben's reputation was at highest, Sir John Suckling, and with him the greater part of the courtiers, set our Shakespeare far above him.

"Beaumont and Fletcher, of whom I am next to speak, had, with the advantage of Shakespeare's wit, which was their precedent, great natural gifts, improved by study: Beaumont especially being so accurate a judge of plays, that Ben Jonson, while he lived, submitted all his writings to his censure, and, 'tis thought, used his judgment in correcting, if not contriving, all his plots. What value he had for him, appears by the verses he writ to him; and therefore I need speak no farther of it. The first play that brought Fletcher and him in esteem was their *Philaster:* for before that, they had written two or three very unsuccessfully, as the like is reported of Ben Jonson, before he writ *Every Man in his Humour.* Their plots were generally more regular than Shakespeare's, especially those which were made before Beaumont's death; and they understood and imitated the conversation of gentlemen much better; whose wild debaucheries, and quickness of wit in repartees, no poet before them could paint as they have done. Humour, which Ben Jonson derived from particular persons, they made it not their business to describe: they represented all the passions very lively, but above all, love. I am apt to believe the English language in them arrived to its highest perfection: what words have since been taken in, are rather superfluous than ornamental. Their plays are now the most pleasant and frequent entertainments of the stage; two of theirs being acted through the year for one of Shakespeare's or Jonson's: the reason is, because there is a certain gaiety in their comedies, and pathos in their more serious plays, which suit generally with all men's humours. Shakespeare's language is likewise a little obsolete, and Ben Jonson's wit comes short of theirs.

"As for Jonson, to whose character I am now arrived, if we look upon him while he was himself (for his last plays were but his dotages), I think him the most learned and judicious writer which any theatre ever had. He was a most severe judge of himself, as well as others. One cannot say he wanted wit, but rather that he was frugal of it. In his works you find little to retrench or alter. Wit, and language, and humour also in some measure, we had before him; but something of art was wanting to the Drama till he came. He managed his strength to more advantage than any who preceded him. You seldom find him making love in any of his scenes, or endeavouring to move the passions; his genius was too sullen and saturnine to do it gracefully, especially when he knew he came after those who had performed both to such an height. Humour was his proper sphere; and in that he delighted most to represent mechanic people. He was deeply conversant in the Ancients, both Greek and Latin, and he borrowed boldly from them: there is scarce a poet or historian among the Roman authors of those times whom he has not translated in *Sejanus* and *Catiline*. But he has done his robberies so openly, that one may see he fears not to be taxed by any law. He invades authors like a monarch; and what would be theft in other poets is only victory in him. With the spoils of these writers he so represents old Rome to us, in its rites, ceremonies, and customs, that if one of their poets had written either of his tragedies, we had seen less of it than in him. If there was any fault in his language, 'twas that he weaved it too closely and laboriously, in his comedies especially: perhaps, too, he did a little too much Romanise our tongue, leaving the words which he translated almost as much Latin as he found them: wherein, though he learnedly followed their language, he did not enough comply with the idiom of ours. If I would compare him with Shakespeare, I must acknowledge him the more correct poet, but Shakespeare the greater wit. Shakespeare was the Homer, or father of our dramatic poets; Jonson was the Virgil, the pattern of elaborate writing; I admire him, but I love Shakespeare. To conclude of him; as he has given us the most correct plays, so in the precepts which he has laid down in his *Discoveries,* we have as many and profitable rules for perfecting the stage, as any wherewith the French can furnish us.

"Having thus spoken of the author, I proceed to the examination of his comedy, *The Silent Woman.* [In his analysis, here omitted, Neander indicates that Jonson has indeed observed the unities of time, place, and action. His greatest praise is reserved for Jonson's skill in characterization and dramatic structure.]

This was the substance of what was then spoken on that occasion; and Lisideius, I think, was going to reply, when he was prevented thus by Crites: "I am confident," said he, "that the most material things that can be said have been already urged on either side; if they have not, I must beg of Lisideius that he will defer his answer till another time: for I confess I have a joint quarrel to you both, because you have concluded, without any reason given for it, that rhyme is proper for the stage. I will not dispute how ancient it hath been among us to write this way; perhaps our ancestors knew no better till Shakespeare's time. I will grant it was not altogether left by him, and that Fletcher and Ben Jonson used it frequently in their Pastorals, and sometimes in other plays. Farther, —I will not argue whether we received it originally from our own countrymen, or from the French; for that is an inquiry of as little benefit, as theirs who, in the midst of the late plague, were not so solicitous to provide against it, as to know whether we had it from the malignity of our own air, or by transportation from Holland. I have therefore only to affirm, that it is not allowable in serious plays; for comedies, I find you already concluding with me. To prove this, I might satisfy myself to tell you, how much in vain it is for you to strive against the stream of the people's inclination; the greatest part of which are prepossessed so much with those excellent plays of Shakespeare, Fletcher, and Ben Jonson, which have been written out of rhyme, that except you could bring them such as were written better in it, and those too by persons of equal reputation with them, it will be impossible for you to gain your cause with them, who will still be judges. This it is to which, in fine, all your reasons must submit. . . . But I will not on this occasion take the advantage of the greater number, but only urge such reasons against rhyme, as I find in the writings of those who have argued for the other way. First, then, I am of opinion that rhyme is unnatural in a play, because dialogue there is presented as the effect of sudden thought: for a play is the imitation of Nature; and since no man, without premeditation, speaks in rhyme, neither ought he to do it on the stage. This hinders not but the fancy may be there elevated to an higher pitch of thought than it is in ordinary discourse; for there is a probability that men of excellent and quick parts may speak noble things *extempore:* but those thoughts are never fettered with the numbers or sound of verse without study, and therefore it cannot be but unnatural to present the most free way of speaking in that which is the most constrained. For this reason, says Aristotle, 'tis best to write tragedy in that kind of verse which is the least such, or which is nearest prose: and this amongst the Ancients was the Iambic, and with us is blank verse, or the measure of verse kept exactly without rhyme. These numbers therefore are fittest for a play; the others for a paper of verses, or a poem; blank verse being as much below them as rhyme is improper for the Drama. And if it be objected that neither are blank verses made *extempore,* yet, as nearest nature, they are still to be preferred.—But there are two particular exceptions, which many besides myself have had to verse; by which it will appear yet more plainly how improper it is in plays. And the first of them is grounded on that very reason for which some have commended rhyme; they say, the quickness of repartees in argumentative scenes receives an ornament from verse. Now what is more unreasonable than to imagine that a man should not only light upon the wit, but the rhyme too, upon the sudden? This nicking of him who spoke before both in sound and measure, is so great an happiness, that you must at least suppose the persons of your play to be born poets: . . . to make verses almost whether they will or no. If they are anything below this, it will look rather like the design of two, than the answer of one: it will appear that your actors hold intelligence together; that they perform their tricks like fortune-tellers, by confederacy. The hand of art will be too visible in it, against that maxim of all professions—*Ars est celare artem;* that it is the greatest perfection of art to keep itself undiscovered. Nor will it serve you to object, that however you manage it, 'tis still known to be a play; and, consequently, the dialogue of two persons understood to be the labour of one poet. For a play is still an imitation of Nature; we know we are to be deceived, and we desire to be so; but no man ever was deceived but with a probability of truth; for who will suffer a gross lie to be fastened on him? Thus we sufficiently understand that the scenes which represent cities and countries to us are not really such, but only painted on boards and canvas; but shall that excuse the ill painture or designment of them? Nay, rather ought they not be laboured with so much the more diligence and exactness, to help the imagination? since the mind of man does naturally tend to truth; and therefore the nearer anything comes to the imitation of it, the more it pleases.

"Thus, you see, your rhyme is uncapable of expressing the greatest thoughts naturally, and the lowest it cannot with any grace: for what is more unbefitting the majesty of verse, than to call a servant, or bid a door be shut in rhyme? and yet you are often forced on this miserable necessity. But verse, you say, circumscribes a quick and luxuriant fancy, which would extend itself too far on every subject, did not the labour which is required to well-turned and polished rhyme, set bounds to it. Yet this argument, if granted, would only prove that we may write better in verse, but not more naturally. Neither is it able to evince that; for he who wants judgment to confine his fancy in blank verse, may want it as much in rhyme: and he who has it will avoid errors in both kinds. . . .

"In our own language we see Ben Jonson confining himself to what ought to be said, even in the liberty of blank verse; and yet Corneille, the most judicious of the French poets, is still varying the same sense an hundred ways, and dwelling eternally on the same subject, though confined by rhyme. Some other exceptions I have to verse; but since these I have named are for the most part already public, I conceive it reasonable they should first be answered."

"It concerns me less than any," said Neander (seeing he had ended), "to reply to this discourse; because when I should have proved that verse may be natural in plays, yet I should always be ready to confess, that those which I have written in this kind come short of that perfection which is required. Yet since you are pleased I should undertake this province, I will do it, though with all imaginable respect and deference, both to that person [Aristotle] from whom you have borrowed your strongest arguments, and to whose judgment, when I have said all, I finally submit. But before I proceed to answer your objections, I must first remember you, that I exclude all Comedy from my defence; and next that I deny not but blank verse may be also used; and content myself only to assert, that in serious plays where the subject and characters are great, and the plot unmixed with mirth, which might allay or divert these concernments which are produced, rhyme is there as natural and more effectual than blank verse.

"And now having laid down this as a foundation,—to begin with Crites,—I must crave leave to tell him, that some of his arguments against rhyme reach no farther than, from the faults or defects of ill rhyme, to conclude against the use of it in general. May not I conclude against blank verse by the same reason? If the words of some poets who write in it are either ill chosen, or ill placed, which makes not only rhyme, but all kind of verse in any language unnatural, shall I, for their vicious affectation, condemn those excellent lines of Fletcher, which are written in that kind? Is there anything in rhyme more constrained than this line in blank verse? *I heaven invoke, and strong resistance make;* where you see both the clauses are placed unnaturally, that is, contrary to the common way of speaking, and that without the excuse of a rhyme to cause it: yet you would think me very ridiculous, if I should accuse the stubbornness of blank verse for this, and not rather the stiffness of the poet. Therefore, Crites, you must either prove that words, though well chosen, and duly placed, yet render not rhyme natural in itself; or that, however natural and easy the rhyme may be, yet it is not proper for a play. If you insist on the former part, I would ask you, what other conditions are required to make rhyme natural in itself, besides an election of apt words, and a right disposition of them? For the due choice of your words expresses your sense naturally, and the due placing them adapts the rhyme to it. If you object that one verse may be made for the sake of another, though both the words and rhyme be apt, I answer, it cannot possibly so fall out; for either there is a dependence of sense betwixt the first line and the second, or there is none: if there be that connection, then in the natural position of the words the latter line must of necessity flow from the former; if there be no dependence, yet still the due ordering of words makes the last line as natural in itself as the other: so that the necessity of a rhyme never forces any but bad or lazy writers to say what they would not otherwise. 'Tis true, there is both care and art required to write in verse. A good poet never establishes the first line till he has sought out such a rhyme as may fit the sense, already prepared to heighten the second: many times the close of the sense falls into the middle of the next verse, or farther off, and he may often prevail himself of the same advantages in English which Virgil had in Latin,—he may break off in the hemistich [half-line], and begin another line. Indeed, the not observing these two last things makes plays which are writ in verse so tedious: for though, most commonly, the sense is to be confined to the couplet, yet nothing that does *perpetuo tenore fluere,* run in the same channel, can please always. 'Tis like the murmuring of a stream, which not varying in the fall, causes at first attention, at last drowsiness. Variety of cadences is the best rule; the greatest help to the actors, and refreshment to the audience.

"If then verse may be made natural in itself, how becomes it unnatural in a play? You say the stage is the representation of nature, and no man in ordinary conversation speaks in rhyme. But you foresaw when you said this, that it might be answered—neither does any man speak in blank verse, or in measure without rhyme. Therefore you concluded, that which is nearest nature is still to be preferred. But you took no notice that rhyme might be made as natural as blank verse, by the well placing of the words, etc. All the difference between them, when they are both correct, is, the sound in one, which the other wants; and if so, the sweetness of it, and all the advantage resulting from it, which are handled in the Preface to *The Rival Ladies,* will yet stand good. As for that place of Aristotle, where he says, plays should be writ in that kind of verse which is nearest prose, it makes little for you; blank verse being properly but measured prose. Now measure alone, in any modern language, does not constitute verse; those of the Ancients in Greek and Latin consisted in quantity of words, and a determinate number of feet. But when, by the inundation of the Goths and Vandals into Italy, new languages were introduced, and barbarously mingled with the Latin, of which the Italian, Spanish, French, and ours (made out of them and the Teutonic) are dialects, a new way of poesy was practised; new, I say, in those countries, for in all probability it was that of the conquerors in their own nations: at least we are able to prove, that the eastern people have used it from all antiquity. This new way consisted in measure or number of feet, and rhyme; the sweetness of rhyme, and observation of accent, supplying the place of quantity in words, which could neither exactly be observed by those Barbarians, who knew not the rules of it, neither was it suitable to their tongues, as it had been to the Greek and Latin. No man is tied in modern poesy to observe any farther rule in the feet of his verse, but that they be dissyllables; whether Spondee, Trochee, or Iambic, it matters not; only he is obliged to rhyme: neither do the Spanish, French, Italian, or Germans, acknowledge at all, or very rarely, any such kind of poesy as blank verse amongst them. Therefore, at most 'tis but a poetic prose, a *sermo pedestris;* and as such, most fit for comedies, where I acknowledge rhyme to be improper. Farther; as to that quotation of Aristotle, our couplet verses may be rendered as near prose as blank verse itself, by using those advantages I lately named,—as breaks in an hemistich, or running the sense into another line,—thereby making art and order appear as loose and free as nature: or not tying ourselves to couplets strictly, we may use the benefit of the Pindaric way practised in *The Siege of Rhodes;* where the numbers vary, and the rhyme is disposed carelessly, and far from often chiming. Neither is that other advantage of the Ancients to be despised, of changing the kind of verse when they please, with the change of the scene, or some new entrance; for they confine not themselves always to iambics, but extend their liberty to all lyric numbers, and sometimes even to hexameter. But I need not go so far to prove that rhyme, as it succeeds to all other offices of Greek and Latin verse, so especially to this of plays, since the custom of nations at this day confirms it; the French, Italian, and Spanish tragedies are generally writ in it; and sure the universal consent of the most civilised parts of the world, ought in this, as it doth in other customs, to include the rest.

"But perhaps you may tell me, I have proposed such a way to make rhyme natural, and consequently proper to plays, as is unpracticable; and that I shall scarce find six or eight lines together in any play, where the words are so placed and chosen as is required to make it natural. I answer, no poet need constrain himself at all times to it. It is enough he makes it his general rule; for I deny not but sometimes there may be a greatness in placing the words otherwise; and sometimes they may sound better; sometimes also the variety itself is excuse enough. But if, for the most part, the words be placed as they are in the negligence of prose, it is sufficient to denominate the way practicable; for we esteem that to be such, which in the trial oftener succeeds than misses. And thus far you may find the practice made good in many plays: where you do not, remember still, that if you cannot find six natural rhymes together, it will be as hard for you to produce as many lines in blank verse, even among the greatest of our poets, against which I cannot make some reasonable exception.

"And this, Sir, calls to my remembrance the beginning of your discourse, where you told us we should never find the audience favourable to this kind of writing, till we could produce as good plays in rhyme as Ben Jonson, Fletcher, and Shakespeare had writ out of it. But it is to raise envy to the living, to compare them with the dead. They are honoured, and almost adored by us, as they deserve; neither do I know any so presumptuous of themselves as to contend with them. Yet give me leave to say thus much, without injury to their ashes; that not only we shall never equal them, but they could never equal themselves, were they to rise and write again. We acknowledge them our fathers in wit; but they have ruined their states themselves, before they came to their children's hands. There is scarce an humour, a character, or any kind of plot, which they have not used. All comes sullied or wasted to us: and were they to entertain this age, they could not now make so plenteous treatments out of such decayed fortunes. This therefore will be a good argument to us, either not to write at all, or to attempt some other way. . . .

"This way of writing in verse they have only left free to us; our age is arrived to a perfection in it, which they never knew; and which (if we may guess by what of theirs we have seen in verse, as *The Faithful Shepherdess,* and *Sad Shepherd*) 'tis probable they never could have reached. For the genius of every age is different; and though ours excel in this, I deny not but to imitate Nature in that perfection which they did in prose, is a greater commendation than to write in verse exactly. As for what you have added— that the people are not generally inclined to like this way,—if it were true, it would be no wonder, that betwixt the shaking off an old habit, and the introducing of a new, there should be difficulty. . . . But if you mean the mixed audience of the populace and the noblesse, I dare confidently affirm that a great part of the latter sort are already favourable to verse; and that no serious plays written since the King's return have been more kindly received by them than *The Siege of Rhodes,* the *Mustapha, The Indian Queen,* and *Indian Emperor.*

"But I come now to the inference of your first argument. You said that the dialogue of plays is presented as the effect of sudden thought, but no man speaks suddenly, or *extempore,* in rhyme; and you inferred from thence, that rhyme, which you acknowledge to be proper to epic poesy, cannot equally be proper to dramatic, unless we could suppose all men born so much more than poets, that verses should be made in them, not by them.

"It has been formerly urged by you, and confessed by me, that since no man spoke any kind of verse *extempore,* that which was nearest Nature was to be preferred. I answer you, therefore, by distinguishing betwixt what is nearest to the nature of Comedy, which is the imitation of common persons and ordinary speaking, and what is nearest the nature of a serious play: this last is indeed the representation of Nature, but 'tis Nature wrought up to a higher pitch. The plot, the characters, the wit, the passions, the descriptions, are all exalted above the level of common converse, as high as the imagination of the poet can carry them, with proportion to verisimility. Tragedy, we know, is wont to image to us the minds and fortunes of noble persons, and to portray these exactly; heroic rhyme is nearest Nature, as being the noblest kind of modern verse. . . . Blank verse is acknowledged to be too low for a poem, nay more, for a paper of verses; but if too low for an ordinary sonnet, how much more for Tragedy, which is by Aristotle, in the dispute betwixt the epic poesy and the dramatic, for many reasons he there alleges, ranked above it?

"But setting this defence aside, your argument is almost as strong against the use of rhyme in poems as in plays; for the epic way is everywhere interlaced with dialogue, or discoursive scenes; and therefore you must either grant rhyme to be improper there, which is contrary to your assertion, or admit it into plays by the same title which you have given it to poems. For though Tragedy be justly preferred above the other, yet there is a great affinity between them, as may easily be discovered in that definition of a play which Lisideius gave us. The *genus* of them is the same, a just and lively image of human nature, in its actions, passions, and traverses of fortune: so is the end—namely, for the delight and benefit of mankind. The characters and persons are still the same, viz., the greatest of both sorts; only the manner of acquainting us with those actions, passions, and fortunes, is different. Tragedy performs it *viva voce,* or by action, in dialogue; wherein it excels the Epic Poem, which does it chiefly by narration, and therefore is not so lively an image of human nature. However, the agreement betwixt them is such, that if rhyme be proper for one, it must be for the other. Verse, 'tis true, is not the effect of sudden thought; but this hinders not that sudden thought may be represented in verse, since those thoughts are such as must be higher than Nature can raise them without premeditation, especially to a continuance of them, even out of verse; and consequently you cannot imagine them to have been sudden either in the poet or in the actors. A play, as I have said, to be like Nature, is to be set above it; as statues which are placed on high are made greater than the life, that they may descend to the sight in their just proportion.

"Perhaps I have insisted too long on this objection; but the clearing of it will make my stay shorter on the rest. You tell us, Crites, that rhyme appears most unnatural in repartees, or short replies: when he who answers (it being presumed he knew not what the other would say, yet) makes up that part of the verse which was left incomplete, and supplies both the sound and measure of it. This, you say, looks rather like the confederacy of two, than the answer of one.

"This, I confess, is an objection which is in every man's mouth, who loves not rhyme: but suppose, I beseech you, the repartee were made only in blank verse, might not part of the same argument be turned against you? for the measure is as often supplied there as it is in rhyme; the latter half of the hemistich as commonly made up, or a second line subjoined as a reply to the former; which any one leaf in Jonson's plays will sufficiently clear to you. You will often find in the Greek tragedians, and in Seneca, that when a scene grows up into the warmth of repartees, which is the close fighting of it, the latter part of the trimeter is supplied by him who answers; and yet it was never observed as a fault in them by any of the ancient or modern critics. The case is the same in our verse, as it was in theirs; rhyme to us being in lieu of quantity to them. But if no latitude is to be allowed a poet, you take from him not only his licence of *quidlibet audendi* ["taking any liberty"], but you tie him up in a straiter compass than you would a philosopher. This is indeed *Musas colere severiores* ["To cultivate the more serious Muses"]. You would have him follow Nature, but he must follow her on foot: you have dismounted him from his Pegasus. But you tell us, this supplying the last half of a verse, or adjoining a whole second to the former, looks more like the design of two, than the answer of one. Suppose we acknowledge it: how comes this confederacy to be more displeasing to you, than in a dance which is well contrived? You see there the united design of many persons to make up one figure: after they have separated themselves in many petty divisions, they rejoin one by one into a gross: the confederacy is plain amongst them, for chance could never produce anything to beautiful; and yet there is nothing in it that shocks your sight. I acknowledge the hand of art appears in repartee, as of necessity it must in all kind of verse. But there is also the quick and poignant brevity of it (which is an high imitation of Nature in those sudden gusts of passion) to mingle with it; and this, joined with the cadency and sweetness of the rhyme, leaves nothing in the soul of the hearer to desire. 'Tis an art which appears; but it appears only like the shadowings of painture, which being to cause the rounding of it, cannot be absent; but while that is considered, they are lost: so while we attend to the other beauties of the matter, the care and labour of the rhyme is carried from us, or at least drowned in its own sweetness, as bees are sometimes buried in their honey. When a poet has found the repartee, the last perfection he can add to it, is to put it into verse. However good the thought may be, however apt the words in which 'tis couched, yet he finds himself at a little unrest, while rhyme is wanting: he cannot leave it till that comes naturally, and then is at ease, and sits down contented.

"From replies, which are the most elevated thoughts of verse, you pass to those which are most mean, and which are common with the lowest of household conversation. In these, you say, the majesty of verse suffers. You instance in the calling of a servant, or commanding a door to be shut, in rhyme. This, Crites, is a good observation of yours, but no argument: for it proves no more but that such thoughts should be waived as often as may be, by the address of the poet. But suppose they are necessary in the places where he uses them, yet there is no need to put them into rhyme. He may place them in the beginning of a verse, and break it off, as unfit, when so debased, for any other use: or granting the worst, —that they require more room than the hemistich will allow, yet still there is a choice to be made of the best words, and least vulgar (provided they be apt), to express such thoughts. Many have blamed rhyme in general, for his fault, when the poet with a little care might have redressed it. But they do it with no more justice than if English Poesy should be made ridiculous for the sake of the Water Poet's [John Taylor's] rhymes. Our language is noble, full, and significant; and I know not why he who is master of it may not clothe ordinary things in it as decently as the Latin, if he use the same diligence in his choice of words: *delectus verborum origo est eloquentiae* ["proper choice of words is the source of eloquence"]. It was the saying of Julius Caesar, one so curious in his, that none of them can be changed but for a worse. One would think, *unlock the door,* was a thing as vulgar as could be spoken; and yet Seneca could make it sound high and lofty in his Latin:

Reserate clusos regii postes laris.
Set wide the palace gates.

"But I turn from this conception, both because it happens not above twice or thrice in any play that those vulgar thoughts are used; and then too (were there no other apology to be made, yet), the necessity of them, which is alike in all kind of writing, may excuse them. For if they are little and mean in rhyme, they are of consequence such in blank verse. Besides that the great eagerness and precipitation with which they are spoken, makes us rather mind the substance than the dress; that for which they are spoken, rather than what is spoken. For they are always the effect of some hasty concernment, and something of consequence depends on them.

"Thus, Crites, I have endeavoured to answer your objections; it remains only that I should vindicate an argument for verse, which you have gone about to overthrow. It had formerly been said that the easiness of blank verse renders the poet too luxuriant, but that the labour of rhyme bounds and circumscribes an over-fruitful fancy; the sense there being commonly confined to the couplet, and the words so ordered that the rhyme naturally follows them, not they the rhyme. To this you answered, that it was no argument to the question in hand; for the dispute was not which way a man may write best, but which is most proper for the subject on which he writes.

"First, give me leave, Sir, to remember you that the Argument against which you raised this objection, was only secondary: it was built on this hypothesis,—that to write in verse was proper for serious plays. Which supposition being granted (as it was briefly made out in that discourse, by showing how verse might be made natural), it asserted, that this way of writing was an help to the poet's judgment, by putting bounds to a wild overflowing fancy. I think, therefore, it will not be hard for me to make good what it was to prove on that supposition. But you add, that were this let pass, yet he who wants judgment in the liberty of his fancy, may as well show the defect of it when he is confined to verse; for he who has judgment will avoid errors, and he who has it not, will commit them in all kinds of writing.

"This argument, as you have taken it from a most acute person [Seneca], so I confess it carries much weight in it: but by using the word judgment here indefinitely, you seem to have put a fallacy upon us. I grant, he who has judgment, that is, so profound, so strong, or rather so infallible a judgment, that he needs no helps to keep it always poised and upright, will commit no faults either in rhyme or out of it. And on the other extreme, he who has a judgment so weak and crazed that no helps can correct or amend it, shall write scurvily out of rhyme, and worse in it. But the first of these judgments is nowhere to be found, and the latter is not fit to write at all. To speak therefore of judgment as it is in the best poets; they who have the greatest proportion of it, want other helps than from it,

within. As for example, you would be loth to say that he who is en-
dued with a sound judgment has no need of History, Geography, or
Moral Philosophy, to write correctly. Judgment is indeed the master-
workman in a play; but he requires many subordinate hands, many
tools to his assistance. And verse I affirm to be one of these; 'tis a
rule and line by which he keeps his building compact and even,
which otherwise lawless imagination would raise either irregularly
or loosely; at least, if the poet commits errors with this help, he
would make greater and more without it: 'tis, in short, a slow and
painful, but the surest kind of working. Ovid, whom you accuse
for luxuriancy in verse, had perhaps been farther guilty of it, had
he writ in prose. And for your instance of Ben Jonson, who, you say,
writ exactly without the help of rhyme; you are to remember, 'tis
only an aid to a luxuriant fancy, which his was not: as he did not
want imagination, so none ever said he had much to spare. Neither
was verse then refined so much, to be an help to that age, as it is to
ours. Thus then the second thoughts being usually the best, as
receiving the maturest digestion from judgment, and the last and
most mature product of those thoughts being artful and laboured
verse, it may well be inferred, that verse is a great help to a luxuriant fancy; and this is what that argument which you opposed was
to evince."

Neander was pursuing this discourse so eagerly that Eugenius
had called to him twice or thrice, ere he took notice that the barge
stood still, and that they were at the foot of Somerset-stairs, where
they had appointed it to land. The company were all sorry to
separate so soon, though a great part of the evening was already
spent; and stood a-while looking back on the water, upon which the
moonbeams played, and made it appear like floating quick-silver:
at last they went up through a crowd of French people, who were
merrily dancing in the open air, and nothing concerned for the noise
of guns which had alarmed the town that afternoon. Walking
thence together to the Piazze, they parted there; Eugenius and Lisideius to some pleasant appointment they had made, and Crites and
Neander to their several lodgings.

Samuel Johnson

(1709–1784)

From PREFACE TO SHAKESPEARE

Though Johnson first proposed a ten-volume edition of Shakespeare's work in 1745, it was not until 1765 that he completed the project, which included the *Preface*. To be sure, his *Dictionary* had interrupted progress, but once it was completed, Johnson again, in 1756, published his proposal, acquired subscribers, and proceeded in his task, not, however, without extensive procrastination and resulting censure. One satirist wrote:

He for subscribers baits his hook,
And takes their cash; but where's the book?
Underlying Dr. Johnson's criticism is the classical assumption that art, by its capacity to move and to please, functions as a formative agent for moral and intellectual development. The writer's task, as he states in his tale *Rasselas,* is not to "number the streaks of the tulip"—that is, to dwell on details for their own sake, however pleasing—but to express universal truths, "just representations of general nature," as he states in his great *Preface.*

THAT praises are without reason lavished on the dead, and that the honours due only to excellence are paid to antiquity, is a complaint likely to be always continued by those, who, being able to add nothing to truth, hope for eminence from the heresies of paradox; or those, who, being forced by disappointment upon consolatory expedients, are willing to hope from posterity what the present age refuses, and flatter themselves that the regard which is yet denied by envy, will be at last bestowed by time.

Antiquity, like every other quality that attracts the notice of mankind, has undoubtedly votaries that reverence it, not from reason, but from prejudice. Some seem to admire indiscriminately whatever has been long preserved, without considering that time has sometimes co-operated with chance; all perhaps are more willing to honour past than present excellence; and the mind contemplates genius through the shades of age, as the eye surveys the sun through artificial opacity. The great contention of criticism is to find the faults of the moderns, and the beauties of the ancients. While an author is yet living we estimate his powers by his worst performance, and when he is dead, we rate them by his best.

To works, however, of which the excellence is not absolute and definite, but gradual and comparative; to works not raised upon principles demonstrative and scientifick, but appealing wholly to observation and experience, no other test can be applied than length of duration and continuance of esteem. What mankind have long possessed they have often examined and compared; and if they persist to value the possession, it is because frequent comparisons have confirmed opinion in its favour. As among the works of nature no man can properly call a river deep, or a mountain high, without the knowledge of many mountains, and many rivers; so in the productions of genius, nothing can be stiled excellent till it has been compared with other works of the same kind. Demonstration immediately displays its power, and has nothing to hope or fear from the flux of years; but works tentative and experimental must be estimated by their proportion to the general and collective ability of man, as it is discovered in a long succession of endeavours. Of the first building that was raised, it might be with certainty determined that it was round or square; but whether it was spacious or lofty must have been referred to time. The Pythagorean scale of numbers was at once discovered to be perfect; but the poems of *Homer* we yet know not to transcend the common limits of human intelligence, but by remarking, that nation after nation, and century after century, has been able to do little more than transpose his incidents, new-name his characters, and paraphrase his sentiments.

The reverence due to writings that have long subsisted arises therefore not from any credulous confidence in the superior wisdom of past ages, or gloomy persuasion of the degeneracy of mankind, but is the consequence of acknowledged and indubitable positions, that what has been longest known has been most considered, and what is most considered is best understood.

The Poet, of whose works I have undertaken the revision, may now begin to assume the dignity of an ancient, and claim the privilege of established fame and prescriptive veneration. He has long outlived his century, the term commonly fixed as the test of literary merit. Whatever advantages he might once derive from personal allusions, local customs, or temporary opinions, have for many years been lost; and every topick of merriment, or motive of sorrow, which the modes of artificial life afforded him, now only obscure the scenes which they once illuminated. The effects of favour and competition are at an end, the tradition of his friendships and his enmities has perished; his works support no opinion with arguments, nor supply any faction with invectives; they can neither indulge vanity nor gratify malignity; but are read without any other reason than the desire of pleasure, and are therefore praised only as pleasure is obtained; yet, thus unassisted by interest or passion, they have past through variations of taste and changes of manners, and, as they devolved from one generation to another, have received new honours at every transmission.

But because human judgment, though it be gradually gaining upon certainty, never becomes infallible; and approbation, though long continued, may yet be only the approbation of prejudice or fashion; it is proper to inquire, by what peculiarities of excellence *Shakespeare* has gained and kept the favour of his countrymen.

Nothing can please many, and please long, but just representations of general nature. Particular manner, can be known to few, and therefore few only can judge how nearly they are copied. The irregular combinations of fanciful invention may delight a-while, by that novelty of which the common satiety of life sends us all in quest; but the pleasures of sudden wonder are soon exhausted, and the mind can only repose on the stability of truth.

Shakespeare is above all writers, at least above all modern writers, the poet of nature; the poet that holds up to his readers

a faithful mirrour of manners and of life. His characters are not
modified by the customs of particular places, unpractised by the
rest of the world; by the peculiarities of studies or professions,
which can operate but upon small numbers; or by the accidents of
transient fashions or temporary opinions: they are the genuine
progeny of common humanity, such as the world will always
supply, and observation will always find. His persons act and
speak by the influence of those general passions and principles
by which all minds are agitated, and the whole system of life is
continued in motion. In the writings of other poets a character is
too often an individual; in those of *Shakespeare* it is commonly
a species.

It is from this wide extension of design that so much instruction
is derived. It is this which fills the plays of *Shakespeare* with
practical axioms and domestic wisdom. It was said of *Euripides,*
that every verse was a precept; and it may be said of *Shakespeare,*
that from his works may be collected a system of civil and
economical prudence. Yet his real power is not shewn in the
splendour of particular passages, but by the progress of his fable,
and the tenour of his dialogue; and he that tries to recommend
him by select quotations, will succeed like the pedant in *Hierocles,*
who, when he offered his house to sale, carried a brick in his pocket
as a specimen.

It will not easily be imagined how much *Shakespeare* excells in
accommodating his sentiments to real life, but by comparing him
with other authors. It was observed of the ancient schools of declamation, that the more diligently they were frequented, the more
was the student disqualified for the world, because he found nothing there which he should ever meet in any other place. The same
remark may be applied to every stage but that of *Shakespeare.* The
theatre, when it is under any other direction, is peopled by such
characters as were never seen, conversing in a language which was
never heard, upon topicks which will never rise in the commerce
of mankind. But the dialogue of this author is often so evidently
determined by the incident which produces it, and is pursued with
so much ease and simplicity, that it seems scarcely to claim the

merit of fiction, but to have been gleaned by diligent selection out of common conversation, and common occurrences.

Upon every other stage the universal agent is love, by whose power all good and evil is distributed, and every action quickened or retarded. To bring a lover, a lady and a rival into the fable; to entangle them in contradictory obligations, perplex them with oppositions of interest, and harrass them with violence of desires inconsistent with each other; to make them meet in rapture and part in agony; to fill their mouths with hyperbolical joy and outrageous sorrow; to distress them as nothing human ever was distressed; to deliver them as nothing human ever was delivered; is the business of a modern dramatist. For this probability is violated, life is misrepresented, and language is depraved. But love is only one of many passions; and as it has no great influence upon the sum of life, it has little operation in the dramas of a poet, who caught his ideas from the living world, and exhibited only what he saw before him. He knew, that any other passion, as it was regular or exorbitant, was a cause of happiness or calamity.

Characters thus ample and general were not easily discriminated and preserved, yet perhaps no poet ever kept his personages more distinct from each other. I will not say with *Pope,* that every speech may be assigned to the proper speaker, because many speeches there are which have nothing characteristical; but perhaps, though some may be equally adapted to every person, it will be difficult to find any that can be properly transferred from the present possessor to another claimant. The choice is right, when there is reason for choice.

Other dramatists can only gain attention by hyperbolical or aggravated characters, by fabulous and unexampled excellence or depravity, as the writers of barbarous romances invigorated the reader by a giant and a dwarf; and he that should form his expectations of human affairs from the play, or from the tale, would be equally deceived. *Shakespeare* has no heroes; his scenes are occupied only by men, who act and speak as the reader thinks that he should himself have spoken or acted on the same occasion: Even where the agency is supernatural the dialogue is level with life. Other writers disguise the most natural passions and most frequent incidents; so that he who contemplates them in the book will not know them in the world: *Shakespeare* approximates the remote, and familiarizes the wonderful; the event which he represents will not happen, but if it were possible, its effects would probably be such as he has assigned; and it may be said, that he has not only shewn human nature as it acts in real exigencies, but as it would be found in trials, to which it cannot be exposed.

This therefore is the praise of *Shakespeare,* that his drama is the mirrour of life; that he who has mazed his imagination, in following the phantoms which other writers raise up before him, may here be cured of his delirious extasies, by reading human sentiments in human language, by scenes from which a hermit may estimate the transactions of the world, and a confessor predict the progress of the passions.

His adherence to general nature has exposed him to the censure of criticks, who form their judgments upon narrow principles. *Dennis* and *Rhymer* think his Romans not sufficiently *Roman;* and *Voltaire* censures his kings as not completely royal. *Dennis* is offended, that *Menenius,* a senator of *Rome,* should play the buffoon; and *Voltaire* perhaps thinks decency violated when the *Danish* Usurper is represented as a drunkard. But *Shakespeare* always makes nature predominate over accident; and if he preserves the essential character, is not very careful of distinctions superinduced and adventitious. His story requires Romans or kings, but he thinks only on men. He knew that *Rome,* like every other city, had men of all dispositions; and wanting a buffoon, he went into the senate-house for that which the senate-house would certainly have afforded him. He was inclined to shew an usurper and a murderer not only odious but despicable, he therefore added drunkenness to his other qualities, knowing that kings love wine like other men, and that wine exerts its natural power upon kings. These are the petty cavils of petty minds; a poet overlooks the casual distinction of country and condition, as a painter, satisfied with the figure, neglects the drapery.

The censure which he has incurred by mixing comick and tragick scenes, as it extends to all his works, deserves more consideration. Let the fact be first stated, and then examined.

Shakespeare's plays are not in the rigorous and critical sense either tragedies or comedies, but compositions of a distinct kind; exhibiting the real state of sublunary nature, which partakes of good and evil, joy and sorrow, mingled with endless variety of proportion and innumerable modes of combination; and expressing the course of the world, in which the loss of one is the gain of another; in which, at the same time, the reveller is hasting to his wine, and the mourner burying his friend; in which the malignity of one is sometimes defeated by the frolick of another; and many mischiefs and many benefits are done and hindered without design.

Out of this chaos of mingled purposes and casualties the ancient poets, according to the laws which custom had prescribed, selected some the crimes of men, and some their absurdities; some the momentous vicissitudes of life, and some the lighter occurrences; some the terrours of distress, and some the gayeties of prosperity. Thus rose the two modes of imitation, known by the names of *tragedy* and *comedy,* compositions intended to promote different ends by contrary means, and considered as so little allied, that I do not recollect among the *Greeks* or *Romans* a single writer who attempted both.

Shakespeare has united the powers of exciting laughter and sorrow not only in one mind, but in one composition. Almost all his plays are divided between serious and ludicrous characters, and, in the successive evolutions of the design, sometimes produce seriousness and sorrow, and sometimes levity and laughter.

That this is a practice contrary to the rules of criticism will be readily allowed; but there is always an appeal open from criticism to nature. The end of writing is to instruct; the end of poetry is to instruct by pleasing. That the mingled drama may convey all the instruction of tragedy or comedy cannot be denied, because it includes both in its alterations of exhibition and approaches nearer than either to the appearance of life, by shewing how great machinations and slender designs may promote or obviate one another, and the high and the low co-operate in the general system by un-avoidable concatenation.

It is objected, that by this change of scenes the passions are in-terrupted in their progression, and that the principal event, being not advanced by a due gradation of preparatory incidents, wants at last the power to move, which constitutes the perfection of dra-matick poetry. This reasoning is so specious, that it is received as true even by those who in daily experience feel it to be false. The interchanges of mingled scenes seldom fail to produce the intended vicissitudes of passion. Fiction cannot move so much, but that the attention may be easily transferred; and though it must be allowed that pleasing melancholy be sometimes interrupted by unwelcome levity, yet let it be considered likewise, that melancholy is often not pleasing, and that the disturbance of one man may be the relief of another; that different auditors have different habitudes; and that, upon the whole, all pleasure consists in variety.

The players, who in their edition divided our authour's works into comedies, histories, and tragedies, seem not to have distin-guished the three kinds by any very exact or definite ideas.

Any action which ended happily to the principal persons, how-ever serious or distressful through its intermediate incidents, in their opinion, constituted a comedy. This idea of a comedy con-tinued long amongst us; and plays were written, which, by chang-ing the catastrophe, were tragedies to-day, and comedies to-morrow.

Tragedy was not in those times a poem of more general dignity or elevation than comedy; it required only a calamitous conclusion, with which the common criticism of that age was satisfied, what-ever lighter pleasure it afforded in its progress.

History was a series of actions, with no other than chronological succession, independent of each other, and without any tendency to introduce or regulate the conclusion. It is not always very nicely distinguished from tragedy. There is not much nearer approach to unity of action in the tragedy of *Antony and Cleopatra,* than in the history of *Richard the Second.* But a history might be continued through many plays; as it had no plan, it had no limits.

Through all these denominations of the drama, *Shakespeare's* mode of composition is the same; an interchange of seriousness and merriment, by which the mind is softened at one time, and exhilarated at another. But whatever be his purpose, whether to gladden or depress, or to conduct the story, without vehemence or emotion, through tracts of easy and familiar dialogue, he never fails to attain his purpose; as he commands us, we laugh or mourn, or sit silent with quiet expectation, in tranquillity without indifference.

When *Shakespeare's* plan is understood, most of the criticisms of *Rhymer* and *Voltaire* vanish away. The play of *Hamlet* is opened, without impropriety, by two sentinels; *Iago* bellows at *Brabantio's* window, without injury to the scheme of the play, though in terms which a modern audience would not easily endure; the character of *Polonius* is seasonable and useful; and the Grave-diggers themselves may be heard with applause.

Shakespeare engaged in dramatick poetry with the world open before him; the rules of the ancients were yet known to few; but publick judgment was unformed; he had no example of such fame as might force him upon imitation, nor criticks of such authority as might restrain his extravagance: He therefore indulged his natural disposition, and his disposition, as *Rhymer* has remarked, led him to comedy. In tragedy he often writes, with great appearance of toil and study, what is written at last with little felicity; but in his comick scenes, he seems to produce without labour what no labour can improve. In tragedy he is always struggling after some occasion to be comick; but in comedy he seems to repose, or to luxuriate, as in a mode of thinking congenial to his nature. In his tragick scenes there is always something wanting, but his comedy often surpasses expectation or desire. His comedy pleases by the thoughts and the language, and his tragedy for the greater part by incident and action. His tragedy seems to be skill, his comedy to be instinct.

The force of his comick scenes has suffered little diminution from the changes made by a century and a half, in manners or in words. As his personages act upon principles arising from genuine passion, very little modified by particular forms, their pleasures and vexations are communicable to all times and to all places; they are natural, and therefore durable; the adventitious peculiarities of personal habits, are only superficial dies, bright and pleasing for a little while, yet soon fading to a dim tinct, without any remains of former lustre; but the discriminations of true passion are the colours of nature; they pervade the whole mass, and can only perish with the body that exhibits them. The accidental compositions of heterogeneous modes are dissolved by the chance which combined them; but the uniform simplicity of primitive qualities neither admits increase, nor suffers decay. The sand heap by one flood is scattered by another, but the rock always continues in its place. The stream of time, which is continually washing the dissoluble fabricks of other poets, passes without injury by the adamant of *Shakespeare*.

If there be, what I believe there is, in every nation, a style which never becomes obsolete, a certain mode of phraseology so consonant and congenial to the analogy and principles of its respective language as to remain settled and unaltered; this style is probably to be sought in the common intercourse of life, among those who speak only to be understood, without ambition of elegance. The polite are always catching modish innovations, and the learned depart from established forms of speech, in hope of finding or making better; those who wish for distinction forsake the vulgar, when the vulgar is right; but there is a conversation above grossness and below refinement, where propriety resides, and where this poet seems to have gathered his comick dialogue. He is therefore more agreeable to the ears of the present age than any other authour equally remote, and among his other excellencies deserves to be studied as one of the original masters of our language.

These observations are to be considered not as unexceptionally constant, but as containing general and predominant truth. *Shakespeare's* familiar dialogue is affirmed to be smooth and clear, yet not wholly without ruggedness or difficulty; as a country may be eminently fruitful, though it has spots unfit for cultivation: His characters are praised as natural, though their sentiments are sometimes forced, and their actions improbable; as the earth upon the whole is spherical, though its surface is varied with protuberances and cavities.

Shakespeare with his excellencies has likewise faults, and faults sufficient to obscure and overwhelm any other merit. I shall shew them in the proportion in which they appear to me, without envious malignity or superstitious veneration. No question can be more innocently discussed than a dead poet's pretensions to renown; and little regard is due to that bigotry which sets candour higher than truth.

His first defect is that to which may be imputed most of the evil in books or in men. He sacrifices virtue to convenience, and is so much more careful to please than to instruct, that he seems to write without any moral purpose. From his writings indeed a system of social duty may be selected, for he that thinks reasonably must think morally; but his precepts and axioms drop casually from him; he makes no just distribution of good or evil, nor is always careful to shew in the virtuous a disapprobation of the wicked; he carries his persons indifferently through right and wrong, and at the close dismisses them without further care, and leaves their examples to operate by chance. This fault the barbarity of his age cannot extenuate; for it is always a writer's duty to make the world better, and justice is a virtue independent of time or place.

The plots are often so loosely formed, that a very slight consideration may improve them, and so carelessly pursued, that he seems not always fully to comprehend his own design. He omits opportunities of instructing or delighting which the train of his story seems to force upon him, and apparently rejects those exhibitions which would be more affecting, for the sake of those which are more easy.

It may be observed, that in many of his plays the latter part is evidently neglected. When he found himself near the end of his work, and, in view of his reward, he shortened the labour to snatch the profit. He therefore remits his efforts where he should most vigorously exert them, and his catastrophe is improbably produced or imperfectly represented.

He had no regard to distinction of time or place, but gives to one age or nation, without scruple, the customs, institutions, and opinions of another, at the expence not only of likelihood, but of possibility. These faults *Pope* has endeavoured, with more zeal than judgment, to transfer to his imagined interpolators. We need not wonder to find *Hector* quoting *Aristotle,* when we see the loves of *Theseus* and *Hippolyta* combined with the *Gothick* mythology of fairies. *Shakespeare,* indeed, was not the only violator of chronology, for in the same age *Sidney,* who wanted not the advantages of learning, has, in his *Arcadia,* confounded the pastoral with the feudal times, the days of innocence, quiet and security, with those of turbulence, violence, and adventure.

In his comick scenes he is seldom very successful, when he engages his characters in reciprocations of smartness and contests of sarcasm; their jests are commonly gross, and their pleasantry licentious; neither his gentlemen nor his ladies have much delicacy, nor are sufficiently distinguished from his clowns by any appearance of refined manners. Whether he represented the real conversation of his time is not easy to determine; the reign of *Elizabeth* is commonly supposed to have been a time of stateliness, formality and reserve; yet perhaps the relaxations of that severity were not very elegant. There must, however, have been always some modes of gayety preferable to others, and a writer ought to chuse the best.

In tragedy his performance seems constantly to be worse, as his labour is more. The effusions of passion which exigence forces out are for the most part striking and energetick; but whenever he solicits his invention, or strains his faculties, the offspring of his throes is tumour, meanness, tediousness, and obscurity.

In narration he affects a disproportionate pomp of diction, and a wearisome train of circumlocution, and tells the incident imperfectly in many words, which might have been more plainly delivered in few. Narration in dramatick poetry is naturally tedious, as it is unanimated and inactive, and obstructs the progress of the action; it should therefore always be rapid, and enlivened by frequent interruption. *Shakespeare* found it an encumbrance, and instead of lightening it by brevity, endeavoured to recommend it by dignity and splendour.

His declamations or set speeches are commonly cold and weak, for his power was the power of nature; when he endeavoured, like other tragick writers, to catch opportunities of amplification, and instead of inquiring what the occasion demanded, to show how much his stores of knowledge could supply, he seldom escapes without the pity or resentment of his reader.

It is incident to him to be now and then entangled with an unwieldy sentiment, which he cannot well express, and will not reject; he struggles with it a while, and if it continues stubborn, comprises it in words such as occur, and leaves it to be disentangled and evolved by those who have more leisure to bestow upon it.

Not that always where the language is intricate the thought is subtle, or the image always great where the line is bulky; the equality of words to things is very often neglected, and trivial sentiments and vulgar ideas disappoint the attention, to which they are recommended by sonorous epithets and swelling figures.

But the admirers of this great poet have never less reason to indulge their hopes of supreme excellence, than when he seems fully resolved to sink them in dejection, and mollify them with tender emotions by the fall of greatness, the danger of innocence, or the crosses of love. He is not long soft and pathetick without some idle conceit, or contemptible equivocation. He no sooner begins to move, than he counteracts himself; and terrour and pity, as they are rising in the mind, are checked and blasted by sudden frigidity.

A quibble is to *Shakespeare,* what luminous vapours are to the traveller; he follows it at all adventures; it is sure to lead him out of his way, and sure to engulf him in the mire. It has some malignant power over his mind, and its fascinations are irresistible. Whatever be the dignity or profundity of his disquisition, whether he be enlarging knowledge or exalting affection, whether he be amusing attention with incidents, or enchaining it in suspense, let but a quibble spring up before him, and he leaves his work unfinished. A quibble is the golden apple for which he will always turn aside from his career, or stoop from his elevation. A quibble, poor and barren as it is, gave him such delight, that he was content to purchase it, by the sacrifice of reason, propriety and truth. A quibble was to him the fatal *Cleopatra* for which he lost the world, and was content to lose it.

It will be thought strange, that, in enumerating the defects of this writer, I have not yet mentioned his neglect of the unities; his violation of those laws which have been instituted and established by the joint authority of poets and criticks.

For his other deviations from the art of writing I resign him to critical justice, without making any other demand in his favour, than that which must be indulged to all human excellence: that his virtues be rated with his failings: But, from the censure which this irregularity may bring upon him, I shall, with due reverence to that learning which I must oppose, adventure to try how I can defend him.

His histories, being neither tragedies nor comedies are not subject to any of their laws; nothing more is necessary to all the praise which they expect, than that the changes of action be so prepared as to be understood, that the incidents be various and affecting, and the characters consistent, natural, and distinct. No other unity is intended, and therefore none is to be sought.

In his other works he has well enough preserved the unity of action. He has not, indeed, an intrigue regularly perplexed and regularly unravelled: he does not endeavour to hide his design only to discover it, for this is seldom the order of real events, and *Shakespeare* is the poet of nature: But his plan has commonly what *Aristotle* requires, a beginning, a middle, and an end; one event is concatenated with another, and the conclusion follows by easy consequence. There are perhaps some incidents that might be spared, as in other poets there is much talk that only fills up time upon the stage; but the general system makes gradual advances, and the end of the play is the end of expectation.

To the unities of time and place he has shewn no regard; and perhaps a nearer view of the principles on which they stand will diminish their value, and withdraw from them the veneration which, from the time of *Corneille,* they have very generally received, by discovering that they have given more trouble to the poet, than pleasure to the auditor.

The necessity of observing the unities of time and place arises from the supposed necessity of making the drama credible. The criticks hold it impossible, that an action of months or years can be possibly believed to pass in three hours; or that the spectator can suppose himself to sit in a theatre, while ambassadors go and return between distant kings, while armies are levied and towns besieged, while an exile wanders and returns, or till he whom they saw courting his mistress, shall lament the untimely fall of his son. The mind revolts from evident falsehood, and fiction loses its force when it departs from the resemblance of reality.

From the narrow limitation of time necessarily arises the contraction of place. The spectator, who knows that he saw the first act at *Alexandria,* cannot suppose that he sees the next at *Rome,* at a distance to which not the dragons of Medea could, in so short a time, have transported him; he knows with certainty that he has not changed his place, and he knows that place cannot change itself; that what was a house cannot become a plain; that what was *Thebes* can never be *Persepolis.*

Such is the triumphant language with which a critick exults over the misery of an irregular poet, and exults commonly without resistance or reply. It is time therefore to tell him by the authority of *Shakespeare,* that he assumes, as an unquestionable principle, a position, which, while his breath is forming it into words, his understanding pronounces to be false. It is false, that any representation is mistaken for reality; that any dramatick fable in its materiality was ever credible, or, for a single moment, was ever credited.

The objection arising from the impossibility of passing the first hour at *Alexandria,* and the next at *Rome,* supposes, that when the play opens, the spectator really imagines himself at *Alexandria,* and believes that his walk to the theatre has been a voyage to *Egypt,* and that he lives in the days of *Antony* and *Cleopatra.* Surely he that imagines this may imagine more. He that can take the stage at one time for the palace of the *Ptolemies,* may take it in half an hour for the promontory of *Actium.* Delusion, if delusion be admitted, has no certain limitation; if the spectator can be once persuaded, that his old acquaintances are *Alexander* and *Caesar,* that a room illuminated with candles is the plain of *Pharsalia,* or the bank of *Granicus,* he is in a state of elevation above the reach of reason, or of truth, and from the heights of empyrean poetry, may despise the circumscriptions of terrestrial nature. There is no reason why a mind thus wandering in extacy should count the clock, or why an hour should not be a century in that calenture of the brains that can make the stage a field.

The truth is, that the spectators are always in their senses, and know, from the first act to the last, that the stage is only a stage, and that the players are only players. They came to hear a certain number of lines recited with just gesture and elegant modulation. The lines relate to some action, and an action must be in some place; but the different actions that complete a story may be in places very remote from each other; and where is the absurdity of allowing that space to represent first *Athens,* and then *Sicily,* which was always known to be neither *Sicily* nor *Athens,* but a modern theatre?

By supposition, as place is introduced, times may be extended; the time required by the fable elapses for the most part between the acts; for, of so much of the action as is represented, the real and poetical duration is the same. If, in the first act, preparations for war against *Mithridates* are represented to be made in *Rome,* the event of the war may, without absurdity, be represented, in the catastrophe, as happening in *Pontus;* we know that there is neither war, nor preparation for war; we know that we are neither in *Rome* nor *Pontus;* that neither *Mithridates* nor *Lucullus* are before us. The drama exhibits successive imitations of successive actions; and why may not the second imitation represent an action that happened years after the first, if it be so connected with it, that nothing but time can be supposed to intervene? Time is, of all modes of existence, most obsequious to the imagination; a lapse of years is as easily conceived as a passage of hours. In contemplation we easily contract the time of real actions, and therefore willingly permit it to be contracted when we only see their imitation.

It will be asked, how the drama moves, if it is not credited. It is credited with all the credit due to a drama. It is credited, whenever it moves, as a just picture of a real original; as representing to the auditor what he would himself feel, if he were to do or suffer what is there feigned to be suffered or to be done. The reflection that strikes the heart is not, that the evils before us are real evils, but that they are evils to which we ourselves may be exposed. If there be any fallacy, it is not that we fancy the players, but that we fancy ourselves unhappy for a moment; but we rather lament the possibility than suppose the presence of misery, as a mother weeps over her babe, when she remembers that death may take it from her. The delight of tragedy proceeds from our consciousness of fiction; if we thought murders and treasons real, they would please no more.

Imitations produce pain or pleasure, not because they are mistaken for realities, but because they bring realities to mind. When the imagination is recreated by a painted landscape, the trees are not supposed capable to give us shade, or the fountains coolness; but we consider, how we should be pleased with such fountains playing beside us, and such woods waving over us. We are agitated in reading the history of *Henry* the Fifth, yet no man takes his book for the field of *Agencourt*. A dramatick exhibition is a book recited with concomitants that encrease or diminish its effect. Familiar comedy is often more powerful in the theatre, than on the page; imperial tragedy is always less. The humour of *Petruchio* may be heightened by grimace; but what voice or what gesture can hope to add dignity or force to the soliloquy of *Cato*.

A play read, affects the mind like a play acted. It is therefore evident, that the action is not supposed to be real; and it follows, that between the acts a longer or shorter time may be allowed to pass, and that no more account of space or duration is to be taken by the auditor of a drama, than by the reader of a narrative, before whom may pass in an hour the life of a hero, or the revolutions of an empire.

Whether *Shakespeare* knew the unities, and rejected them by design, or deviated from them by happy ignorance, it is, I think, impossible to decide, and useless to enquire. We may reasonably suppose, that when he rose to notice, he did not want the counsels and admonitions of scholars and cricks, and that he at last deliberately persisted in a practice, which he might have begun by chance. As nothing is essential to the fable, but unity of action, and as the unities of time and place arise evidently from false assumptions, and, by circumscribing the extent of the drama, lessen its variety, I cannot think it much to be lamented, that they were not known by him, or not observed: Nor, if such another poet could arise, should I very vehemently reproach him, that his first act passed at *Venice,* and his next in *Cyprus.* Such violations of rules merely positive, become the comprehensive genius of *Shakespeare* . . .

Yet when I speak thus slightly of dramatick rules, I cannot but recollect how much wit and learning may be produced against me; before such authorities I am afraid to stand, not that I think the present question one of those that are to be decided by mere authority, but because it is to be suspected, that these precepts have not been so easily received but for better reasons than I have yet been able to find. The result of my enquiries, in which it would be ludicrous to boast of impartiality, is, that the unities of time and place are not essential to a just drama, that though they may sometimes conduce to pleasure, they are always to be sacrificed to the nobler beauties of variety and instruction; and that a play, written with nice observation of critical rules, is to be contemplated as an elaborate curiosity, as the product of superfluous and ostentatious art, by which is shewn, rather what is possible, than what is necessary.

He that, without diminution of any other excellence, shall preserve all the unities unbroken, deserves the like applause with the architect, who shall display all the orders of architecture in a citadel, without any deduction from its strength; but the principal beauty of a citadel is to exclude the enemy; and the greatest graces of a play, are to copy nature and instruct life.

Perhaps what I have here not dogmatically but deliberately written, may recall the principles of the drama to a new examination. I am almost frighted at my own temerity; and when I estimate the fame and the strength of those that maintain the contrary opinion, am ready to sink down in reverential silence; as *Aeneas* withdrew from the defence of *Troy,* when he saw *Neptune* shaking the wall, and *Juno* heading the besiegers.

Those whom my arguments cannot persuade to give their approbation to the judgment of *Shakespeare,* will easily, if they consider the condition of his life, make some allowance for his ignorance.

Every man's performances, to be rightly estimated, must be compared with the state of the age in which he lived, and with his own particular opportunities; and though to the reader a book be not worse or better for the circumstances of the authour, yet as there is always a silent reference of human works to human abilities, and as the enquiry, how far man may extend his designs, or how high he may rate his native force, is of far greater dignity than in what rank we shall place any particular performance, curiosity is always busy to discover the instruments, as well as to survey the workmanship, to know how much is to be ascribed to original powers, and how much to casual and adventitious help. The palaces of *Peru* or *Mexico* were certainly mean and incommodious habitations, if compared to the houses of *European* monarchs; yet who could forbear to view them with astonishment, who remembered that they were built without the use of iron?

The *English* nation, in the time of *Shakespeare,* was yet struggling to emerge from barbarity. The philology of *Italy* had been transplanted hither in the reign of *Henry* the Eighth; and the learned languages had been successfully cultivated by *Lilly, Linacer, and More;* by *Pole, Cheke,* and *Gardiner;* and afterwards by *Smith, Clerk, Haddon,* and *Ascham.* Greek was now taught to boys in the principal schools; and those who united elegance with learning, read, with great diligence, the *Italian* and *Spanish* poets. But literature was yet confined to professed scholars, or to men and women of high rank. The publick was gross and dark; and to be able to read and write, was an accomplishment still valued for its rarity.

Nations, like individuals, have their infancy. A people newly awakened to literary curiosity, being yet unacquainted with the true state of things, knows not how to judge of that which is proposed as its resemblance. Whatever is remote from common appearances is always welcome to vulgar, as to childish credulity; and of a country unenlightened by learning, the whole people is the vulgar. The study of those who then aspired to plebian learning was laid out upon adventures, giants, dragons, and enchantments. *The Death of Arthur* was the favourite volume. . . .

[In the brief section that follows—here omitted—Johnson discusses the sources of Shakespeare's plots.]

His plots, whether historical or fabulous, are always crowded with incidents, by which the attention of a rude people was more easily caught than by sentiment or argumentation; and such is the power of the marvellous even over those who despise it, that every man finds his mind more strongly seized by the tragedies of *Shakespeare* than of any other writer; others please us by particular speeches, but he always makes us anxious for the event, and has perhaps excelled all but Homer in securing the first purpose of a writer, by exciting restless and unquenchable curiosity and compelling him that reads his work to read it through.

The shows and bustle with which his plays abound have the same original. As knowledge advances, pleasure passes from the eye to the ear, but returns, as it declines, from the ear to the eye. Those to whom our author's labours were exhibited had more skill in pomps or processions than in poetical language, and perhaps wanted some visible and discriminated events, as comments on the dialogue. He knew how he should most please; and whether his practice is more agreeable to nature, or whether his example has prejudiced the nation, we still find that on our stage something must be done as well as said, and inactive declamation is very coldly heard, however musical or elegant, passionate or sublime.

Voltaire expresses his wonder, that our author's extravagances are endured by a nation, which has seen the tragedy of *Cato*. Let him be answered, that *Addison* speaks the language of poets, and *Shakespeare,* of men. We find in *Cato* innumerable beauties which enamour us of its authour, but we see nothing that acquaints us with human sentiments or human actions; we place it with the fairest and the noblest progeny which judgment propagates by conjunction with learning, but *Othello* is the vigorous and vivacious offspring of observation impregnated by genius. *Cato* affords a splendid exhibition of artificial and fictitious manners, and delivers just and noble sentiments, in diction easy, elevated and harmonious, but its hopes and fears communicate no vibration to the heart; the composition refers us only to the writer; we pronounce the name of *Cato,* but we think on *Addison.*

The work of a correct and regular writer is a garden accurately formed and diligently planted, varied with shades and scented with flowers. The composition of *Shakespeare* is a forest in which oaks extend their branches and pines tower in the air, interspersed sometimes with weeds and brambles and sometimes giving shelter to myrtles and to roses; filling the eye with awful pomp and gratifying the mind with endless diversity. Other poets display cabinets of precious rarities minutely finished, wrought into shape, and polished into brightness. *Shakespeare* opens a mine which contains gold and diamonds in unexhaustible plenty, though clouded by incrustations, debased by impurities, and mingled with a mass of meaner minerals. . . .

[In the remainder of the *Preface,* Johnson discusses Shakespeare's life and previous editions of Shakespeare's plays.]

III

THE NINETEENTH
CENTURY:
ROMANTICISM
AND CLASSICAL
HUMANISM

Preface

I

For the English neo-classicists, truth rested on rational principles which were self-evident to any intelligent man. Upon such a basis, critics assumed that a work, to be valuable as an "imitation" of Nature, should embody general forms, the universal truths, which all men could recognize. The ancient writers, Pope states, had grasped these truths and had systematized them, for aesthetic ends, as rules of art:

> Those Rules of old discover'd, not devis'd,
> Are Nature still, but Nature methodiz'd . . .

The value of a work, then, rested upon its correspondence to Nature (by which was meant human nature—man's rational and moral essence—as well as the harmonious cosmos, within which man strives to fulfill his ideal nature), which had been the same for the ancients:

> Unerring Nature! still divinely bright,
> One clear, unchang'd, and universal light,
> Life, force, and beauty, must to all impart,
> At once the source, and end, and test of art.

The ancients, then, were the proper objects of study and imitation:

> Learn hence for ancient rules a just esteem;
> To copy Nature is to copy them.

Though the major neo-classical critics never insisted on strict adherence to rules, their faith in man's unchanging nature was to be questioned in the eighteenth century as the result of a new approach which has come to be called "historicism." The recognition that man's manner of thinking and feeling changes with different historical periods, and the study of the conditions which give rise to the literature of a specific period may be seen earlier, for example, in Thomas Rymer's *Tragedies of the Last Age* (1678), but with Giambattista Vico's *New Science* (1725), the historical approach gained new impetus. (In his *History of Modern Criticism,* René Wellek doubts the influence of Vico in England before the nineteenth century, but Thomas Blackwell's *Enquiry into the Life and Writings of Homer,* 1735, and Thomas Warton's *History of English Poetry,* 1774-81, clearly indicate the new approach.) This resulted in a cultural relativism emphasizing the uniqueness of each historical period. In Germany, this produced *Kulturgeschichte* ("cultural history"), formally inaugurated by Johann Gottfried Herder at the end of the century. Its intent was to study art as the product of its age, an idea still strong today.

During the century, the new historicism, in conjunction with the effects of British empiricism, undermined the neo-classical assumption concerning universal standards of judgment. A new interest in the literature of other countries and an awareness of their inherent differences, not measurable by neo-classical criteria, testified to the inevitable abandonment of all rules, for how could Chinese tragedy or Icelandic verse be judged by standards established by sixteenth-century Italians or eighteenth-century Englishmen? Though admiration of the ancients did not weaken, it was absurd to assume that one could use standards based on Greek and Roman literature or that one could write like Homer or Horace, since cultural conditions had produced, in the eighteenth century, men and conditions far different from those in classical antiquity; moreover, the truths discovered by the ancients might not be operable for the modern men of the Enlightenment. In short, man could no longer assume that his objective, ideal nature—as reason had revealed it to the ancients and to the neo-classicists—was self-evident.

II

In addition to the new cultural perspective, there was, during the eighteenth century, a progressive change in man's awareness of the place of feeling in his experience. Early in the century, the Earl of Shaftesbury, in a philosophical work entitled *Characteristics of Men, Manners, Opinions, and Times* (1711), postulated that man possessed a "moral sense" which directed him toward truth and virtue—a view of man's innate capacity for good directly challenging Hobbes's contention that man is motivated by self-interest. Shaftesbury's interpreters believed this to be an individual's "sensibility," that quality which expresses itself through feeling. The consequences of this attitude may be seen in the "drama of sensibility," of which Sir Richard Steele's *The Conscious Lovers* (1722) is typical. The bourgeois audience—encouraged to shed tears at the sudden conversions of villains, at the extraordinary goodness of the hero who, in his inevitable triumph over adversity, is always magnanimous—demonstrates its own moral sense when confronted by the good, the true, and the beautiful. The virtue of such a response—much discussed in connection with Rousseau's idea that the "natural" man, essentially good, may rely on his feelings—is a major idea leading to Wordsworth's famous discussion of poetry as the "spontaneous overflow of powerful feeling" (after long contemplation) and to the rise of primitivism (the cult of the "noble savage," the child, and the rustic—all unspoiled by civilization).

The emphasis on feeling in the eighteenth century (which may be traced not only in the arts but also in wide popularity of the Methodist movement, founded by John Wesley in the 1730's) may also be seen in the way Longinus' *On the Sublime* was interpreted. The neo-classicists had themselves quoted Longinus as one who emphasized not "rules" or "correctness" based on rational principles but excellencies of style achieved by the writer of genius. However, they were not always attracted to Longinus' idea that art must evoke the passions and "transport" the reader to achieve its proper effect.

For the romantics, intensity of feeling became the touchstone of judgment, though not generally divorced from moral considerations. Byron, for example, called poetry "the expression of excited passion," "the lava of the imagination"; Hazlitt, who admired Longinus, called intensity of expression "gusto," by which he meant "the power or passion defining any object"; and Keats, influenced by Hazlitt, wrote, in a famous letter to his brothers: "The excellence of every art is its intensity, capable of making all disagreeables evaporate, from their being in close relationship with Beauty and Truth," a statement which closely approximates Hazlitt's "gusto" and Longinus' "sublime."

In short, criticism now centered on the expressive qualities of the work rather than on its capacity to imitate an ideal Nature. When Keats wrote, "I am certain of nothing but the holiness of the Heart's affections and the truth of the Imagination," he uttered a central doctrine of romanticism: faith in one's feelings and in the creative mind to reveal reality, to bring about a sympathetic identification with Nature, as Keats suggests in his phrase "Negative Capability"—the capacity to negate the self, to obliterate the distinction between subject and object.

III

Such attitudes imply a rejection of the primary significance of man's rational faculty. As early as 1651, in *The Leviathan,* Thomas Hobbes postulated philosophical empiricism, which was to bring about such extraordinary changes in the following century. In his work, Hobbes wrote that "there is no conception in a man's mind, which hath not at first, totally or by parts, been begotten upon the organs of sense." Following Hobbes, in the *Essay Concerning Human Understanding* (1690), a work read widely, John Locke made the mind a passive receiver of impressions. Denying the existence of innate ideas, Locke stated that we acquire ideas from the "impressions" that concrete objects make on our minds, which at birth are, as he says, blank sheets of paper. Since all ideas come from these impressions, knowledge is possible only from experience.

In the work of David Hume (*Treatise of Human Nature,* 1739-40), British empiricism reached its climax, for he postulated that we can know only our own impressions and those ideas (weak copies of those impressions) derived from them. Cause and effect relationships, he indicates, have no actual existence in nature; long experience of past "coincidental" events may enable us to predict a future event, but there is no certainty that it will always occur in precisely the same way. As Walter Jackson Bate writes:

> In the philosophy of Hume more than any other writer, the tradition of classical rationalism, which underlies the thought of antiquity, the Middle Ages, and Renaissance humanism, and the great rationalistic systems of the seventeenth century, came to its conclusion. In his writings, human reason was dissected with such devastating effect that philosophy has never since quite recovered the traditional classical confidence in reason.

With the distrust of human reason in its capacity to reveal the nature of reality, literary discussion gradually shifted in its emphasis from neo-classical concern with general, universal forms to individual, particular experience. The shift is observable in the drama, for example, where critical concern with the psychology of individual characters replaced discussions of "types" according to the classical theory of decorum.

Ironically, empirical philosophy had, in discrediting the notion of abstract, universal forms of truth, also discredited man's creative capacity, for the empiricists had emphasized the mind's passive state while receiving impressions. However, the German philosopher Immanuel Kant developed, in *The Critique of Pure Reason* (1781), a theory that the mind had structure, or "categories," which ordered sensations and which provided man with the concepts with which to understand experience. In short, the mind was a "creative" instrument. Combined with "associationist" psychology, as developed by David Hartley in *Observations on Man* (1749), which contended that man's capacity for universal sympathy may be derived ultimately from simple, then more complex, associations of impressions, post-Kantean philosophy pointed directly toward the romantic distinction between imagination—which for Coleridge enabled man to construct new organic realities and to identify himself with them; and reason—which categorized reality in disembodied abstractions. This division is established by Shelley, for example, at the very opening of his *Defence of Poetry*.

IV

Unlike the continent, England did not have a self-conscious romantic "movement." The term "romantic," used earlier to refer to the qualities of romances, or tales, first appeared in its modern meaning in the criticism of A. W. von Schlegel (1767-1848) and his younger brother, Friedrich (1772-1829), who were the first to distinguish between the "classic" and the "romantic," an activity which has become the favorite pastime of critics ever since. In England, the distinction, already implicit in eighteenth-century criticism, was popularized by Madame de Staël's *De l'Allemagne* in 1813. In 1815, a translation of the Schlegels' *Dramatic Lectures* also appeared in England. It was not until the 1850's, however, that the term began to appear in literary histories. Earlier the poets, though not aware that they were "romantics," were, to be sure, conscious of their rejection of neo-classical poetry, about which Robert Southey (with Wordsworth and Coleridge, one of the "Lake Poets") said in 1807: "The time which elapsed from the days of Dryden to those of Pope is the dark age of English poetry."

With the publication of the *Lyrical Ballads* (1798), one of the great landmarks in English poetry, romanticism found its first important practitioners in Wordsworth and Coleridge. In Wordsworth's famous "Preface" to the second edition (1800), the absence of neo-classical terminology is striking: no longer is there talk of "rules," "correctness," separation of genres, "imitation" of the ancients, etc. But what is also striking is the remarkable similarity to neo-classical thought in such a passage as this:

Aristotle, I have been told, has said that poetry is the most philosophic of all writing; it is so: its object is truth, not individual and
local, but general and operative . . .

The *Lyrical Ballads* and the "Preface" were to set off considerable controversy over the questions of subject matter and poetic
diction, questions which Coleridge would take up later in his
Biographia Literaria, which in part was conceived as a rejection
of Wordsworth's conception of the imagination as a more com-
plicated activity of the mind than fancy (rather than fundamentally different, as Coleridge contended) and a critique of
Wordsworth's theory of poetic diction.

V

In a society increasingly concerned with progress and empire,
Matthew Arnold saw the necessity of reasserting the values of
classical humanistic thought in order, as he says, "to do away with
classes," with the inequality which "materializes the upper class"
—the "Barbarians"; "vulgarizes the middle class"—the "Philistines"; "brutalizes the lower class." This elimination of inequality
is what "culture" seeks to do. As defined in Arnold's essay "Sweetness and Light," from *Culture and Anarchy* (1869), culture is the
"activity of mind" (David Perkins' phrase) that consists "in *becoming* something rather than in *having* something, in an inward condition of the mind and spirit, not in an outward set of circumstances."
Literature has the unique capacity to set into motion man's total
being—his emotions, will, and reason—in quest of the meaning of
life. In its capacity to bring into activity those qualities which may
produce greater awareness and sympathy, literature is essentially
a moral force. It is, Arnold insists, a "criticism of life," for culture,
with its "single-minded love of perfection," wishes "to make reason
and the will of God prevail." However the "harmonious expansion
of human nature," in both mind and spirit, requires—as Arnold
states in *The Function of Criticism*—"disinterestedness," that
quality which liberates one from motives of self-interest. Without

it, the attainment of "full perfection of our humanity" is not possible.

The "pursuit of perfection," says Arnold, "is the pursuit of sweetness and light"—of beauty, harmony, intelligence—the ideals of the Greeks. In exercising his craft, the critic—literary or otherwise—must make these ideals prevail, for it is his moral imperative: "He who works for machinery, he who works for hatred, works only for confusion."

William Wordsworth

(1770–1850)

Preface to the LYRICAL BALLADS

To regard Wordworth's "Preface" to the second edition of the *Lyrical Ballads* (1800) as the "manifesto" of the Romantic Movement is a convenience of literary historians intent on dramatizing the commonplace, for in the preface Wordsworth spoke only for himself in defense of his poetic practice; indeed, Coleridge was later to reject some of his friend's theories. Moreover, no "movement" existed, if by that we mean a self-conscious group of poets aware of their role in history. Perhaps it may be said that the eighteenth century "produced" Wordsworth rather than that he "inaugurated" anything, for virtually all of Wordsworth's critical theories advanced in the "Preface" have their sources in the proceeding century. Nevertheless, in its fusion of eloquence and vision, the "Preface" is a notable movement.

———◆———

THE first volume of these Poems has already been submitted to general perusal. It was published, as an experiment, which, I hoped, might be of some use to ascertain, how far, by fitting to metrical arrangement a selection of the real language of men in a state of vivid sensation, that sort of pleasure and that quantity of pleasure may be imparted, which a Poet may rationally endeavour to impart.

I had formed no very inaccurate estimate of the probable effect of those Poems: I flattered myself that they who should be pleased with them would read them with more than common pleasure: and, on the other hand, I was well aware, that by those who should dislike them, they would be read with more than common dislike. The result has differed from my expectation in this only, that a greater number have been pleased than I ventured to hope I should please.

Several of my Friends are anxious for the success of these Poems, from a belief, that, if the views with which they were composed were indeed realized, a class of Poetry would be produced, well adapted to interest mankind permanently, and not unimportant in the quality, and in the multiplicity of its moral relations: and on this account they have advised me to prefix a systematic defence of the theory upon which the Poems were written. But I was unwilling to undertake the task, knowing that on this occasion the Reader would look coldly upon my arguments, since I might be suspected of having been principally influenced by the selfish and foolish hope of *reasoning* him into an approbation of these particular Poems: and I was still more unwilling to undertake the task, because, adequately to display the opinions, and fully to enforce the arguments, would require a space wholly disproportionate to a preface. For, to treat the subject with the clearness and coherence of which it is susceptible, it would be necessary to give a full account of the present state of the public taste in this country, and to determine how far this taste is healthy or depraved; which, again, could not be determined, without pointing out in what manner language and the human mind act and re-act on each other, and without retracing the revolutions, not of literature alone, but likewise of society itself. I have therefore altogether declined to enter regularly upon this defence; yet I am sensible, that there would be something like impropriety in abruptly obtruding upon the Public, without a few words of introduction, Poems so materially different from those upon which general approbation is at present bestowed.

It is supposed, that by the act of writing in verse an Author makes a formal engagement that he will gratify certain known habits of association; that he not only thus apprises the Reader that certain classes of ideas and expressions will be found in his book, but that others will be carefully excluded. This exponent or symbol held forth by metrical language must in different eras of literature have excited very different expectations: for example, in the age of Catullus, Terence, and Lucretius, and that of Statius or Claudian; and in our own country, in the age of Shakespeare and

Beaumont and Fletcher, and that of Donne and Cowley, or Dryden, or Pope. I will not take upon me to determine the exact import of the promise which, by the act of writing in verse, an Author in the present day makes to his reader: but it will undoubtedly appear to many persons that I have not fulfilled the terms of an engagement thus voluntarily contracted. They who have been accustomed to the gaudiness and inane phraseology of many modern writers, if they persist in reading this book to its conclusion, will, no doubt, frequently have to struggle with feelings of strangeness and awkwardness: they will look round for poetry, and will be induced to inquire by what species of courtesy these attempts can be permitted to assume that title. I hope therefore the reader will not censure me for attempting to state what I have proposed to myself to perform; and also (as far as the limits of a preface will permit) to explain some of the chief reasons which have determined me in the choice of my purpose: that at least he may be spared any unpleasant feeling of disappointment, and that I myself may be protected from one of the most dishonourable accusations which can be brought against an Author; namely, that of an indolence which prevents him from endeavouring to ascertain what is his duty, or, when his duty is ascertained, prevents him from performing it.

The principal object, then, proposed in these Poems was to choose incidents and situations from common life, and to relate or describe them, throughout, as far as was possible in a selection of language really used by men, and, at the same time, to throw over them a certain colouring of imagination, whereby ordinary things should be presented to the mind in an unusual aspect; and, further, and above all, to make these incidents and situations interesting by tracing in them, truly though not ostentatiously, the primary laws of our nature: chiefly, as far as regards the manner in which we associate ideas in a state of excitement. Humble and rustic life was generally chosen, because, in that condition, the essential passions of the heart find a better soil in which they can attain their maturity, are less under restraint, and speak a plainer and more emphatic language; because in that condition of life our elementary feelings coexist in a state of greater simplicity, and, consequently, may be more accurately contemplated, and more forcibly communicated; because the manners of rural life germinate from those elementary feelings, and, from the necessary character of rural occupations, are more easily comprehended, and are more durable; and, lastly, because in that condition the passions of men are incorporated with the beautiful and permanent forms of nature. The language, too, of these men has been adopted (purified indeed from what appear to be its real defects, from all lasting and rational causes of dislike or disgust) because such men hourly communicate with the best objects from which the best part of language is originally derived; and because, from their rank in society and the sameness and narrow circle of their intercourse, being less under the influence of social vanity, they convey their feelings and notions in simple and unelaborated expressions. Accordingly, such a language, arising out of repeated experience and regular feelings, is a more permanent, and a far more philosophical language, than that which is frequently substituted for it by Poets, who think that they are conferring honour upon themselves and their art, in proportion as they separate themselves from the sympathies of men, and indulge in arbitrary and capricious habits of expression, in order to furnish food for fickle tastes, and fickle appetites, of their own creation.[1]

I cannot, however, be insensible to the present outcry against the triviality and meanness, both of thought and language, which some of my contemporaries have occasionally introduced into their metrical compositions; and I acknowledge that this defect, where it exists, is more dishonourable to the Writer's own character than false refinement or arbitrary innovation, though I should contend at the same time, that it is far less pernicious in the sum of its consequences. From such verses the Poems in these volumes will be found distinguished at least by one mark of difference, that each of them has a worthy *purpose*. Not that I always began to

[1] It is worth while here to observe, that the affecting parts of Chaucer are almost always expressed in language pure and universally intelligible even to this day. [Wordsworth]

write with a distinct purpose formerly conceived; but habits of meditation have, I trust, so prompted and regulated my feelings, that my descriptions of such objects as strongly excite those feelings, will be found to carry along with them a *purpose*. If this opinion be erroneous, I can have little right to the name of a Poet. For all good poetry is the spontaneous overflow of powerful feelings: and though this be true, Poems to which any value can be attached were never produced on any variety of subjects but by a man who, being possessed of more than usual organic sensibility, had also thought long and deeply. For our continued influxes of feeling are modified and directed by our thoughts, which are indeed the representatives of all our past feelings; and, as by contemplating the relation of these general representatives to each other, we discover what is really important to men, so, by the repetition and continuance of this act, our feelings will be connected with important subjects, till at length, if we be originally possessed of much sensibility, such habits of mind will be produced that, by obeying blindly and mechanically the impulses of those habits, we shall describe objects, and utter sentiments, of such a nature, and in such connexion with each other, that the understanding of the Reader must necessarily be in some degree enlightened, and his affections strengthened and purified.

It has been said that each of these poems has a purpose. Another circumstance must be mentioned which distinguishes these Poems from the popular Poetry of the day; it is this, that the feeling therein developed gives importance to the action and situation, and not the action and situation to the feeling.

A sense of false modesty shall not prevent me from asserting, that the Reader's attention is pointed to this mark of distinction, far less for the sake of these particular Poems than from the general importance of the subject. The subject is indeed important! For the human mind is capable of being excited without the application of gross and violent stimulants; and he must have a very faint perception of its beauty and dignity who does not know this, and who does not further know, that one being is elevated above another, in proportion as he possesses this capability. It has therefore appeared to me, that to endeavour to produce or enlarge this capability is one of the best services in which, at any period, a Writer can be engaged; but this service, excellent at all times, is especially so at the present day. For a multitude of causes, unknown to former times, are now acting with a combined force to blunt the discriminating powers of the mind, and, unfitting it for all voluntary exertion, to reduce it to a state of almost savage torpor. The most effective of these causes are the great national events which are daily taking place, and the increasing accumulation of men in cities, where the uniformity of their occupations produces a craving for extraordinary incident, which the rapid communication of intelligence hourly gratifies. To this tendency of life and manners the literature and theatrical exhibitions of the country have conformed themselves. The invaluable works of our elder writers, I had almost said the works of Shakespeare and Milton, are driven into neglect by frantic novels, sickly and stupid German Tragedies, and deluges of idle and extravagant stories in verse.— When I think upon this degrading thirst after outrageous stimulation, I am almost ashamed to have spoken of the feeble endeavour made in these volumes to counteract it; and, reflecting upon the magnitude of the general evil, I should be oppressed with no dishonourable melancholy, had I not a deep impression of certain inherent and indestructible qualities of the human mind, and likewise of certain powers in the great and permanent objects that act upon it, which are equally inherent and indestructible; and were there not added to this impression a belief, that the time is approaching when the evil will be systematically opposed, by men of greater powers, and with far more distinguished success.

Having dwelt thus long on the subjects and aim of these Poems, I shall request the Reader's permission to apprise him of a few circumstances relating to their *style,* in order, among other reasons, that he may not censure me for not having performed what I never attempted. The Reader will find that personifications of abstract ideas rarely occur in these volumes; and are utterly rejected, as an ordinary device to elevate the style, and raise it above prose. My purpose was to imitate, and, as far as possible, to

adopt the very language of men; and assuredly such personifications do not make any natural or regular part of that language.
They are, indeed, a figure of speech occasionally prompted by passion, and I have made use of them as such; but have endeavoured
utterly to reject them as a mechanical device of style, or as a family
language which Writers in metre seem to lay claim to by prescrip-
tion. I have wished to keep the Reader in the company of flesh and
blood, persuaded that by so doing I shall interest him. Others who
pursue a different track will interest him likewise; I do not interfere with their claim, but wish to prefer a claim of my own. There
will also be found in these volumes little of what is usually
called poetic diction; as much pains has been taken to avoid it as is
ordinarily taken to produce it; this has been done for the reason already alleged, to bring my language near to the language of men;
and further, because the pleasure which I have proposed to myself
to impart, is of a kind very different from that which is supposed
by many persons to be the proper object of poetry. Without being
culpably particular, I do not know how to give my Reader a more
exact notion of the style in which it was my wish and intention to
write, than by informing him that I have at all times endeavoured
to look steadily at my subject; consequently, there is I hope in
these Poems little falsehood of description, and my ideas are expressed in language fitted to their respective importance. Something must have been gained by this practice, as it is friendly to
one property of all good poetry, namely, good sense: but it has
necessarily cut me off from a large portion of phrases and figures
of speech which from father to son have long been regarded as the
common inheritance of Poets. I have also thought it expedient to
restrict myself still further, having abstained from the use of many
expressions, in themselves proper and beautiful, but which have
been foolishly repeated by bad Poets, till such feelings of disgust
are connected with them as it is scarcely possible by any art of
association to overpower.

   If in a poem there should be found a series of lines, or even a
single line, in which the language, though naturally arranged, and
according to the strict laws of metre, does not differ from that of

prose, there is a numerous class of critics, who, when they stumble upon these prosaisms, as they call them, imagine that they have made a notable discovery, and exult over the Poet as over a man ignorant of his own profession. Now these men would establish a canon of criticism which the Reader will conclude he must utterly reject, if he wishes to be pleased with these volumes. And it would be a most easy task to prove to him, that not only the language of a large portion of every good poem, even of the most elevated character, must necessarily, except with reference to the metre, in no respect differ from that of good prose, but likewise that some of the most interesting parts of the best poems will be found to be strictly the languge of prose when prose is well written. The truth of this assertion might be demonstrated by innumerable passages from almost all the poetical writings, even of Milton himself. To illustrate the subject in a general manner, I will here adduce a short composition of Gray, who was at the head of those who, by their reasonings, have attempted to widen the space of separation betwixt Prose and Metrical composition, and was more than any other man curiously elaborate in the structure of his own poetic diction.

> In vain to me the smiling mornings shine,
> And reddening Phœbus lifts his golden fire:
> The birds in vain their amorous descant join,
> Or cheerful fields resume their green attire.
> These ears, alas! for other notes repine;
> *A different object do these eyes require;*
> *My lonely anguish melts no heart but mine;*
> *And in my breast the imperfect joys expire;*
> Yet morning smiles the busy race to cheer,
> And new-born pleasure brings to happier men;
> The fields to all their wonted tribute bear;
> To warm their little loves the birds complain,
> *I fruitless mourn to him that cannot hear,*
> *And weep the more because I weep in vain.*

It will easily be perceived, that the only part of this Sonnet which is of any value is the lines printed in Italics; it is equally obvious, that, except in the rhyme, and in the use of the single word "fruit-less" for fruitlessly, which is so far a defect, the language of these lines does in no respect differ from that of prose.

By the foregoing quotation it has been shown that language of Prose may yet be well adapted to Poetry; and it was previously as-serted, that a large portion of the language of every good poem can in no respect differ from that of good Prose. We will go further. It may be safely affirmed, that there neither is, nor can be, any *essential* difference between the language of prose and metrical composition. We are fond of tracing the resemblance between Poetry and Painting, and, accordingly, we call them Sisters: but where shall we find bonds of connexion sufficiently strict to typify the affinity betwixt metrical and prose composition? They both speak by and to the same organs; the bodies in which both of them are clothed may be said to be of the same substance, their affections are kindred, and almost identical, not necessarily differing even in degree; Poetry[2] sheds no tears "such as Angels weep," but natu-ral and human tears; she can boast of no celestial ichor that dis-tinguishes her vital juices from those of prose; the same human blood circulates through the veins of them both.

If it be affirmed that rhyme and metrical arrangement of them-selves constitute a distinction which overturns what has just been said on the strict affinity of metrical language with that of prose, and paves the way for other artificial distinctions which the mind voluntarily admits, I answer that the language of such Poetry as is here recommended is, as far as is possible, a selection of the lan-guage really spoken by men; that this selection, wherever it is made with true taste and feeling, will of itself form a distinction far greater than would at first be imagined, and will entirely sepa-

[2] I here use the word "Poetry" (though against my own judgement) as opposed to the word Prose, and synonymous with metrical composition. But much confusion has been introduced into criticism by this con-tradistinction of Poetry and Prose, instead of the more philosophical one of Poetry and Matter of Fact, or Science. The only strict antithesis to Prose is Metre; nor is this, in truth, a *strict* anithesis, because lines and passages of metre so naturally occur in writing prose, that it would be scarcely possible to avoid them, even were it desirable. [Wordsworth]

rate the composition from the vulgarity and meanness of ordinary life; and, if metre be superadded thereto, I believe that a dissimilitude will be produced altogether sufficient for the gratification of a rational mind. What other distinction would we have? Whence is it to come? And where is it to exist? Not, surely, where the Poet speaks through the mouths of his characters: it cannot be necessary here, either for elevation of style, or any of its supposed ornaments: for, if the Poet's subject be judiciously chosen, it will naturally, and upon fit occasion, lead him to passions the language of which, if selected truly and judiciously, must necessarily be dignified and variegated, and alive with metaphors and figures. I forbear to speak of an incongruity which would shock the intelligent Reader, should the Poet interweave any foreign splendour of his own with that which the passion naturally suggests: it is sufficient to say that such addition is unnecessary. And, surely, it is more probable that those passages, which with propriety abound with metaphors and figures, will have their due effect, if, upon other occasions where the passions are of a milder character, the style also be subdued and temperate.

But, as the pleasure which I hope to give by the Poems now presented to the Reader must depend entirely on just notions upon this subject, and, as it is in itself of high importance to our taste and moral feelings, I cannot content myself with these detached remarks. And if, in what I am about to say, it shall appear to some that my labour is unnecessary, and that I am like a man fighting a battle without enemies, such persons may be reminded, that, whatever be the language outwardly holden by men, a practical faith in the opinions which I am wishing to establish is almost unknown. If my conclusions are admitted, and carried as far as they must be carried if admitted at all, our judgments concerning the works of the greatest Poets both ancient and modern will be far different from what they are at present, both when we praise, and when we censure: and our moral feelings influencing and influenced by these judgements will, I believe, be corrected and purified.

Taking up the subject, then, upon general grounds, let me ask, what is meant by the word Poet? What is a Poet? To whom does he address himself? And what language is to be expected from him?—He is a man speaking to men: a man, it is true, endowed with more lively sensibility, more enthusiasm and tenderness, who has a greater knowledge of human nature, and a more comprehensive soul, than are supposed to be common among mankind; a man pleased with his own passions and volitions, and who rejoices more than other men in the spirit of life that is in him; delighting to contemplate similar volitions and passions as manifested in the goings-on of the Universe, and habitually impelled to create them where he does not find them. To these qualities he has added a disposition to be affected more than other men by absent things as if they were present; an ability of conjuring up in himself passions, which are indeed far from being the same as those produced by real events, yet (especially in those parts of the general sympathy which are pleasing and delightful) do more nearly resemble the passions produced by real events, than anything which, from the motions of their own minds merely, other men are accustomed to feel in themselves:—whence, and from practice, he has acquired a greater readiness and power in expressing what he thinks and feels, and especially those thoughts and feelings which, by his own choice, or from the structure of his own mind, arise in him without immediate external excitement.

But whatever portion of this faculty we may suppose even the greatest Poet to possess, there cannot be a doubt that the language which it will suggest to him, must often, in liveliness and truth, fall short of that which is uttered by men in real life, under the actual pressure of those passions, certain shadows of which the Poet thus produces, or feels to be produced, in himself.

However exalted a notion we would wish to cherish of the character of a Poet, it is obvious, that while he describes and imitates passions, his employment is in some degree mechanical, compared with the freedom and power of real and substantial action and suffering. So that it will be the wish of the Poet to bring his feelings near to those of the persons whose feelings he describes, nay, for short spaces of time, perhaps, to let himself slip into an entire delusion, and even confound and identify his own feelings with theirs; modifying only the language which is thus suggested to him by a consideration that he describes for a particular purpose, that of giving pleasure. Here, then, he will apply the principle of selection which has been already insisted upon. He will depend upon this for removing what would otherwise be painful or disgusting in the passion; he will feel that there is no necessity to trick out or to elevate nature: and, the more industriously he applies this principle, the deeper will be his faith that no words, which *his* fancy or imagination can suggest, will be to be compared with those which are the emanations of reality and truth.

But it may be said by those who do not object to the general spirit of these remarks, that, as it is impossible for the Poet to produce upon all occasions language as exquisitely fitted for the passion as that which the real passion itself suggests, it is proper that he should consider himself as in the situation of a translator, who does not scruple to substitute excellencies of another kind for those which are unattainable by him; and endeavours occasionally to surpass his original, in order to make some amends for the general inferiority to which he feels that he must submit. But this would be to encourage idleness and unmanly despair. Further, it is the language of men who speak of what they do not understand; who talk of Poetry as of a matter of amusement and idle pleasure; who will converse with us as gravely about a *taste* for Poetry, as they express it, as if it were a thing as indifferent as a taste for rope-dancing, or Frontiniac or Sherry. Aristotle, I have been told, has said, that Poetry is the most philosophic of all writing: it is so: its object is truth, not individual and local, but general, and operative; not standing upon external testimony, but carried alive into the heart by passion; truth which is its own testimony, which gives competence and confidence to the tribunal to which it appeals, and receives them from the same tribunal. Poetry is the image of man and nature. The obstacles which stand in the way of the fidelity of the Biographer and Historian, and of their consequent utility, are incalculably greater than those which are to be encountered by the Poet who comprehends the dignity of his art. The Poet writes under one restriction only, namely, the necessity of giving immediate pleasure to a human Being possessed of that information which may be expected from him, not as a lawyer, a physician, a mariner, an astronomer, or a natural philosopher, but as a Man. Except this one restriction, there is no object standing between the Poet and the image of things; between this, and the Biographer and Historian, there are a thousand.

Nor let this necessity of producing immediate pleasure be considered as a degradation of the Poet's art. It is far otherwise. It is an acknowledgement of the beauty of the universe, an acknowledgement the more sincere, because not formal, but indirect; it is a task light and easy to him who looks at the world in the spirit of love: further, it is a homage paid to the native and naked dignity of man, to the grand elementary principle of pleasure, by which he knows, and feels, and lives, and moves. We have no sympathy but what is propagated by pleasure: I would not be misunderstood; but wherever we sympathize with pain, it will be found that the sympathy is produced and carried on by subtle combinations with pleasure. We have no knowledge, that is, no general principles drawn from the contemplation of particular facts, but what has been built up by pleasure, and exists in us by pleasure alone. The Man of science, the Chemist and Mathematician, whatever difficulties and disgusts they may have had to struggle with, know and feel this. However painful may be the objects with which the Anatomist's knowledge is connected, he feels that his knowledge is pleasure; and where he has no pleasure he has no knowledge. What then does the Poet? He considers man and the objects that surround him as acting and reacting upon each other, so as to produce an infinite complexity of pain and pleasure; he considers man in his own nature and in his ordinary life as contemplating this with a certain quantity of immediate knowledge, with certain convictions, intuitions, and deductions, which from habit acquire the quality of intuitions; he considers him as looking upon this complex scene of ideas and sensations, and finding everywhere objects that immediately excite in him sympathies which, from the necessities of his nature, are accompanied by an overbalance of enjoyment.

To this knowledge which all men carry about with them, and to these sympathies in which, without any other discipline than that of our daily life, we are fitted to take delight, the Poet principally directs his attention. He considers man and nature as essentially adapted to each other, and the mind of man as naturally the mirror of the fairest and most interesting properties of nature. And thus the Poet, prompted by this feeling of pleasure, which accompanies him through the whole course of his studies, converses with general nature, with affections akin to those, which, through labour and length of time, the Man of science has raised up in himself, by conversing with those particular parts of nature which are the objects of his studies. The knowledge both of the Poet and the Man of science is pleasure; but the knowledge of the one cleaves to us as a necessary part of our existence, our natural and unalienable inheritance; the other is a personal and individual acquisition, slow to come to us, and by no habitual and direct sympathy connecting us with our fellow-beings. The Man of science seeks truth as a remote and unknown benefactor; he cherishes and loves it in his solitude: the Poet singing a song in which all human beings join with him, rejoices in the presence of truth as our visible friend and hourly companion. Poetry is the breath and finer spirit of all knowledge; it is the impassioned expression which is in the countenance of all Science. Emphatically may it be said of the Poet, as Shakespeare hath said of man, "that he looks before and after." He is the rock of defence for human nature; an upholder and preserver, carrying everywhere with him relationship and love. In spite of difference of soil and climate, of language and manners, of laws and customs: in spite of things silently gone out of mind, and things violently destroyed; the Poet binds together by passion and knowledge the vast empire of human society, as it is spread over the whole earth, and over all time. The objects of the Poet's thoughts are everywhere; though the eyes and senses of man are, it is true, his favourite guides, yet he will follow wheresoever he can find an atmosphere of sensation in which to move his wings. Poetry is the first and last of all knowledge—it is as immortal as the heart of man. If the labours of Men of science should ever create any material revolution, direct or indirect, in our condition, and in the impressions which we habitually receive, the Poet will sleep then no more than at present; he will be ready to follow the steps of the Man of science, not only in those general indirect effects, but he will be at his side, carrying sensation into the midst of the objects of the science itself. The remotest discoveries of the Chemist, the Botanist, or Mineralogist, will be as proper objects of the Poet's art as any upon which it can be employed, if the time should ever come when these things shall be familiar to us, and the relations under which they are contemplated by the followers of these respective sciences shall be manifestly and palpably material to us as enjoying and suffering beings. If the time should ever come when what is now called science, thus familiarized to men, shall be ready to put on, as it were, a form of flesh and blood, the Poet will lend his divine spirit to aid the transfiguration, and will welcome the Being thus produced, as a dear and genuine inmate of the household of man.—It is not, then, to be supposed that any one, who holds that sublime notion of Poetry which I have attempted to convey, will break in upon the sanctity and truth of his pictures by transitory and accidental ornaments, and endeavour to excite admiration of himself by arts, the necessity of which must manifestly depend upon the assumed meanness of his subject.

What has been thus far said applies to Poetry in general; but especially to those parts of composition where the Poet speaks through the mouths of his characters; and upon this point it appears to authorize the conclusion that there are few persons of good sense, who would not allow that the dramatic parts of composition are defective, in proportion as they deviate from the real language of nature, and are coloured by a diction of the Poet's own, either peculiar to him as an individual Poet or belonging simply to Poets in general; to a body of men who, from the circumstance of their compositions being in metre, it is expected will employ a particular language.

It is not, then, in the dramatic parts of composition that we look for this distinction of language; but still it may be proper and necessary where the Poet speaks to us in his own person and character. To this I answer by referring the Reader to the description before given of a Poet. Among the qualities there enumerated as principally conducing to form a Poet, is implied nothing differing in kind from other men, but only in degree. The sum of what was said is, that the Poet is chiefly distinguished from other men by a greater promptness to think and feel without immediate external excitement, and a greater power in expressing such thoughts and feelings as are produced in him in that manner. But these passions and thoughts and feelings are the general passions and thoughts and feelings of men. And with what are they connected? Undoubtedly with our moral sentiments and animal sensations, and with the causes which excite these; with the operations of the elements, and the appearances of the visible universe; with storm and sunshine, with the revolutions of the seasons, with cold and heat, with loss of friends and kindred, with injuries and resentments, gratitude and hope, with fear and sorrow. These, and the like, are the sensations and objects which the Poet describes, as they are the sensations of other men, and the objects which interest them. The Poet thinks and feels in the spirit of human passions. How, then, can his language differ in any material degree from that of other men who feel vividly and see clearly? It might be *proved* that it is impossible. But supposing that this were not the case, the Poet might then be allowed to use a peculiar language when expressing his feelings for his own gratification, or that of men like himself. But Poets do not write for Poets alone, but for men. Unless therefore we are advocates for that admiration which subsists upon ignorance, and that pleasure which arises from hearing what we do not understand, the Poet must descend from this supposed height; and, in order to excite rational sympathy, he must express himself as other men express themselves. To this it may be added, that while he is only selecting from the real language of men, or, which amounts to the same thing, composing accurately in the spirit of such selection, he is treading upon safe ground, and we know what we are to expect from him. Our feelings are the same with respect to metre; for, as it may be proper to remind the Reader, the distinction of metre is regular and uniform, and not, like that which is produced by what is usually called POETIC DICTION, arbitrary, and subject to infinite caprices upon which no calculation whatever can be made. In the one case, the Reader is utterly at the mercy of the Poet, respecting what imagery or diction he may choose to connect with the passion; whereas, in the other, the metre obeys certain laws, to which the Poet and Reader both willingly submit because they are certain, and because no interference is made by them with the passion, but such as the concurring testimony of ages has shown to heighten and improve the pleasure which co-exists with it.

It will now be proper to answer an obvious question, namely, Why, professing these opinions, have I written in verse? To this, in addition to such answer as is included in what has been already said, I reply, in the first place, Because, however I may have restricted myself, there is still left open to me what confessedly constitutes the most valuable object of all writing, whether in prose or verse; the great and universal passions of men, the most general and interesting of their occupations, and the entire world of nature before me—to supply endless combinations of forms and imagery. Now, supposing for a moment that whatever is interesting in these objects may be as vividly described in prose, why should I be condemned for attempting to superadd to such description the charm which, by the consent of all nations, is acknowledged to exist in metrical language? To this, by such as are yet unconvinced, it may be answered that a very small part of the pleasure given by Poetry depends upon the metre, and that it is injudicious to write in metre, unless it be accompanied with the other artificial distinctions of style with which metre is usually accompanied, and that, by such deviation, more will be lost from the shock which will thereby be given to the Reader's associations than will be counterbalanced by any pleasure which he can derive from the general power of numbers. In answer to those who still contend for the necessity of accompanying metre with certain appropriate colours of style in order to the accomplishment of its appropriate end, and who also, in my opinion, greatly underrate the power of metre in itself, it might, perhaps, as far as relates to these Volumes, have been almost sufficient to observe, that poems are extant, written upon more humble subjects, and in a still more naked and simple style, which have continued to give pleasure from generation to generation. Now, if nakedness and simplicity be a defect, the fact here mentioned affords a strong presumption that poems somewhat less naked and simple are capable of affording pleasure at the present day; and, what I wish *chiefly* to attempt, at present, was to justify myself for having written under the impression of this belief.

But various causes might be pointed out why, when the style is manly and the subject of some importance, words metrically arranged will long continue to impart such a pleasure to mankind as he who proves the extent of that pleasure will be desirous to impart. The end of Poetry is to produce excitement in co-existence with an overbalance of pleasure; but, by the supposition, excitement is an unusual and irregular state of the mind; ideas and feelings do not, in that state, succeed each other in accustomed order. If the words, however, by which this excitement is produced be in themselves powerful, or the images and feelings have an undue proportion of pain connected with them, there is some danger that the excitement may be carried beyond its proper bounds. Now the co-presence of something regular, something to which the mind has been accustomed in various moods and in a less excited state, cannot but have great efficacy in tempering and restraining the passion by an inter-texture of ordinary feeling, and of feeling not strictly and necessarily connected with the passion. This is unquestionably true; and hence, though the opinion will at first appear paradoxical, from the tendency of metre to divest language, in a certain degree, of its reality, and thus to throw a sort of half-consciousness of unsubstantial existence over the whole composition, there can be little doubt but that more pathetic situations and sentiments, that is, those which have a greater proportion of pain connected with them, may be endured in metrical composition, especially in rhyme, than in prose. The metre of the old ballads is very artless; yet they contain many passages which would illustrate this opinion; and, I hope, if the following Poems be attentively perused, similar instances will be found in them. This opinion may be further illustrated by appealing to the Reader's own experience of the reluctance with which he comes to the re-perusal of the distressful parts of *Clarissa Harlowe,* or *The Gamester;* while Shakespeare's writings, in the most pathetic scenes, never act upon us, as pathetic, beyond the bounds of pleasure—an effect which, in a much greater degree than might at first be imagined, is to be ascribed to small, but continual and regular impulses of pleasurable surprise from the metrical arrangement.—On the other hand (what it must be allowed will much more frequently happen) if the Poet's words should be incommensurate with the passion, and inadequate to raise the Reader to a height of desirable excitement, then (unless the Poet's choice of his metre has been grossly injudicious), in the feelings of pleasure which the Reader has been accustomed to connect with metre in general, and in the feeling, whether cheerful or melancholy, which he has been accustomed to connect with that particular movement of metre, there will be found something which will greatly contribute to impart passion to the words, and to effect the complex end which the Poet proposes to himself.

If I had undertaken a SYSTEMATIC defence of the theory here maintained, it would have been my duty to develop the various causes upon which the pleasure received from metrical language depends. Among the chief of these causes is to be reckoned a principle which must be well known to those who have made any of the Arts the object of accurate reflection; namely, the pleasure which the mind derives from the perception of similitude in dissimilitude. This principle is the great spring of the activity of our minds, and their chief feeder. From this principle the direction of the sexual appetite, and all the passions connected with it, take their origin: it is the life of our ordinary conversation; and upon the accuracy with which similitude in dissimilitude, and dissimilitude in similitude are perceived, depend our taste and our moral feelings. It would not be a useless employment to apply this principle to the consideration of metre, and to show that metre is hence enabled to afford much pleasure, and to point out in what manner that pleasure is produced. But my limits will not permit me to enter upon this subject, and I must content myself with a general summary.

I have said that poetry is the spontaneous overflow of powerful feelings: it takes its origin from emotion recollected in tranquillity: the emotion is contemplated till, by a species of reaction, the tranquillity gradually disappears, and an emotion, kindred to that which was before the subject of contemplation, is gradually produced, and does itself actually exist in the mind. In this mood successful composition generally begins, and in a mood similar to this it is carried on; but the emotion, of whatever kind, and in whatever degree, from various causes, is qualified by various pleasures, so that in describing any passions whatsoever, which are voluntarily described, the mind will, upon the whole, be in a state of enjoyment. If Nature be thus cautious to preserve in a state of enjoyment a being so employed, the Poet ought to profit by the lesson held forth to him, and ought especially to take care, that, whatever passions he communicates to his Reader, those passions, if his Reader's mind be sound and vigorous, should always be accompanied with an overbalance of pleasure. Now the music of harmonious metrical language, the sense of difficulty overcome, and the blind association of pleasure which has been previously received from works of rhyme or metre of the same or similar construction, an indistinct perception perpetually renewed of language closely resembling that of real life, and yet, in the circumstance of metre, differing from it so widely—all these imperceptibly make up a complex feeling of delight, which is of the most important use in tempering the painful feeling always found intermingled with powerful descriptions of the deeper passions. This effect is always produced in pathetic and impassioned poetry; while, in lighter compositions, the ease and gracefulness with which the Poet manages his numbers are themselves confessedly a principal source of the gratification of the Reader. All that it is *necessary* to say, however, upon this subject, may be effected by affirming, what few persons will deny, that, of two descriptions, either of passions, manners, or characters, each of them equally well executed, the one in prose and the other in verse, the verse will be read a hundred times where the prose is read once.

Having thus explained a few of my reasons for writing in verse, and why I have chosen subjects from common life, and endeavoured to bring my language near to the real language of men, if I have been too minute in pleading my own cause, I have at the same time been treating a subject of general interest; and for this reason a few words shall be added with reference solely to these particular poems, and to some defects which will probably be found in them. I am sensible that my associations must have sometimes been particular instead of general, and that, consequently, giving to things a false importance, I may have sometimes written upon unworthy subjects; but I am less apprehensive on this account, than that my language may frequently have suffered from those arbitrary connexions of feelings and ideas with particular words and phrases, from which no man can altogether protect himself. Hence I have no doubt, that, in some instances, feelings, even of the ludicrous, may be given to my Readers by expressions which appeared to me tender and pathetic. Such faulty expressions, were I convinced they were faulty at present, and that they must necessarily continue to be so, I would willingly take all reasonable pains to correct. But it is dangerous to make these alterations on the simple authority of a few individuals, or even of certain classes of men; for where the understanding of an Author is not convinced, or his feelings altered, this cannot be done without great injury to himself: for his own feelings are his stay and support; and, if he set them aside in one instance, he may be induced to repeat this act till his mind shall lose all confidence in itself, and become utterly debilitated. To this it may be added, that the critic ought never to forget that he is himself exposed to the same errors as the Poet, and, perhaps, in a much greater degree: for there can be no presumption in saying of most readers, that it is not probable they will be so well acquainted with the various stages of meaning through which words have passed, or with the fickleness of stability of the relations of particular ideas to each other; and, above all, since they are so much less interested in the subject, they may decide lightly and carelessly.

Long as the Reader has been detained, I hope he will permit me to caution him against a mode of false criticism which has been applied to Poetry, in which the language closely resembles that of life and nature. Such verses have been triumphed over in parodies, of which Dr. Johnson's stanza is a fair specimen:—

> I put my hat upon my head
> · And walked into the Strand,
> And there I met another man
> Whose hat was in his hand.

Immediately under these lines let us place one of the most justly admired stanzas of the "Babes in the Wood."

> These pretty Babes with hand in hand
> Went wandering up and down;
> But never more they saw the Man
> Approaching from the Town.

In both these stanzas the words, and the order of the words, in no respect differ from the most unimpassioned conversation. There are words in both, for example, "the Strand," and "the Town," connected with none but the most familiar ideas; yet the one stanza we admit as admirable, and the other as a fair example of the superlatively contemptible. Whence arises this difference? Not from the metre, not from the language, not from the order of the words; but the *matter* expressed in Dr. Johnson's stanza is contemptible. The proper method of treating trivial and simple verses, to which Dr. Johnson's stanza would be a fair parallelism, is not to say, this is a bad kind of poetry, or, this is not poetry; but, this wants sense; it is neither interesting in itself nor can *lead* to anything interesting; the images neither originate in that sane state of feeling which arises out of thought, nor can excite thought or feeling in the Reader. This is the only sensible manner of dealing with such verses. Why trouble yourself about the species till you have previously decided upon the genus? Why take pains to prove that an ape is not a Newton, when it is self-evident that he is not a man?

One request I must make of my reader, which is, that in judging these Poems he would decide by his own feelings genuinely, and not by reflection upon what will probably be the judgement of others. How common is it to hear a person say, I myself do not object to this style of composition, or this or that expression, but, to such and such classes of people it will appear mean or ludicrous! This mode of criticism, so destructive of all sound unadulterated judgement, is almost universal: let the Reader then abide, independently, by his own feelings, and, if he finds himself affected, let him not suffer such conjectures to interfere with his pleasure.

If an Author, by any single composition, has impressed us with respect for his talents, it is useful to consider this as affording a presumption, that on other occasions where we have been displeased, he, nevertheless, may not have written ill or absurdly; and further, to give him so much credit for this one composition as may induce us to review what has displeased us, with more care than we should otherwise have bestowed upon it. This is not only an act of justice, but, in our decisions upon poetry especially, may conduce, in a high degree, to the improvement of our own taste; for an *accurate* taste in poetry, and in all the other arts, as Sir Joshua Reynolds has observed, is an *acquired* talent, which can only be produced by thought and a long continued intercourse with the best models of composition. This is mentioned, not with so ridiculous a purpose as to prevent the most inexperienced Reader from judging for himself (I have already said that I wish him to judge for himself), but merely to temper the rashness of decision, and to suggest, that, if Poetry be a subject on which much time has not been bestowed, the judgement may be erroneous; and that, in many cases, it necessarily will be so.

Nothing would, I know, have so effectually contributed to further the end which I have in view, as to have shown of what kind the pleasure is, and how that pleasure is produced, which is confessedly produced by metrical composition essentially different from that which I have here endeavoured to recommend: for the

Reader will say that he has been pleased by such composition; and what more can be done for him? The power of any art is limited; and he will suspect, that, if it be proposed to furnish him with new friends, that can be only upon condition of his abandoning his old friends. Besides, as I have said, the Reader is himself conscious of the pleasure which he has received from such composition, composition to which he has peculiarly attached the endearing name of Poetry; and all men feel an habitual gratitude, and something of an honourable bigotry, for the objects which have long continued to please them: we not only wish to be pleased, but to be pleased in that particular way in which we have been accustomed to be pleased. There is in these feelings enough to resist a host of arguments; and I should be the less able to combat them successfully, as I am willing to allow, that, in order entirely to enjoy the Poetry which I am recommending, it would be necessary to give up much of what is ordinarily enjoyed. But, would my limits have permitted me to point out how this pleasure is produced, many obstacles might have been removed, and the Reader assisted in perceiving that the powers of language are not so limited as he may suppose; and that it is possible for poetry to give other enjoyments, of a purer, more lasting, and more exquisite nature. This part of the subject has not been altogether neglected, but it has not been so much my present aim to prove, that the interest excited by some other kinds of poetry is less vivid, and less worthy of the nobler powers of the mind, as to offer reasons for presuming, that if my purpose were fulfilled, a species of poetry would be produced, which is genuine poetry; in its nature well adapted to interest mankind permanently, and likewise important in the multiplicity and quality of its moral relations.

From what has been said, and from a perusal of the Poems, the Reader will be able clearly to perceive the object which I had in view: he will determine how far it has been attained; and, what is a much more important question, whether it be worth attaining: and upon the decision of these two questions will rest my claim to the approbation of the Public.

Samuel Taylor Coleridge

(1772–1834)

From the BIOGRAPHIA LITERARIA

A scholar of great reputation, George Saintsbury, once suggested that for the title of "greatest critic" he would select three candidates: Aristotle, Longinus, and Coleridge. Arthur Symons named the *Biographia Literaria* as "the greatest book on criticism in English." In recent years, however, the question of plagiarism has been raised, by René Wellek, for example, since it has been discovered that Coleridge "borrowed" heavily for certain of his theories in the first volume from the German philosophers—Schelling and Kant, in particular—in some cases taking entire passages with little or no change. Though this has resulted, understandably, in some revision of judgment by certain scholars, others (such as Richard Harter Fogle in his recent *The Idea of Coleridge's Criticism*, 1961) find in Coleridge a critic of striking originality, "a genuinely organic thinker," as Fogle says, "whose mind is a totality and who aims always at synthesis."

The *Biographia Literaria* (published in 1817 with a dedication to Wordsworth) is not, strictly speaking, a literary biography. The first volume consists almost entirely of an attempt to distinguish between imagination and fancy. The second (from which the following selections are drawn) is devoted principally to critiques of Wordsworth and Shakespeare.

For thirteen years, Coleridge had talked of doing such a work. In its completed form, the *Biographia Literaria*, despite its fragmented genius, remains the most influential single critical work in English.

CHAPTER XIV

Occasion of the Lyrical Ballads, and the objects originally proposed—Preface to the second edition—The ensuing controversy, its causes and acrimony—Philosophic definitions of a poem and poetry with scholia.

DURING the first year [1797] that Mr. Wordsworth and I were neighbours, our conversations turned frequently on the two cardinal points of poetry, the power of exciting the sympathy of the reader by a faithful adherence to the truth of nature, and the power of giving the interest of novelty by the modifying colours of imagination. The sudden charm, which accidents of light and shade, which moon-light or sunset diffused over a known and familiar landscape, appeared to represent the practicability of combining both. These are the poetry of nature. The thought suggested itself—(to which of us I do not recollect)—that a series of poems might be composed of two sorts. In the one, the incidents and agents were to be, in part at least, supernatural; and the excellence aimed at was to consist in the interesting of the affections by the dramatic truth of such emotions, as would naturally accompany such situations, supposing them real. And real in this sense they have been to every human being who, from whatever source of delusion, has at any time believed himself under supernatural agency. For the second class, subjects were to be chosen from ordinary life; the characters and incidents were to be such as will be found in every village and its vicinity, where there is a meditative and feeling mind to seek after them, or to notice them, when they present themselves.

In this idea originated the plan of the *Lyrical Ballads;* in which it was agreed, that my endeavours should be directed to persons and characters supernatural, or at least romantic; yet so as to transfer from our inward nature a human interest and a semblance of truth sufficient to procure for these shadows of imagination that willing suspension of disbelief for the moment, which constitutes poetic faith. Mr. Wordsworth, on the other hand, was to propose to himself as his object, to give the charm of novelty to things of every day, and to excite a feeling analogous to the supernatural, by awakening the mind's attention to the lethargy of custom, and directing it to the loveliness and the wonders of the world before us; an inexhaustible treasure, but for which, in consequence of the film of familiarity and selfish solicitude, we have eyes, yet see not, ears that hear not, and hearts that neither feel nor understand.

With this view I wrote *The Ancient Mariner,* and was preparing among other poems, *The Dark Ladie,* and the *Christabel,* in which I should have more nearly realized my ideal, than I had done in my first attempt. But Mr. Wordsworth's industry had proved so much more successful, and the number of his poems so much greater, that my compositions, instead of forming a balance, appeared rather an interpolation of heterogeneous matter. Mr. Wordsworth added two or three poems written in his own character, in the impassioned, lofty, and sustained diction, which is characteristic of his genius. In this form the *Lyrical Ballads* were published; and were presented by him, as an experiment, whether subjects, which from their nature rejected the usual ornaments and extra-colloquial style of poems in general, might not be so managed in the language of ordinary life as to produce the pleasurable interest, which it is the peculiar business of poetry to impart. To the second edition he added a preface of considerable length; in which, notwithstanding some passages of apparently a contrary import, he was understood to contend for the extension of this style to poetry of all kinds, and to reject as vicious and indefensible all phrases and forms of speech that were not included in what he (unfortunately, I think, adopting an equivocal expression) called the language of real life. From this preface, prefixed to poems in which it was impossible to deny the presence of original genius, however mistaken its direction might be deemed, arose the whole long-continued controversy [on Wordsworth's theory of poetic diction]. For from the conjunction of perceived power with supposed heresy I explain the inveteracy and in some instances, I grieve to say, the acrimonious passions, with which the controversy has been conducted by the assailants.

Had Mr. Wordsworth's poems been the silly, the childish things, which they were for a long time described as being: had they been really distinguished from the compositions of other poets merely by meanness of language and inanity of thought; had they indeed contained nothing more than what is found in the parodies and pretended imitations of them; they must have sunk at once, a dead weight, into the slough of oblivion, and have dragged the preface along with them. But year after year increased the number of

Mr. Wordsworth's admirers. They were found too not in the lower classes of the reading public, but chiefly among young men of strong sensibility and meditative minds; and their admiration (inflamed perhaps in some degree by opposition) was distinguished by its intensity, I might almost say, by its religious fervour. These facts, and the intellectual energy of the author, which was more or less consciously felt, where it was outwardly and even boisterously denied, meeting with sentiments of aversion to his opinions, and of alarm at their consequences, produced an eddy of criticism, which would of itself have borne up the poems by the violence with which it whirled them round and round. With many parts of this preface in the sense attributed to them and which the words undoubtedly seem to authorize, I never concurred; but on the contrary objected to them as erroneous in principle, and as contradictory (in appearance at least) both to other parts of the same preface, and to the author's own practice in the greater part of the poems themselves. Mr. Wordsworth in his recent collection has, I find, degraded this prefatory disquisition to the end of his second volume, to be read or not at the reader's choice. But he has not, as far as I can discover, announced any change in his poetic creed. At all events, considering it as the source of a controversy, in which I have been honoured more than I deserve by the frequent conjunction of my name with his, I think it expedient to declare once for all, in what points I coincide with the opinions supported in that preface, and in what points I altogether differ. But in order to render myself intelligible I must previously, in as few words as possible, explain my views, first, of a Poem; and secondly, of Poetry itself, in kind, and in essence.

The office of philosophical disquisition consists in just distinction; while it is the privilege of the philosopher to preserve himself constantly aware, that distinction is not division. In order to obtain adequate notions of any truth, we must intellectually separate its distinguishable parts; and this is the technical process of philosophy. But having so done, we must then restore them in our conceptions to the unity, in which they actually co-exist; and this is the result of philosophy. A poem contains the same elements as a prose composition; the difference therefore must consist in a different combination of them, in consequence of a different object being proposed. According to the difference of the object will be the difference of the combination. It is possible, that the object may be merely to facilitate the recollection of any given facts or observations by artificial arrangement; and the composition will be a poem, merely because it is distinguished from prose by metre, or by rhyme, or by both conjointly. In this, the lowest sense, a man might attribute the name of a poem to the well-known enumeration of the days in the several months;

"Thirty days hath September,
April, June, and November," &c.

and others of the same class and purpose. And as a particular pleasure is found in anticipating the recurrence of sounds and quantities, all compositions that have this charm super-added, whatever be their contents, *may* be entitled poems.

So much for the superficial form. A difference of object and contents supplies an additional ground of distinction. The immediate purpose may be the communication of truths; either of truth absolute and demonstrable, as in works of science; or of facts experienced and recorded, as in history. Pleasure, and that of the highest and most permanent kind, may result from the attainment of the end; but it is not itself the immediate end. In other works the communication of pleasure may be the immediate purpose; and though truth, either moral or intellectual, ought to be the ultimate end, yet this will distinguish the character of the author, not the class to which the work belongs. Blest indeed is that state of society, in which the immediate purpose would be baffled by the perversion of the proper ultimate end; in which no charm of diction or imagery could exempt the *Bathyllus* even of an Anacreon, or the *Alexis* of Virgil, from disgust and aversion!

But the communication of pleasure may be the immediate object of a work not metrically composed; and that object may have been in a high degree attained, as in novels and romances. Would then the mere superaddition of metre, with or without rhyme, entitle these to the name of poems? The answer is, that nothing can permanently please, which does not contain in itself the reason why it is so, and not otherwise. If metre be superseded, all other parts must be made consonant with it. They must be such, as to justify the perpetual and distinct attention to each part, which an exact correspondent recurrence of accent and sound are calculated to excite. The final definition then, so deduced, may be thus worded. A poem is that species of composition, which is opposed to works of science, by proposing for its *immediate* object pleasure, not truth; and from all other species—(having *this* object in common with it)—it is discriminated by proposing to itself such delight from the *whole,* as is compatible with a distinct gratification from each component *part.*

Controversy is not seldom excited in consequence of the disputants attaching each a different meaning to the same word; and in few instances has this been more striking, than in disputes concerning the present subject. If a man chooses to call every composition a poem, which is rhyme, or measure, or both, I must leave his opinion uncontroverted. The distinction is at least competent to characterize the writer's intention. If it were subjoined, that the whole is likewise entertaining or affecting, as a tale, or as a series of interesting reflections, I of course admit this as another fit ingredient of a poem, and an additional merit. But if the definition sought for be that of a *legitimate* poem, I answer it must be one, the parts of which mutually support and explain each other; all in their proportion harmonizing with, and supporting the purpose and known influences of metrical arrangement. The philosophic critics of all ages coincide with the ultimate judgment of all countries, in equally denying the praises of a just poem, on the one hand, to a series of striking lines or distiches, each of which, absorbing the whole attention of the reader to itself, becomes disjoined from its context, and forms a separate whole, instead of a harmonizing part; and on the other hand, to an unsustained composition, from which the reader collects rapidly the general result unattracted by the component parts. The reader should be carried forward, not merely or chiefly by the mechanical impulse of curiosity, or by a restless desire to arrive at the final solution; but by the pleasureable activity of mind excited by the attractions of the journey itself. Like the motion of a serpent, which the Egyptians made the emblem of intellectual power; or like the path of sound through the air;—at every step he pauses and half recedes, and from the retrogressive movement collects the force which again carries him onward. . . .

But if this should be admitted as a satisfactory character of a poem, we have still to seek for a definition of poetry. The writings of Plato, and Jeremy Taylor, and the *Theoria Sacra* of Burnet, furnish undeniable proofs that poetry of the highest kind may exist without metre, and even without the contradistinguishing objects of a poem. The first chapter of Isaiah—(indeed a very large portion of the whole book)—is poetry in the most emphatic sense; yet it would be not less irrational than strange to assert, that pleasure, and not truth was the immediate object of the prophet. In short, whatever specific import we attach to the word, Poetry, there will be found involved in it, as a necessary consequence, that a poem of any length neither can be, nor ought to be, all poetry. Yet if an harmonious whole is to be produced, the remaining parts must be preserved in keeping with the poetry; and this can be no otherwise effected than by such a studied selection and artificial arrangement, as will partake of one, though not a peculiar property of poetry. And this again can be no other than the property of exciting a more continuous and equal attention than the language of prose aims at, whether colloquial or written.

My own conclusions on the nature of poetry, in the strictest use of the word, have been in part anticipated in some of the remarks on the Fancy and Imagination in the early part of this work. What is poetry?—is so nearly the same question with, what is a poet? —that the answer to the one is involved in the solution of the other. For it is a distinction resulting from the poetic genius itself, which sustains and modifies the images, thoughts, and emotions of the poet's own mind.

The poet, described in ideal perfection, brings the whole soul of man into activity, with the subordination of its faculties to each other according to their relative worth and dignity. He diffuses a tone and spirit of unity, that blends, and (as it were) *fuses,* each into each, by that synthetic and magical power, to which I would exclusively appropriate the name of Imagination. This power, first put in action by the will and understanding, and retained under their irremissive, though gentle and unnoticed, control, *laxis effertur habenis* ["is carried along with loose reins"], reveals itself in the balance or reconcilement of opposite or discordant qualities: of sameness, with difference; of the general with the concrete; the idea with the image; the individual with the representative; the sense of novelty and freshness with old and familiar objects; a more than usual state of emotion with more than usual order; judgment ever awake and steady self-possession with enthusiasm and feeling profound or vehement; and while it blends and harmonizes the natural and the artificial, still subordinates art to nature; the manner to the matter; and our admiration of the poet to our sympathy with the poetry. Doubtless, as Sir John Davies observes of the soul—(and his words may with slight alteration be applied, and even more appropriately, to the poetic Imagination)—

Doubtless this could not be, but that she turns
    Bodies to *spirit* by sublimation strange,
As fire converts to fire the things it burns,
    As we our food into our nature change.

From their gross matter she abstracts *their* forms,
    And draws a kind of quintessence from things;
Which to her proper nature she transforms
    To bear them light on her celestial wings.

Thus does she, when from *individual states*
    She doth abstract the universal kinds;
Which then re-clothed in divers names and fates
    Steal access through the senses to our minds.

Finally, Good Sense is the Body of poetic genius, Fancy its Drapery, Motion its Life, and Imagination the Soul that is everywhere, and in each; and forms all into one graceful and intelligent whole.

CHAPTER XVII

*Examination of the tenets peculiar to Mr. Wordsworth—Rustic life
(above all, low and rustic life) especially unfavourable to the formation
of a human diction—The best parts of language the product of philosophers not of clowns or shepherds—Poetry essentially ideal and generic
—The language of Milton as much the language of real life, yea, incom-
parably more so than that of the cottager.*

As far then as Mr. Wordsworth in his preface contended, and
most ably contended, for a reformation in our poetic diction, as
far as he has evinced the truth of passion, and the dramatic
propriety of those figures and metaphors in the original poets,
which, stripped of their justifying reasons, and converted into mere
artifices of connection or ornament, constitute the characteristic
falsity in the poetic style of the moderns; and as far as he has,
with equal acuteness and clearness, pointed out the process by
which this change was effected, and the resemblances between that
state into which the reader's mind is thrown by the pleasurable
confusion of thought from an unaccustomed train of words and
images; and that state which is induced by the natural language
of impassioned feeling; he undertook a useful task, and deserves
all praise, both for the attempt and for the execution. The provo-
cations to this remonstrance in behalf of truth and nature were still
of perpetual recurrence before and after the publication of this
preface. I cannot likewise but add, that the comparison of such
poems of merit, as have been given to the public within the last ten
or twelve years, with the majority of those produced previously
to the appearance of that preface, leave no doubt on my mind,
that Mr. Wordsworth is fully justified in believing his efforts to
have been by no means ineffectual. Not only in the verses of those
who have professed their admiration of his genius, but even of those
who have distinguished themselves by hostility to his theory, and
depreciation of his writings, are the impressions of his principles
plainly visible. It is possible, that with these principles others may

have been blended, which are not equally evident; and some which are unsteady and subvertible from the narrowness or imperfection of their basis. But it is more than possible, that these errors of defect or exaggeration, by kindling and feeding the controversy, may have conduced not only to the wider propagation of the accompanying truths, but that, by their frequent presentation to the mind in an excited state, they may have won for them a more permanent and practical result. A man will borrow a part from his opponent the more easily, if he feels himself justified in continuing to reject a part. While there remain important points in which he can still feel himself in the right, in which he still finds firm footing for continued resistance, he will gradually adopt those opinions, which were the least remote from his own convictions, as not less congruous with his own theory than with that which he reprobates. In like manner with a kind of instinctive prudence, he will abandon by little and little his weakest posts, till at length he seems to forget that they had ever belonged to him, or affects to consider them at most as accidental and "petty annexments," the removal of which leaves the citadel unhurt and unendangered.

My own differences from certain supposed parts of Mr. Wordsworth's theory ground themselves on the assumption, that his words had been rightly interpreted, as purporting that the proper diction for poetry in general consists altogether in a language taken, with due exceptions, from the mouths of men in real life, a language which actually constitutes the natural conversation of men under the influence of natural feelings. My objection is, first, that in any sense this rule is applicable only to certain classes of poetry; secondly, that even to these classes it is not applicable, except in such a sense, as hath never by any one (as far as I know or have read,) been denied or doubted; and lastly, that as far as, and in that degree in which it is practicable, it is yet as a rule useless, if not injurious, and therefore either need not, or ought not to be practised. The poet informs his reader, that he had generally chosen low and rustic life; but not as low and rustic, or in order to repeat that pleasure of doubtful moral effect, which persons of elevated rank and of superior refinement oftentimes derive from a happy imitation of the rude unpolished manners and discourse of their inferiors. For the pleasure so derived may be traced to three exciting causes. The first is the naturalness, in fact, of the things represented. The second is the apparent naturalness of the representation, as raised and qualified by an imperceptible infusion of the author's own knowledge and talent, which infusion does, indeed, constitute it an imitation as distinguished from a mere copy. The third cause may be found in the reader's conscious feeling of his superiority awakened by the contrast presented to him; even as for the same purpose the kings and great barons of yore retained, sometimes actual clowns and fools, but more frequently shrewd and witty fellows in that character. These, however, were not Mr. Wordsworth's objects. *He* chose low and rustic life, "because in that condition the essential passions of the heart find a better soil, in which they can attain their maturity, are less under restraint, and speak a plainer and more emphatic language; because in that condition of life our elementary feelings coexist in a state of greater simplicity, and consequently may be more accurately contemplated, and more forcibly communicated; because the manners of rural life germinate from those elementary feelings; and from the necessary character of rural occupations are more easily comprehended, and are more durable; and lastly, because in that condition the passions of men are incorporated with the beautiful and permanent forms of nature."

Now it is clear to me, that in the most interesting of the poems, in which the author is more or less dramatic, as *The Brothers, Michael, Ruth, The Mad Mother,* and others, the persons introduced are by no means taken from low or rustic life in the common acceptation of those words! and it is not less clear, that the sentiments and language, as far as they can be conceived to have been really transferred from the minds and conversation of such persons, are attributable to causes and circumstances not necessarily connected with "their occupations and abode." The thoughts, feelings, language, and manners of the shepherd-farmers in the vales of Cumberland and Westmoreland, as far as they are actually adopted in those poems, may be accounted for from causes, which will and do produce the same results in every state of life, whether in town or country. As the two principal I rank that independence, which raises a man above servitude, or daily toil for the profit of others, yet not above the necessity of industry and a frugal simplicity of domestic life; and the accompanying unambitious, but solid and religious, education, which has rendered few books familiar, but the Bible, and the Liturgy or Hymn book. To this latter cause, indeed, which is so far accidental, that it is the blessing of particular countries and a particular age, not the product of particular places or employments, the poet owes the show of probability, that his personages might really feel, think, and talk with any tolerable resemblance to his representation. It is an excellent remark of Dr. Henry More's, that "a man of confined education, but of good parts, by constant reading of the Bible will naturally form a more winning and commanding rhetoric than those that are learned: the intermixture of tongues and of artificial phrases debasing *their* style."

It is, moreover, to be considered that to the formation of healthy feelings, and a reflecting mind, negations involve impediments not less formidable than sophistication and vicious intermixture. I am convinced, that for the human soul to prosper in rustic life a certain vantage-ground is pre-requisite. It is not every man that is likely to be improved by a country life or by country labours. Education, or original sensibility, or both, must pre-exist, if the changes, forms, and incidents of nature are to prove a sufficient stimulant. And where these are not sufficient, the mind contracts and hardens by want of stimulants: and the man becomes selfish, sensual, gross, and hard-hearted. Let the management of the Poor Laws in Liverpool, Manchester, or Bristol be compared with the ordinary dispensation of the poor rates in agricultural villages, where the farmers are the overseers and guardians of the poor. If my own experience has not been particularly unfortunate, as well as that of the many respectable country clergymen with whom I have conversed on the subject, the result would engender more than scepticism concerning the desirable influences of low and rustic life in and for itself. Whatever may be concluded on the other side, from the stronger local attachments and enterprising spirit of the Swiss, and other mountaineers, applies to a particular mode of pastoral life, under forms of property that permit and beget manners truly republican, not to rustic life in general, or to the absence of artificial cultivation. On the contrary the mountaineers, whose manners have been so often eulogized, are in general better educated and greater readers than men of equal rank elsewhere. But where this is not the case, as among the peasantry of North Wales, the ancient mountains, with all their terrors and all their glories, are pictures to the blind, and music to the deaf.

I should not have entered so much into detail upon this passage, but here seems to be the point, to which all the lines of difference converge as to their source and centre;—I mean, as far as, and in whatever respect, my poetic creed *does* differ from the doctrines promulgated in this preface. I adopt with full faith, the principle of Aristotle, that poetry, as poetry, is essentially ideal, that it avoids and excludes all accident; that its apparent individualities of rank, character, or occupation must be representative of a class; and that the persons of poetry must be clothed with generic attributes, with the common attributes of the class: not with such as one gifted individual might possibly possess, but such as from his situation it is most probable before-hand that he would possess. If my premises are right and my deductions legitimate, it follows that there can be no poetic medium between the swains of Theocritus and those of an imaginary golden age.

The characters of the vicar and the shepherd-mariner in the poem of *The Brothers,* and that of the shepherd of Green-head Ghyll in the *Michael,* have all the verisimilitude and representative quality, that the purposes of poetry can require. They are persons of a known and abiding class, and their manners and sentiments the natural product of circumstances common to the class. Take *Michael* for instance. . . . [From the poem, Coleridge here cites a passage of some 38 lines beginning "An old man stout of heart and strong of limb. . . ."] On the other hand, in the poems which are pitched in a lower key, as the *Harry Gill,* and *The Idiot Boy,* the feelings are those of human nature in general; though the poet has judiciously laid the scene in the country, in order to place himself in the vicinity of interesting images, without the necessity of ascribing a sentimental perception of their beauty to the persons of his drama. In *The Idiot Boy,* indeed, the mother's character is not so much the real and native product of a "situation where the essential passions of the heart find a better soil, in which they can attain their maturity and speak a plainer and more emphatic language," as it is an impersonation of an instinct abandoned by judgment. Hence the two following charges seem to me not wholly groundless: at least, they are the only plausible objections, which I have heard to that fine poem. The one is, that the author has not, in the poem itself, taken sufficient care to preclude from the reader's fancy the disgusting images of ordinary morbid idiocy, which yet it was by no means his intention to represent. He has even by the "burr, burr, burr," uncounteracted by any preceding description of the boy's beauty, assisted in recalling them. The other is, that the idiocy of the boy is so evenly balanced by the folly of the mother, as to present to the general reader rather a laughable burlesque on the blindness of anile dotage, than an analytic display of maternal affection in its ordinary workings.

In *The Thorn,* the poet himself acknowledges in a note the necessity of an introductory poem, in which he should have portrayed the character of the person from whom the words of the poem are supposed to proceed: a superstitious man moderately imaginative, of slow faculties and deep feelings, "a captain of a small trading vessel, for example, who, being past the middle age of life, had retired upon an annuity, or small independent income, to some village or country town of which he was not a native, or in which he had not been accustomed to live. Such men having nothing to do become credulous and talkative from indolence." But in a poem, still more in a lyric poem—and the Nurse in *Romeo and Juliet* alone prevents me from extending the remark even to dramatic poetry, if indeed even the Nurse can be deemed altogether a case in point—it is not possible to imitate truly a dull and garrulous discourser, without repeating the effects of dullness and garrulity. . . .

If then I am compelled to doubt the theory, by which the choice of characters was to be directed, not only *a priori,* from grounds of reason, but both from the few instances in which the poet himself need be supposed to have been governed by it, and from the comparative inferiority of those instances; still more must I hesitate in my assent to the sentence which immediately follows the former citation; and which I can neither admit as particular fact, nor as general rule. "The language, too, of these men has been adopted (purified indeed from what appear to be its real defects, from all lasting and rational causes of dislike or disgust) because such men hourly communicate with the best objects from which the best part of language is originally derived; and because, from their rank in society and the sameness and narrow circle of their intercourse, being less under the action of social vanity, they convey their feelings and notions in simple and unelaborated expressions." To this I reply; that a rustic's language, purified from all provincialism and grossness, and so far reconstructed as to be made consistent with the rules of grammar—(which are in essence no other than the laws of universal logic, applied to psychological materials)—will not differ from the language of any other man of common sense, however learned or refined he may be, except as far as the notions, which the rustic has to convey, are fewer and more indiscriminate. This will become still clearer, if we add the consideration—(equally important though less obvious)—that the rustic, from the more imperfect development of his faculties, and from the lower state of their cultivation, aims almost solely to convey insulated facts, either those of his scanty experience or his traditional belief; while the educated man chiefly seeks to discover and express those connections of things, or those relative bearings of fact to fact, from which some more or less general law is deducible. For facts are valuable to a wise man, chiefly as they lead to the discovery of the in-dwelling law, which is the true being of things, the sole solution of their modes of existence, and in the knowledge of which consists our dignity and our power.

As little can I agree with the assertion, that from the objects with which the rustic hourly communicates the best part of language is formed. For first, if to communicate with an object implies such an acquaintance with it, as renders it capable of being discriminately reflected on, the distinct knowledge of an uneducated rustic would furnish a very scanty vocabulary. The few things and modes of action requisite for his bodily conveniences would alone be individualized; while all the rest of nature would be expressed by a small number of confused general terms. Secondly, I deny that the words and combinations of words derived from the objects, with which the rustic is familiar, whether with distinct or confused knowledge, can be justly said to form the best part of language. It is more than probable, that many classes of the brute creation possess discriminating sounds, by which they can convey to each other notices of such objects as concern their food, shelter, or safety. Yet we hesitate to call the aggregate of such sounds a language, otherwise than metaphorically. The best part of human language, properly so called, is derived from reflection on the acts of the mind itself. It is formed by a voluntary appropriation of fixed symbols to internal acts, to processes and results of imagination, the greater part of which have no place in the consciousness of uneducated man; though in civilized society, by imitation and passive remembrance of what they hear from their religious instructors and other superiors, the most uneducated share in the harvest which they neither sowed, nor reaped. If the history of the phrases in hourly currency among our peasants were traced, a person not previously aware of the fact would be surprised at finding so large a number, which three or four centuries ago were the exclusive property of the universities and the schools; and, at the commencement of the Reformation, had been transferred from the school to the pulpit, and thus gradually passed into common life. The extreme difficulty, and often the impossibility, of finding words for the simplest moral and intellectual processes of the languages of uncivilized tribes has proved perhaps the weightiest obstacle to the progress of our most zealous and adroit missionaries. Yet these tribes are surrounded by the same nature as our peasants are; but in still more impressive forms; and they are, moreover, obliged to particularize many more of them. When, therefore, Mr. Wordsworth adds, "accordingly, such a language"—(meaning, as before, the language of rustic life purified from provincialism)—"arising out of repeated experience and regular feelings, is a more permanent, and a far more philosophical language, than that which is frequently substituted for it by Poets, who think that they are conferring honour upon themselves and their art in proportion as they indulge in arbitrary and capricious habits of expression;" it may be answered, that the language, which he has in view, can be attributed to rustics with no greater right, than the style of Hooker or Bacon to Tom Brown or Sir Roger L'Estrange. Doubtless, if what is peculiar to each were omitted in each, the result must needs be the same. Further, that the poet, who uses an illogical diction, or a style fitted to excite only the low and changeable pleasure of wonder by means of groundless novelty, substitutes a language of folly and vanity, not for that of the rustic, but for that of good sense and natural feeling.

Here let me be permitted to remind the reader, that the positions, which I controvert, are contained in the sentences—"a selection of the real language of men;"—"the language of these men" (that is, men in low and rustic life) "has been adopted; I have proposed to myself to imitate, and, as far as is possible, to adopt the very language of men."

"Between the language of prose and that of metrical composition, there neither is, nor can be, any *essential difference:*" it is against these exclusively that my opposition is directed.

I object, in the very first instance, to an equivocation in the use of the word "real." Every man's language varies, according to the extent of his knowledge, the activity of his faculties, and the depth or quickness of his feelings. Every man's language has, first, its individualities; secondly, the common properties of the class to which he belongs; and thirdly, words and phrases of universal use. The language of Hooker, Bacon, Bishop Taylor, and Burke differs from the common language of the learned class only by the superior number and novelty of the thoughts and relations which they had to convey. The language of Algernon Sidney differs not at all from that, which every well-educated gentleman would wish to write, and (with due allowances for the undeliberateness, and less connected train, of thinking natural and proper to conversation) such as he would wish to talk. Neither one nor the other differ half as much from the general language of cultivated society, as the language of Mr. Wordsworth's homeliest composition differs from that of a common peasant. For "real" therefore, we must substitute ordinary, or *lingua communis*. And this, we have proved, is no more to be found in the phraseology of low and rustic life than in that of any other class. Omit the peculiarities of each and the result of course must be common to all. And assuredly the omissions and changes to be made in the language of rustics, before it could be transferred to any species of poem, except the drama or other professed imitation, are at least as numerous and weighty, as would be required in adapting to the same purpose the ordinary language of tradesmen and manufacturers. Not to mention, that the language so highly extolled by Mr. Wordsworth varies in every county, nay in every village, according to the accidental character of the clergyman, the existence or non-existence of schools; or even, perhaps, as the exciseman, publican, and barber happen to be, or not to be, zealous politicians, and readers of the weekly newspaper *pro bono publico*. Anterior to cultivation the *lingua communis* of every country, as Dante has well observed, exists every where in parts, and no where as a whole.

Neither is the case rendered at all more tenable by the addition of the words, "in a state of excitement." For the nature of a man's words, where he is strongly affected by joy, grief, or anger, must necessarily depend on the number and quality of the general truths, conceptions and images, and of the words expressing them, with which his mind had been previously stored. For the property of passion is not to create; but to set in increased activity. At least, whatever new connections of thoughts or images, or— (which is equally, if not more than equally, the appropriate effect of strong excitement)—whatever generalizations of truth or expe-

rience the heat of passion may produce; yet the terms of their con-
veyance must have pre-existed in his former conversations, and are
only collected and crowded together by the unusual stimulation. It
is indeed very possible to adopt in a poem the unmeaning repetitions, habitual phrases, and other blank counters, which an un-
furnished or confused understanding interposes at short intervals,
in order to keep hold of his subject, which is still slipping from
him, and to give him time for recollection; or, in mere aid of
vacancy, as in the scanty companies of a country stage the same
player pops backwards and forwards, in order to prevent the
appearance of empty spaces, in the procession of Macbeth, or
Henry VIII. But what assistance to the poet, or ornament to the
poem, these can supply, I am at a loss to conjecture. Nothing
assuredly can differ either in origin or in mode more widely
from the apparent tautologies of intense and turbulent feeling,
in which the passion is greater and of longer endurance than to
be exhausted or satisfied by a single representation of the image
or incident exciting it. Such repetitions I admit to be a beauty of
the highest kind; as illustrated by Mr. Wordsworth himself from the
song of Deborah. *At her feet he bowed, he fell, he lay down: at
her feet he bowed, he fell: where he bowed, there he fell down
dead.* [Judges 5: 27.]

John Keats

(1795–1821)

From the LETTERS

Of Keats' speculations on the poet and poetry, T. S. Eliot has written: "There is hardly one statement of Keats about poetry which . . . will not be found to be true." The following selections have been arranged not in chronological order but in accordance with subject matter. Unsystematic as Keats' insights were, they reveal an unusually perceptive intelligence which gives the letters, as Lionel Trilling states, "a unique place in literature."

———◆———

TO JOHN TAYLOR
[publisher of Keats' *Endymion*]

27 February 1818

[The nature of poetry]

. . . IN POETRY I have a few Axioms, and you will see how far I am from their Centre. 1st. I think Poetry should surprise by a fine excess and not by Singularity—it should strike the Reader as a wording of his own highest thoughts, and appear almost a Remembrance— 2nd. Its touches of Beauty should never be half way thereby making the reader breathless instead of content: the rise, the progress, the setting of imagery should like the Sun come natural to him—shine over him and set soberly although in magnificence leaving him in the Luxury of twilight—but it is easier to think what Poetry should be than to write it—and this leads me on to another axiom. That if Poetry comes not as naturally as the Leaves to a tree it had better not come at all. . . .

TO GEORGE AND GEORGIANA KEATS

19 March 1819

. . . The greater part of Men make their way with the same in-
stinctiveness, the same unwandering eye from their purposes, the
same animal eagerness as the Hawk. The Hawk wants a Mate, so
does the Man—look at them both; they set about it and procure
one in the same manner. They want both a nest and they both
set about one in the same manner—they get their food in the
same manner— The noble animal Man for his amusement smokes
his pipe—the Hawk balances about the Clouds—that is the only
difference of their leisures. This it is that makes the Amusement of Life—to a speculative Mind. I go among the Fields
and catch a glimpse of a Stoat or a fieldmouse peeping out of
the withered grass—the creature hath a purpose and its eyes
are bright with it. I go amongst the buildings of a city and I
see a Man hurrying along—to what? the Creature has a purpose
and his eyes are bright with it. But then, as Wordsworth says, "we
have all one human heart"—there is an electric fire in human nature tending to purify—so that among these human creatures there
is continually some birth of a new heroism. . . . Even here,
though I myself am pursuing the same instinctive course as the
veriest human animal you can think of (I am, however, young,
writing at random), straining at particles of light in the midst of a
great darkness, without knowing the bearing of any one assertion,
of any one opinion—yet may I not in this be free from sin? May
there not be superior beings amused with any graceful, though
instinctive attitude my mind may fall into, as I am entertained with
the alertness of a Stoat or the anxiety of a Deer? Though a quarrel in the Streets is a thing to be hated, the energies displayed in
it are fine; the commonest Man shows a grace in his quarrel— By
a superior being our reasonings may take the same tone—though
erroneous they may be fine.— This is the very thing in which consists poetry; and if so it is not so fine a thing as philosophy— For
the same reason that an eagle is not so fine a thing as a truth. . . .

TO RICHARD WOODHOUSE
[A close friend of Keats]

27 October 1818

[*The nature of the poet*]

. . . As to the poetical Character itself (I mean that sort of which, if I am anything, I am a Member; that sort of distinguished from the Wordsworthian or egotistical sublime; which is a thing per se and stands alone) it is not itself—it has no self—it is everything and nothing— It has no character—it enjoys light and shade; it lives in gusto, be it foul or fair, high or low, rich or poor, mean or elevated— It has as much delight in conceiving an Iago as an Imogen. What shocks the virtuous philosopher, delights the camelion Poet. It does no harm from its relish of the dark side of things any more than from its taste for the bright one; because they both end in speculation. A Poet is the most unpoetical of any thing in existence; because he has no Identity—he is continually infor[ming] and filling some other Body— The Sun, the Moon, the Sea and Men and Women who are creatures of impulse are poetical and have about them an unchangeable attribute—the poet has none; no identity—he is certainly the most unpoetical of all God's Creatures. If then he has no self, and if I am a Poet, where is the Wonder that I should say I would write no more? Might I not at that very instant have been cogitating on the Characters of Saturn and Ops? It is a wretched thing to confess; but is a very fact that not one word I ever utter can be taken for granted as an opinion growing out of my identical nature— how can it, when I have no nature? When I am in a room with People if I ever am free from speculating on creations of my own brain, then not myself goes home to myself: but the identity of every one in the room begins to press upon me [so] that I am in a very little time annihilated—not only among Men; it would be the same in a Nursery of children. . . .

TO BENJAMIN BAILEY
[a student at Oxford]

22 November 1817

[*The nature of the imagination*]

. . . Men of Genius are great as certain etherial Chemicals op-
erating on the Mass of neutral intellect—but they have not any
individuality, any determined Character. . . . I am certain of
nothing but of the holiness of the Heart's affections and the truth
of Imagination— What the imagination seizes as Beauty must
be truth . . . The Imagination may be compared to Adam's
dream—he awoke and found it truth. I am the more zealous in
this affair because I have never yet been able to perceive how
anything can be known for truth by consequitive reasoning—and
yet it must be. Can it be that even the greatest Philosopher
ever arrived at his goal without putting aside numerous objections?
However it may be, O for a Life of Sensations rather than of
Thoughts! It is 'a Vision in the form of Youth' a Shadow of
reality to come—and this consideration has further convinced me
for it has come as auxiliary to another favorite Speculation of
mine, that we shall enjoy ourselves here after by having what we
called happiness on Earth repeated in a finer tone and so repeated.
And yet such a fate can only befall those who delight in Sensation
rather than hunger as you after Truth. Adam's dream [in *Paradise
Lost*] will do here and seems to be a conviction that Imagination
and its empyreal reflection is the same as human Life and its
Spiritual reflection. But as I was saying—the simple imaginative
Mind may have its rewards in the repeti[ti]on of its own silent
Working coming continually on the Spirit with a fine Suddenness
—to compare great things with small—have you never by being
Surprised with an old Melody—in a delicious place—by a delicious
voice, fe[l]t over again your very Speculations and Surmises at
the time it first operated on your Soul—do you not remember

forming to yourself the singer's face more beautiful [than] it was possible and yet with the elevation of the Moment you did not think so—even then you were mounted on the Wings of Imagination so high—that the Prototype must be here after—that delicious face you will see. . . .

TO GEORGE AND THOMAS KEATS

27 December 1817

[*Negative Capability*]

. . . The excellence of every art is its intensity, capable of making all disagreeables evaporate, from their being in close relationship with Beauty and Truth. Examine "King Lear," and you will find this exemplified throughout . . . Several things dove-tailed in my mind, and at once it struck me what quality went to form a Man of Achievement, especially in Literature, and which Shakespeare possessed so enormously—I mean *Negative Capability,* that is, when a man is capable of being in uncertainties, mysteries, doubts, without any irritable reaching after fact and reason—Coleridge, for instance, would let go by a fine isolated verisimilitude caught from the Penetralium of mystery, from being incapable of remaining content with half-knowledge. This pursued through volumes would perhaps take us no further than this, that with a great poet the sense of Beauty overcomes every other consideration, or rather obliterates all consideration. . . .

TO JOHN HAMILTON REYNOLDS
[a young clerk who wrote poetry]

3 February 1818

[*On Wordsworth*]

It may be said that we ought to read our Contemporaries—that Wordsworth &c. should have their due from us. But, for the sake of a few fine imaginative or domestic passages, are we to be bullied

into a certain Philosophy engendered in the whims of an Egotist.
—Every man has his speculations, but every man does not brood
and peacock over them till he makes a false coinage and deceives
himself. Many a man can travel to the very bourne of Heaven,
and yet want confidence to put down his half-seeing. Sancho will
invent a Journey heavenward as well as anybody. We hate poetry
that has a palpable design upon us—and if we do not agree, seems
to put its hand in its breeches pocket. Poetry should be great and
unobtrusive, a thing which enters into one's soul, and does not
startle it or amaze it with itself, but with its subject.—How beautiful are the retired flowers! how would they lose their beauty were
they to throng into the highway crying out, "admire me I am a
violet!—dote upon me I am a primrose!" Modern poets differ
from the Elizabethans in this. Each of the moderns like an Elector
of Hanover governs his petty state, and knows how many straws
are swept daily from the Causeways in all his dominions and has a
continual itching that all the Housewives should have their coppers
well scoured: the antients were Emperors of vast Provinces, they
had only heard of the remote ones and scarcely cared to visit
them.—I will cut all this—I will have no more of Wordsworth
or [Leigh] Hunt in particular. . . . Old Matthew spoke to
[Wordsworth] some years ago on some nothing, and because he
happens in an Evening Walk to imagine the figure of the Old Man
—he must stamp it down in black and white, and it is henceforth
sacred—I don't mean to deny Wordsworth's grandeur and Hunt's
merit, but I mean to say we need not be teazed with grandeur
and merit when we can have them uncontaminated and unobtrusive. . . .

Matthew Arnold

(1822–1888)

THE FUNCTION OF CRITICISM
AT THE PRESENT TIME

First published in 1864 (in the following year reprinted in *Essays in Criticism*), Arnold's *Function of Criticism* has been called by Lionel Trilling "the classic statement in English of the role of intelligence in the modern world, of an intelligence truly objective and disinterested."

Certain of the ideas expressed here were later to be restated and systematized by Irving Babbitt and Paul Elmer More, the "New Humanists." Arnold's influence may also be seen in such critics as F. R. Leavis and T. S. Eliot, who draws upon this essay for his own account of the function of criticism.

———————◆———————

MANY objections have been made to a proposition which, in some remarks of mine on translating Homer, I ventured to put forth; a proposition about criticism, and its importance at the present day. I said that "of the literature of France and Germany, as of the intellect of Europe in general, the main effort, for now many years, has been a critical effort; the endeavour, in all branches of knowledge, theology, philosophy, history, art, science, to see the object as in itself it really is." I added, that owing to the operation in English literature of certain causes, "almost the last thing for which one would come to English literature is just that very thing which now Europe most desires,—criticism;" and that the power and value of English literature was thereby impaired. More than one rejoinder declared that the importance I here assigned to criticism was excessive, and asserted the inherent superiority of the creative effort of the human spirit over its critical effort. And

the other day, having been led by [an] excellent notice of Wordsworth, published in the *North British Review,* to turn again to
his biography, I found, in the words of this great man, whom I, for
one, must always listen to with the profoundest respect, a sentence
passed on the critic's business, which seems to justify every possible
disparagement of it. Wordsworth says in one of his letters:—

"The writers in these publications" [the Reviews], "while they
prosecute their inglorious employment, cannot be supposed to be in
a state of mind very favourable for being affected by the finer influences of a thing so pure as genuine poetry."

And a trustworthy reporter of his conversation quotes a more
elaborate judgment to the same effect:—

"Wordsworth holds the critical power very low, infinitely lower
than the inventive; and he said to-day that if the quantity of time
consumed in writing critiques on the works of others were given to
original composition, of whatever kind it might be, it would be
much better employed; it would make a man find out sooner his
own level, and it would do infinitely less mischief. A false or malicious criticism may do much injury to the minds of others; a stupid
invention, either in prose or verse, is quite harmless."

It is almost too much to expect of poor human nature, that a
man capable of producing some effect in one line of literature,
should, for the greater good of society, voluntarily doom himself
to impotence and obscurity in another. Still less is this to be expected from men addicted to the composition of the "false or
malicious criticism" of which Wordsworth speaks. However, everybody would admit that a false or malicious criticism had better
never have been written. Everybody, too, would be willing to admit, as a general proposition, that the critical faculty is lower than
the inventive. But is it true that criticism is really, in itself, a baneful and injurious employment? is it true that all time given to
writing critiques on the works of others would be much better employed if it were given to original composition, of whatever kind
this may be? Is it true that Johnson had better have gone on
producing more *Irenes* instead of writing his *Lives of the Poets?*
nay, is it certain that Wordsworth himself was better employed

in making his Ecclesiastical Sonnets than when he made his celebrated Preface, so full of criticism, and criticism of the works of
others? Wordsworth was himself a great critic, and it is to be
sincerely regretted that he has not left us more criticism; Goethe
was one of the greatest critics, and we may sincerely congratulate
ourselves that he has left us so much criticism. Without wasting
time over the exaggeration which Wordsworth's judgment on
criticism clearly contains, or over an attempt to trace the causes,
—not difficult, I think, to be traced,—which may have led
Wordsworth to this exaggeration, a critic may with advantage seize
an occasion for trying his own conscience, and for asking himself
of what real service, at any given moment, the practice of criticism
either is, or may be made, to his own mind and spirit, and to the
minds and spirits of others.

The critical power is of lower rank than the creative. True; but
in assenting to this proposition, one or two things are to be kept in
mind. It is undeniable that the exercise of a creative power, that a
free creative activity, is the true function of man; it is proved to be
so by man's finding in it his true happiness. But it is undeniable,
also, that men may have the sense of exercising this free creative
activity in other ways than in producing great works of literature
or art; if it were not so, all but a very few men would be shut out
from the true happiness of all men; they may have it in well-
doing, they may have it in learning, they may have it even in
criticising. This is one thing to be kept in mind. Another is, that
the exercise of the creative power in the production of great works
of literature or art, however high this exercise of it may rank, is not
at all epochs and under all conditions possible; and that therefore
labour may be vainly spent in attempting it, and may with more
fruit be used in preparing for it, in rendering it possible. This
creative power works with elements, with materials; what if it
has not those materials, those elements, ready for its use? In that
case it must surely wait till they are ready. Now, in literature,—I
will limit myself to literature, for it is about literature that the
question arises,—the elements with which the creative power
works are ideas; the best ideas on every matter which literature

touches, current at the time; at any rate we may lay it down as certain that in modern literature no manifestation of the creative power not working with these can be very important or fruitful. And I say *current* at the time, not merely accessible at the time; for creative literary genius does not principally show itself in discovering new ideas, that is rather the business of the philosopher; the grand work of literary genius is a work of synthesis and exposition, not of analysis and discovery; its gift lies in the faculty of being happily inspired by a certain intellectual and spiritual atmosphere, by a certain order of ideas, when it finds itself in them; of dealing divinely with these ideas, presenting them in the most effective and attractive combinations, making beautiful works with them, in short. But it must have the atmosphere, it must find itself amidst the order of ideas, in order to work freely; and these it is not so easy to command. This is why great creative epochs in literature are so rare; this is why there is so much that is unsatisfactory in the productions of many men of real genius; because, for the creation of a master-work of literature two powers must concur, the power of the man and the power of the moment, and the man is not enough without the moment; the creative power has, for its happy exercise, appointed elements, and those elements are not in its own control.

Nay, they are more within the control of the critical power. It is the business of the critical power, as I said in the words already quoted, "in all branches of knowledge, theology, philosophy, history, art, science, to see the object as in itself it really is." Thus it tends, at last, to make an intellectual situation of which the creative power can profitably avail itself. It tends to establish an order of ideas, if not absolutely true, yet true by comparison with that which it displaces; to make the best ideas prevail. Presently these new ideas reach society, the touch of truth is the touch of life, and there is a stir and growth everywhere; out of this stir and growth come the creative epochs of literature.

Or, to narrow our range, and quit these considerations of the general march of genius and of society,—considerations which are apt to become too abstract and impalpable,—every one can see that a poet, for instance, ought to know life and the world before dealing with them in poetry; and life and the world being in modern times, very complex things, the creation of a modern poet, to be worth much, implies a great critical effort behind it; else it would be a comparatively poor, barren, and short-lived affair. This is why Byron's poetry had so little endurance in it, and Goethe's so much; both had a great productive power, but Goethe's was nourished by a great critical effort providing the true materials for it, and Byron's was not; Goethe knew life and the world, the poet's necessary subjects, much more comprehensively and thoroughly than Byron. He knew a great deal more of them, and he knew them much more as they really are.

It has long seemed to me that the burst of creative activity in our literature, through the first quarter of this century, had about it in fact something premature; and that from this cause its productions are doomed, most of them, in spite of the sanguine hopes which accompanied and do still accompany them, to prove hardly more lasting than the productions of far less splendid epochs. And this prematureness comes from its having proceeded without having its proper data, without sufficient materials to work with. In other words, the English poetry of the first quarter of this century, with plenty of energy, plenty of creative force, did not know enough. This makes Byron so empty of matter, Shelley so incoherent, Wordsworth even, profound as he is, yet so wanting in completeness and variety. Wordsworth cared little for books, and disparaged Goethe. I admire Wordsworth, as he is, so much that I cannot wish him different; and it is vain, no doubt, to imagine such a man different from what he is, to suppose that he *could* have been different; but surely the one thing wanting to make Wordsworth an even greater poet than he is,—his thought richer, and his influence of wider application,—was that he should have read more books, among them, no doubt, those of that Goethe whom he disparaged without reading him. But to speak of books and reading may easily lead to a misunderstanding here. It was not really books and reading that lacked to our poetry at this epoch; Shelley had plenty of reading, Coleridge had immense reading. Pindar and Sophocles—as we all say so glibly, and often with so little discernment of the real import of what we are saying—had not many books; Shakespeare was no deep reader. True; but in the Greece of Pindar and Sophocles, in the England of Shakespeare, the poet lived in a current of ideas in the highest degree animating and nourishing to the creative power; society was, in the fullest measure, permeated by fresh thought, intelligent and alive; and this state of things is the true basis for the creative power's exercise, in this it finds its data, its materials, truly ready for its hand; all the books and reading in the world are only valuable as they are helps to this. Even when this does not actually exist, books and reading may enable a man to construct a kind of semblance of it in his own mind, a world of knowledge and intelligence in which he may live and work; this is by no means an equivalent to the artist for the nationally diffused life and thought of the epochs of Sophocles or Shakespeare; but, besides that it may be a means of preparation for such epochs, it does really constitute, if many share in it, a quickening and sustaining atmosphere of great value. Such an atmosphere the many-sided learning and the long and widely-combined critical effort of Germany formed for Goethe, when he lived and worked. There was no national glow of life and thought there, as in the Athens of Pericles or the England of Elizabeth. That was the poet's weakness. But there was a sort of equivalent for it in the complete culture and unfettered thinking of a large body of Germans. That was his strength. In the England of the first quarter of this century there was neither a national glow of life and thought, such as we had in the age of Elizabeth, nor yet a culture and a force of learning and criticism such as were to be found in Germany. Therefore the creative power of poetry wanted, for success in the highest sense, materials and a basis; a thorough interpretation of the world was necessarily denied to it.

At first sight it seems strange that out of the immense stir of the French Revolution and its age should not have come a crop of works of genius equal to that which came out of the stir of the great productive time of Greece, or out of that of the Renascence, with its powerful episode the Reformation. But the truth is that the stir of the French Revolution took a character which essentially distinguished it from such movements as these. These were, in the main, disinterestedly intellectual and spiritual movements; movements in which the human spirit looked for its satisfaction in itself and in the increased play of its own activity: the French Revolution took a political, practical character. The movement, which went on in France, under the old *régime,* from 1700 to 1789, was far more really akin than that of the Revolution itself to the movement of the Renascence; the France of Voltaire and Rousseau told far more powerfully upon the mind of Europe than the France of the Revolution. Goethe reproached this last expressly with having "thrown quiet culture back." Nay, and the true key to how much in our Byron, even in our Wordsworth, is this!—that they had their source in a great moment of feeling, not in a great movement of mind. This Revolution—the object of so much blind love and so much blind hatred,—found indeed its motive-power in the intelligence of men, and not in the practical sense;—this is what distinguishes it from the English Revolution of Charles the First's time; this is what makes it a more spiritual event than our Revolution, an event of much more powerful and world-wide interest, though practically less successful—it appeals to an order of ideas which are universal, certain, permanent. 1789 asked of a thing, Is it rational? 1642 asked of a thing, Is it legal? or, when it went furthest, Is it according to conscience? This is the English fashion, a fashion to be treated, within its own sphere, with the highest respect; for its success, within its own sphere, has been prodigious. But what is law in one place is not law in another; what is law here to-day is not law even here to-morrow; and as for conscience, what is binding on one man's conscience is not binding on another's, the old woman who threw her stool at the head of the surpliced minister in St. Giles's Church at Edinburgh obeyed an impulse to which millions of the human race may be permitted to remain strangers. But the prescriptions of reason are absolute, unchanging, of universal validity; *to count by tens is the easiest way of counting*—that is a proposition of which every one, from here to the Antipodes, feels the force; at least I should say so if we did not live in a country where it is not impossible that any morning we may find a letter in the *Times* declaring that a decimal coinage is an absurdity. That a whole nation should have been penetrated with an enthusiasm for pure reason, and with an ardent zeal for making its prescriptions triumph, is a very remarkable thing, when we consider how little of mind, or anything so worthy and quickening as mind, comes into the motives which alone, in general, *impel* great masses of men. In spite of the extravagant direction given to this enthusiasm, in spite of the crimes and follies in which it lost itself, the French Revolution derives from the force, truth, an universality of the ideas which it took for its law, and from the passion with which it could inspire a multitude for these ideas, a unique and still living power; it is—it will probably long remain —the greatest, the most animating event in history. And as no sincere passion for the things of the mind, even though it turn out in many respects an unfortunate passion, is ever quite thrown away and quite barren of good, France has reaped from hers one fruit, the natural and legitimate fruit, though not precisely the grand fruit she expected: she is the country in Europe where *the people* is most alive.

But the mania for giving an immediate political and practical application to all these fine ideas of the reason was fatal. Here an Englishman is in his element: on this theme we can all go for hours. And all we are in the habit of saying on it has undoubtedly a great deal of truth. Ideas cannot be too much prized in and for themselves, cannot be too much lived with; but to transport them abruptly into the world of politics and practice, violently to revolutionise this world to their bidding,—that is quite another thing. There is the world of ideas and there is the world of practice; the French are often for suppressing the one and the English the other; but neither is to be suppressed. A member of the House of Commons said to me the other day: "That a thing is an anomaly, I consider to be no objection to it whatever." I venture to think he was wrong; that a thing is an anomaly *is* an objection to it, but absolutely and in the sphere of ideas: it is not necessarily, under such and such circumstances, or at such and such a moment, an objection to it in the sphere of politics and practice. Joubert has said beautifully: "C'est la force et le droit qui réglent toutes choses dans le monde; la force en attendant le droit." (Force and right are the governors of this world; force till right is ready.) *Force till right is ready;* and till right is ready, force, the existing order of things, is justified, is the legitimate ruler. But right is something moral, and implies inward recognition, free assent of the will; we are not ready for right,—*right,* so far as we are concerned, *is not ready,*—until we have attained this sense of seeing it and willing it. The way in which for us it may change and transform force, the existing order of things, and become, in its turn, the legitimate ruler of the world, will depend on the way in which, when our time comes, we see it and will it. Therefore for other people enamoured of their own newly discerned right, to attempt to impose it upon us as ours, and violently to substitute their right for our force, is an act of tyranny, and to be resisted. It sets at nought the second great half of our maxim, *force till right is ready.* This was the grand error of the French Revolution; and its movement of ideas, by quitting the intellectual sphere and rushing furiously into the political sphere, ran, indeed, a prodigious and memorable course, but produced no such intellectual fruit as the movement of ideas of the Renascence, and created, in opposition to itself, what I may call an *epoch of concentration.* The great force of that epoch of concentration was England; and the great voice of that epoch of concentration was Burke. It is the fashion to treat Burke's writings on the French Revolution as superannuated and conquered by the event; as the eloquent but unphilosophical tirades of bigotry and prejudice. I will not deny that they are often disfigured by the violence and passion of the moment, and that in some directions Burke's view was bounded, and his observation therefore at fault, but on the whole, and for those who can make the needful corrections, what distinguishes these writings is their profound, permanent, fruitful, philosophical truth, they contain the true philosophy of an epoch of concentration, dissipate the heavy atmosphere which its own nature is apt to engender round it, and make its resistance rational instead of mechanical.

But Burke is so great because, almost alone in England, he brings thought to bear upon politics, he saturates politics with thought; it is his accident that his ideas were at the service of an epoch of concentration, not of an epoch of expansion; it is his characteristic that he so lived by ideas, and had such a source of them welling up within him, that he could float even an epoch of concentration and English Tory politics with them. It does not hurt him that Dr. Price and the Liberals were enraged with him; it does not even hurt him that George the Third and the Tories were enchanted with him. His greatness is that he lived in a world which neither English Liberalism nor English Toryism is apt to enter;—the world of ideas, not the world of catchwords and party habits. So far is it from being really true of him that he "to party gave up what was meant for mankind," that at the very end of his fierce struggle with the French Revolution, after all his invectives against its false pretensions, hollowness, and madness, with his sincere conviction of its mischievousness, he can close a memorandum on the best means of combating it, some of the last pages he ever wrote,—the *Thoughts on French Affairs,* in December 1791,—with these striking words:—

"The evil is stated, in my opinion, as it exists. The remedy must be where power, wisdom, and information, I hope, are more united with good intentions than they can be with me. I have done with this subject, I believe, for ever. It has given me many anxious moments for the last two years. *If a great change is to be made in human affairs, the minds of men will be fitted to it; the general opinions and feelings will draw that way. Every fear, every hope will forward it; and then they who persist in opposing this mighty current in human affairs, will appear rather to resist the decrees of Providence itself, than the mere designs of men. They will not be resolute and firm, but perverse and obstinate.*"

That return of Burke upon himself has always seemed to me one of the finest things in English literature, or indeed in any literature. That is what I call living by ideas: when one side of a question has long had your earnest support, when all your feelings are engaged, when you hear all round you no language but one, when your party talks this language like a steam-engine and can imagine no other,—still to be able to think, still to be irresistibly carried, if so it be, by the current of thought to the opposite side of the question, and, like Balaam, to be unable to speak anything *but what the Lord has put in your mouth*. I know nothing more striking, and I must add that I know nothing more un-English.

For the Englishman in general is like my friend the Member of Parliament, and believes, point-blank, that for a thing to be an anomaly is absolutely no objection to it whatever. He is like the Lord Auckland of Burke's day, who, in a memorandum on the French Revolution, talks of "certain miscreants, assuming the name of philosophers, who have presumed themselves capable of establishing a new system of society." The Englishman has been called a political animal, and he values what is political and practical so much that ideas easily become objects of dislike in his eyes, and thinkers "miscreants," because ideas and thinkers have rashly meddled with politics and practice. This would be all very well if the dislike and neglect confined themselves to ideas transported out of their own sphere, and meddling rashly with practice; but they are inevitably extended to ideas as such, and to the whole life of intelligence; practice is everything, a free play of the mind is nothing. The notion of the free play of the mind upon all subjects being a pleasure in itself, being an object of desire, being an essential provider of elements without which a nation's spirit, whatever compensations it may have for them, must, in the long run, die of inanition, hardly enters into an Englishman's thoughts. It is noticeable that the word *curiosity,* which in other languages is used in a good sense, to mean, as a high and fine quality of man's nature, just this disinterested love of a free play of the mind on all subjects, for its own sake,—it is noticeable, I say, that this word has in our language no sense of the kind, no sense but a rather bad and disparaging one. But criticism, real criticism, is essentially the exercise of this very quality; it obeys an instinct prompting it to try to know the best that is known and thought in the world, irrespectively of practice, politics, and everything of the kind; and to value knowledge and thought as they approach this best, without the intrusion of any other considerations whatever. This is an instinct for which there is, I think, little original sympathy in the practical English nature, and what there was of it has undergone a long benumbing period of check and suppression in the epoch of concentration which followed the French Revolution.

But epochs of concentration cannot well endure for ever; epochs of expansion, in the due course of things, follow them. Such an epoch of expansion seems to be opening in this country. In the first place all danger of a hostile forcible pressure of foreign ideas upon our practice has long disappeared; like the traveller in the fable, therefore, we begin to wear our cloak a little more loosely. Then, with a long peace the ideas of Europe steal gradually and amicably in, and mingle, though in infinitesimally small quantities at a time, with our own notions. Then, too, in spite of all that is said about the absorbing and brutalising influence of our passionate material progress, it seems to me indisputable that this progress is likely, though not certain, to lead in the end to an apparition of intellectual life; and that man, after he has made himself perfectly comfortable and has now to determine what to do with himself next, may begin to remember that he has a mind, and that the mind may be made the source of great pleasure. I grant it is mainly the privilege of faith, at present, to discern this end to our railways, our business, and our fortune-making; but we shall see if, here as elsewhere, faith is not in the end the true prophet. Our ease, our travelling, and our unbounded liberty to hold just as hard and securely as we please to the practice to which our notions have given birth, all tend to beget an inclination to deal a little more freely with these notions themselves, to canvass them a little, to penetrate a little into their real nature. Flutterings of curiosity, in the foreign sense of the word, appear amongst us, and it is in these that criticism must look to find its account. Criticism first; a time of true creative activity, perhaps,—which, as I have said, must inevitably be preceded amongst us by a time of criticism,—hereafter, when criticism has done its work.

It is of the last importance that English criticism should clearly discern what rules for its course, in order to avail itself of the field now opening to it, and to produce fruit for the future, it ought to take. The rule may be summed up in one word—*disinterestedness.* And how is criticism to show disinterestedness? By keeping aloof from what is called "the practical view of things"; by resolutely following the law of its own nature, which is to be a free play of the mind on all subjects which it touches; by steadily refusing to lend itself to any of those ulterior, political, practical considerations about ideas, which plenty of people will be sure to attach to them, which perhaps ought often to be attached to them, which in this country at any rate are certain to be attached to them quite sufficiently, but which criticism has really nothing to do with. Its business is, as I have said, simply to know the best that is known and thought in the world, and by in its turn making this known, to create a current of true and fresh ideas. Its business is to do this with inflexible honesty, with due ability; but its business is to do no more, and to leave alone all questions of practical consequences and applications, questions which will never fail to have due prominence given to them. Else criticism, besides being really false to its own nature, merely continues in the old rut which it has hitherto followed in this country, and will certainly miss the chance now given to it. For what is at present the bane of criticism in this country? It is that practical considerations cling to it and stifle it; it subserves interests not its own; our organs of criticism are organs of men and parties having practical ends to serve, and with them those practical ends are the first thing and the play of mind the second; so much play of mind as is compatible with the prosecution of those practical ends is all that is wanted. An organ like the *Revue des Deux Mondes,* having for its main function to understand and utter the best that is known and thought in the world, existing, it may be said, as just an organ for a free play of the mind, we have not; but we have the *Edinburgh Review,* existing as an organ of the old Whigs, and for as much play of the mind as may suit its being that; we have the *Quarterly Review,* existing as an organ of the Tories, and for as much play of mind as may suit its being that; we have the *British Quarterly Review,* existing as an organ of the political Dissenters, and for as much play of mind as may suit its being that; we have the *Times,* existing as an organ of the common, satisfied, well-to-do Englishman, and for as much play of mind as may suit its being that. And so on through all the various fractions, political and religious, of our society; every fraction has, as such, its organ of criticism, but the notion of combining all fractions in the common pleasure of a free disinterested play of mind meets with no favour. Directly this play of mind wants to have more scope, and to forget the pressure of practical considerations a little, it is checked, it is made to feel the chain. We saw this the other day in the extinction, so much to be regretted, of the *Home and Foreign Review;* perhaps in no organ of criticism in this country was there so much knowledge, so much play of mind; but these could not save it. The *Dublin Review* subordinates play of mind to the practical business of English and Irish Catholicism, and lives. It must needs be that men should act in sects and parties, that each of these sects and parties should have its organ, and should make this organ subserve the interests of its action; but it would be well, too, that there should be a criticism, not the minister of these interests, not their enemy, but absolutely and entirely independent of them. No other criticism will ever attain any real authority or make any real way towards its end,—the creating a current of true and fresh ideas.

It is because criticism has so little kept in the pure intellectual sphere, has so little detached itself from practice, has been so directly polemical and controversial, that it has so ill accomplished, in this country, its best spiritual work; which is to keep man from a self-satisfaction which is retarding and vulgarising, to lead him towards perfection, by making his mind dwell upon what is excellent in itself, and the absolute beauty and fitness of things. A polemical practical criticism makes men blind even to the ideal imperfection of their practice, makes them willingly assert its ideal perfection, in order the better to secure it against attack; and clearly this is narrowing and baneful for them. If they were reassured on the practical side, speculative considerations of ideal perfection they might be brought to entertain, and their spiritual horizon would thus gradually widen. Sir Charles Adderley [Conservative in politics] says to the Warwickshire farmers:

"Talk of the improvement of breed! Why, the race we ourselves represent, the men and women, the old Anglo-Saxon race, are the best breed in the whole world. . . . The absence of a too enervating climate, too unclouded skies, and a too luxurious nature, has produced so vigorous a race of people, and has rendered us so superior to all the world."

Mr. Roebuck [a Liberal reformer] says to the Sheffield cutlers:

"I look around me and ask what is the state of England? Is not property safe? Is not every man able to say what he likes? Can you not walk from one end of England to the other in perfect security? I ask you whether, the world over or in past history, there is anything like it? Nothing. I pray that our unrivalled happiness may last."

Now obviously there is a peril for poor human nature in words and thoughts of such exuberant self-satisfaction, until we find ourselves safe in the streets of the Celestial City.

> *Das wenige verschwindet leicht dem Blicke*
> *Der vorwärts sieht, wie viel noch übrig bleibt—*
> > *[Iphigenie auf Tauris, I, ii]*

says Goethe; "the little that is done seems nothing when we look forward and see how much we have yet to do." Clearly this is a better line of reflection for weak humanity, so long as it remains on this earthly field of labour and trial.

But neither Sir Charles Adderley nor Mr. Roebuck is by nature inaccessible to considerations of this sort. They only lose sight of them owing to the controversial life we all lead, and the practical form which all speculation takes with us. They have in view opponents whose aim is not ideal, but practical; and in their zeal to uphold their own practice against these innovators, they go so far as even to attribute to this practice an ideal perfection. Somebody has been wanting to introduce a six-pound franchise, or to abolish church-rates, or to collect agricultural statistics by force, or to diminish local self-government. How natural, in reply to such proposals, very likely improper or ill-timed, to go a little beyond the mark and to say stoutly, "Such a race of people as we stand, so superior to all the world! The old Anglo-Saxon race, the best breed in the whole world! I pray that our unrivalled happiness may last! I ask you whether, the world over or in past history, there is anything like it?" And so long as criticism answers this dithyramb by insisting that the old Anglo-Saxon race would be still more superior to all others if it had no church-rates, or that our unrivalled happiness would last yet longer with a six-pound franchise, so long will the strain, "The best breed in the whole world!" swell louder and louder, everything ideal and refining will be lost out of sight, and both the assailed and their critics will remain in a sphere, to say the truth, perfectly unvital, a sphere in which spiritual progression is impossible. But let criticism leave church-rates and the franchise alone, and in the most candid spirit, without a single lurking thought of practical innovation, confront with our dithyramb this paragraph on which I stumbled in a newspaper immediately after reading Mr. Roebuck:

"A shocking child murder has just been committed at Nottingham. A girl named Wragg left the workhouse there on Saturday morning with her young illegitimate child. The child was soon afterwards found dead on Mapperly Hills, having been strangled. Wragg is in custody."

Nothing but that; but, in juxtaposition with the absolute eulogies of Sir Charles Adderley and Mr. Roebuck, how eloquent, how suggestive are those few lines! "Our old Anglo-Saxon breed, the best in the whole world!"—how much that is harsh and ill-favoured there is in this best! *Wragg!* If we are to talk of ideal perfection, of "the best in the whole world," has any one reflected what a touch of grossness in our race, what an original short-coming in the more delicate spiritual perceptions, is shown by the natural growth amongst us of such hideous names,—Higginbottom, Stiggins, Bugg! In Ionia and Attica they were luckier in this respect than "the best race in the world"; by the Ilissus there was no Wragg, poor thing! And "our unrivalled happiness";—what an element of grimness, bareness, and hideousness mixes with it and blurs it; the workhouse, the dismal Mapperly Hills,—how dismal those who have seen them will remember;—the gloom, the smoke, the cold, the strangled illegitimate child! "I ask you whether, the world over or in past history, there is anything like it?" Perhaps not, one is inclined to answer; but at any rate, in that case, the world is very much to be pitied. And the final touch,—short, bleak and inhuman: *Wragg is in custody.* The sex lost in the confusion of our unrivalled happiness; or (shall I say?) the superfluous Christian name lopped off by the straightforward vigour of our old Anglo-Saxon breed! There is profit for the spirit in such contrasts as this; criticism serves the cause of perfection by establishing them. By eluding sterile conflict, by refusing to remain in the sphere where alone narrow and relative conceptions have any worth and validity, criticism may diminish its momentary importance, but only in this way has it a chance of gaining admittance for those wider and more perfect conceptions to which all its duty is really owed. Mr. Roebuck will have a poor opinion of an adversary who replies to his defiant songs of triumph only by murmuring under his breath, *Wragg is in custody;* but in no other way will these songs of triumph be induced gradually to moderate themselves, to get rid of what in them is excessive and offensive, and to fall into a softer and truer key.

It will be said that it is a very subtle and indirect action which I am thus prescribing for criticism, and that, by embracing in this manner the Indian virtue of detachment and abandoning the sphere of practical life, it condemns itself to a slow and obscure work. Slow and obscure it may be, but it is the only proper work of criticism. The mass of mankind will never have any ardent zeal for seeing things as they are; very inadequate ideas will always satisfy them. On these inadequate ideas reposes, and must repose, the general practice of the world. That is as much as saying that whoever sets himself to see things as they are will find himself one of a very small circle; but it is only by this small circle resolutely doing its own work that adequate ideas will ever get current at all. The rush and roar of practical life will always have a dizzying and attracting effect upon the most collected spectator, and tend to draw him into its vortex; most of all will this be the case where that life is so powerful as it is in England. But it is only by remaining collected, and refusing to lend himself to the point of view of the practical man, that the critic can do the practical man any service; and it is only by the greatest sincerity in pursuing his own course, and by at last convincing even the practical man of his sincerity, that he can escape misunderstandings which perpetually threaten him.

For the practical man is not apt for fine distinctions, and yet in these distinctions truth and the highest culture greatly find their account. But it is not easy to lead a practical man,—unless you reassure him as to your practical intentions, you have no chance of leading him,—to see that a thing which he has always been used to look at from one side only, which he greatly values, and which, looked at from that side, quite deserves, perhaps, all the prizing and admiring which he bestows upon it,—that this thing, looked at from another side, may appear much less beneficent and beautiful, and yet retain all its claims to our practical allegiance. Where shall we find language innocent enough, how shall we make the spotless purity of our intentions evident enough, to enable us to say to the political Englishman that the British Constitution itself, which, seen from the practical side, looks such a magnificent organ of progress and virtue, seen from the speculative side,—with its compromises, its love of facts, its horror of theory, its studied avoidance of clear thoughts,—that, seen from this side, our august Constitution sometimes looks,—forgive me, shade of Lord Somers [who defended the Constitution—d. 1716]!—a colossal machine for the manufacture of Philistines? How is Cobbett [a political writer] to say this and not be misunderstood, blackened as he is with the smoke of a lifelong conflict in the field of political practice? how is Mr. Carlyle to say it and not be misunderstood, after his furious raid into this field with his *Latter-day Pamphlets?* how is Mr. Ruskin, after his pugnacious political economy? I say, the critic must keep out of the region of immediate practice in the political, social, humanitarian sphere if he wants to make a beginning for that more free speculative treatment of things, which may perhaps one day make its benefits felt even in this sphere, but in a natural and thence irresistible manner.

Do what he will, however, the critic will still remain exposed to frequent misunderstandings, and nowhere so much as in this country. For here people are particularly indisposed even to comprehend that without this free disinterested treatment of things, truth and the highest culture are out of the question. So immersed are they in practical life, so accustomed to take all their notions from this life and its processes, that they are apt to think that truth and culture themselves can be reached by the processes of this life, and that it is an impertinent singularity to think of reaching them in any other. "We are all *terrae filii* ['sons of the earth']," cries their eloquent advocate; "all Philistines together. Away with the notion of proceeding by any other course than the course dear to the Philistines; let us have a social movement, let us organise and combine a party to pursue truth and new thought, let us call it *the liberal party,* and let us all stick to each other, and back each other up. Let us have no nonsense about independent criticism, and intellectual delicacy, and the few and the many. Don't let us trouble ourselves about foreign thought; we shall invent the whole thing for ourselves as we go along. If one of us speaks well, applaud him; if one of us speaks ill, applaud him too; we are all in the same movement, we are all liberals, we are all in pursuit of truth." In this way the pursuit of truth becomes really a social, practical, pleasurable affair, almost requiring a chairman, a secretary, and advertisements; with the excitement of an occasional scandal, with a little resistance to give the happy sense of difficulty overcome; but, in general, plenty of bustle and very little thought. To act is so easy, as Goethe says; to think is so hard! It is true that the critic has many temptations to go with the stream, to make one of the party movement, one of these *terrae filii;* it seems ungracious to refuse to be a *terrae filius* when so many excellent people are; but the critic's duty is to refuse, or, if resistance is vain, at least to cry with Obermann: *Périssons en résistant* ["Let us perish while resisting"].

[The following section, here omitted, deals with a controversy over Arnold's criticism of a theological work by John William Colenso, Bishop of Natal, who had attacked the literal interpretation of the Bible. Arnold insisted that the volume lacked clarity and scholarship.]

If I have insisted so much on the course which criticism must take where politics and religion are concerned, it is because, where these burning matters are in question, it is most likely to go astray. In general, its course is determined for it by the idea which is the law of its being; the idea of a disinterested endeavour to learn and propagate the best that is known and thought in the world, and thus to establish a current of fresh and true ideas. By the very nature of things, as England is not all the world, much of the best that is known and thought in the world cannot be of English growth, must be foreign; by the nature of things, again, it is just this that we are least likely to know, while English thought is streaming in upon us from all sides, and takes excellent care that we shall not be ignorant of its existence; the English critic, therefore, must dwell much on foreign thought, and with particular heed on any part of it, which, while significant and fruitful in itself, is for any reason specially likely to escape him. Judging is often spoken of as the critic's one business, and so in some sense it is; but the judgment which almost insensibly forms itself in a fair and clear mind, along with fresh knowledge, is the valuable one; and thus knowledge, and ever fresh knowledge, must be the critic's great concern for himself; and it is by communicating fresh knowledge, and letting his own judgment pass along with it,—but insensibly, and in the second place, not the first, as a sort of companion and clue, not as an abstract lawgiver,—that he will generally do most good to his readers. Sometimes, no doubt, for the sake of establishing an author's place in literature, and his relation to a central standard (and if this is not done, how are we to get at our *best in the world?*) criticism may have to deal with a subject-matter so familiar that fresh knowledge is out of the question, and then it must be all judgment; an enunciation and detailed application of principles. Here the great safeguard is never to let oneself become abstract, always to retain an intimate and lively consciousness of the truth of what one is saying, and, the moment this fails us, to be sure that something is wrong. Still, under all circumstances, this mere judgment and application of principles is, in itself, not the most satisfactory work to the critic; like mathematics, it is tautological, and cannot well give us, like fresh learning, the sense of creative activity.

But stop, someone will say; all this talk is of no practical use to us whatever; this criticism of yours is not what we have in our minds when we speak of criticism; when we speak of critics and criticism, we mean critics and criticism of the current English literature of the day; when you offer to tell criticism its function, it is to this criticism that we expect you to address yourself. I am sorry for it, for I am afraid I must disappoint these expectations. I am bound by my own definition of criticism: *a disinterested endeavor to learn and propagate the best that is known and thought in the world.* How much of current English literature comes into this "best that is known and thought in the world"? Not very much, I fear; certainly less, at this moment, than of the current literature of France or Germany. Well, then, am I to alter my definition of criticism, in order to meet the requirements of a number of practicing English critics, who, after all, are free in their choice of a business? That would be making criticism lend itself just to one of those alien practical considerations which, I have said, are so fatal to it. One may say, indeed, to those who have to deal with the mass—so much better disregarded—of current English literature, that they may at all events endeavor, in dealing with this, to try it, so far as they can, by the standard of the best that is known and thought in the world; one may say, that to get anywhere near this standard, every critic should try and possess one great literature, at least, besides his own; and the more unlike his own, the better. But, after all, the criticism I am really concerned with—the criticism which alone can much help us for the future, the criticism which, throughout Europe, is at the present day meant, when so much stress is laid on the importance of criticism and the critical spirit—is a criticism which regards Europe as being, for intellectual and spiritual purposes, one great confederation, bound to a joint action and working to a common result, and whose members have, for their proper outfit, a knowledge of Greek, Roman, and Eastern antiquity, and of one another. Special, local, and temporary advantages being put out of account, that modern nation will in the intellectual and spiritual sphere make most progress, which most thoroughly carries out this program. And what is that but saying that we too, all of us, as individuals, the more thoroughly we carry it out, shall make the more progress?

There is so much inviting us!—what are we to take? what will nourish us in growth toward perfection? That is the question which, with the immense field of life and of literature lying before him, the critic has to answer; for himself first, and afterwards for others. In this idea of the critics business the essays brought together in the following pages have had their origin; in this idea, widely different as are their subjects, they have, perhaps, their unity.

I conclude with what I said at the beginning: to have the sense of creative activity is the great happiness and the great proof of being alive, and it is not denied to criticism to have it; but then criticism must be sincere, simple, flexible, ardent, ever widening its knowledge. Then it may have, in no contemptible measure, a joyful sense of creative activity; a sense which a man of insight and conscience will prefer to what he might derive from a poor, starved, fragmentary, inadequate creation. And at some epochs no other creation is possible.

Still, in full measure, the sense of creative activity belongs only to genuine creation; in literature we must never forget that. But what true man of letters ever can forget it? It is no such common matter for a gifted nature to come into possession of a current of true and living ideas, and to produce amidst the inspiration of them, that we are likely to underrate it. The epochs of Æschylus and Shakespeare make us feel their pre-eminence. In an epoch like those is, no doubt, the true life of literature; there is the promised land, towards which criticism can only beckon. That promised land it will not be ours to enter, and we shall die in the wilderness: but to have desired to enter it, to have saluted it from afar, is already, perhaps, the best distinction among contemporaries; it will certainly be the best title to esteem with posterity.

Selected Bibliography

GENERAL

Abrams, M. H. *The Mirror and the Lamp: Romantic Theory and the Critical Tradition*. New York, 1953. Reprinted by Norton Library [paperback]. New York, 1958.

Atkins, J. W. H. *English Literary Criticism:* I, *The Medieval Phase*. Cambridge, 1943; II, *The Renascence*. London, 1947; III, *The Seventeenth and Eighteenth Centuries*. London, 1951.

————. *Literary Criticism in Antiquity:* I, *Greek;* II, *Graeco-Roman*. Cambridge, 1934.

Baldwin, Charles Sears. *Renaissance Literary Theory and Practice*. New York, 1939.

Bate, Walter Jackson. *Prefaces to Criticism*. Anchor Books [paperback]. New York, 1959.

————. *From Classic to Romantic: Premises of Taste in Eighteenth-Century England*. Cambridge, Mass., 1946. Reprinted as Harper Torchbook [paperback], 1961.

Bosker, Aisso. *Literary Criticism in the Age of Johnson*. Revised edition. New York, 1953.

Daiches, David. *Critical Approaches to Literature*. Englewood Cliffs, New Jersey, 1956.

Greene, W. C. "The Greek Criticism of Poetry, a Reconsideration," in *Perspectives of Criticism*, ed. Harry Levin. Cambridge, Mass., 1950.

Saintsbury, George. *A History of Criticism*, 3 vols., 3rd ed. New York, 1902-17.

Spingarn, J. E. *A History of Literary Criticism in the Renaissance*, second edition. New York, 1908.

Warren, Jr., Alba H. *English Poetic Theory, 1825-1865*. Princeton, 1950.

Weinberg, Bernard. *A History of Literary Criticism in the Italian Renaissance*, 2 vols. Chicago, 1961.

Wellek, René. *A History of Modern Criticism: 1750-1950:* I, *The Later Eighteenth Century;* II, *The Romantic Age*. New Haven, 1955.

Wimsatt, Jr., William K. and Cleanth Brooks. *Literary Criticism: A Short History*. New York, 1957.

ARISTOTLE

Cooper, Lane. *The Poetics of Aristotle, Its Meaning and Influence.* London, 1924.

Else, Gerald Frank. *Aristotle's Poetics: the Argument.* Cambridge, Mass., 1957.

Fergusson, Francis. "On the Poetics," *Tulane Drama Review,* vol. 4, no. 4 (May, 1960), 23-32.

Herrick, M. T. *The Poetics of Aristotle in England.* New Haven, 1930.

House, Humphrey. *Aristotle's Poetics: A Course of Eight Lectures.* London, 1956.

Lucas, F. L. *Tragedy in Relation to Aristotle's "Poetics."* London, 1928. (pp. 91ff.)

Ransom, John Crowe. "The Literary Criticism of Aristotle," in *Lectures in Criticism,* ed. Elliott Coleman. Harper Torchbook [paperback]. New York, 1961.

ARNOLD

Garrod, H. W. *Poetry and the Criticism of Life.* Cambridge, Mass., 1931.

James, D. G. *Matthew Arnold and the Decline of English Romanticism.* Oxford, 1961.

Leavis, F. R. "Revaluations (XI): Arnold as Critic," *Scrutiny,* VII (December, 1938), 319-32. Reprinted in *The Importance of Scrutiny,* ed. Eric Bentley. New York, 1948.

Perkins, David. "Arnold and the Function of Literature," *Journal of English Literary History,* XVIII (1951), 287-309.

Trilling, Lionel. *Matthew Arnold.* New York, 1949.

COLERIDGE

Bate, Walter Jackson. "Coleridge on the Function of Art," in *Perspectives of Criticism,* ed. Harry Levin. Cambridge, Mass., 1950.

Fogle, Richard H. *The Idea of Coleridge's Criticism.* Berkeley and Los Angeles, 1962.

Leavis, F. R. "Coleridge in Criticism," *Scrutiny,* IX (1940), 57-69. Reprinted in *The Importance of Scrutiny,* ed. Eric Bentley. New York, 1948.

Raysor, Thomas M. "Coleridge's Criticism of Wordsworth," *PMLA,* XXXIV (June, 1939), 496-510.

Richards, I. A. *Coleridge on Imagination.* London, 1924.

Thorp, C. D. "Coleridge as Aesthetician and Critic," *Journal of the History of Ideas,* I (1944), 387-414.

DRYDEN

Eliot, T. S. *John Dryden: The Poet, The Dramatist, The Critic.* New York, 1932.

Huntley, Frank L. "On the Persons of Dryden's *Essay of Dramatic Poesy," Modern Language Notes,* LXIII (1948), 88-95.

Legouis, Pierre. "Corneille and Dryden as Dramatic Critics," in *Seventeenth Century Studies Presented to Sir Herbert Grierson.* Oxford, 1938.

Trowbridge, Hoyt. "The Place of the Rules in Dryden's Criticism," *Modern Philology,* XLIV (Nov., 1946), 84-96.

Williamson, George. "The Occasion of 'An Essay of Dramatic Poesy,' " *Modern Philology,* XLIV (August, 1946), 1-9.

HORACE

Goad, Caroline. *Horace in English Literature of the Eighteenth Century.* New Haven, 1918.

Herrick, Marvin T. *The Fusion of Horatian and Aristotelian Literary Criticism,* 1531-1555. Urbana, 1946.

KEATS

Bate, Walter Jackson. *Negative Capability.* Cambridge, Mass., 1939.

Caldwell, John. *John Keats' Fancy.* Ithaca, N.Y., 1945.

Davies, R. T. "Was 'Negative Capability' Enough for Keats? A Reassessment of the Evidence in the Letters," *Studies in Philology,* LV (1958), 176-85.

Thorp, C. D. *The Mind of John Keats.* Oxford, 1926.

Trilling, Lionel. "Introduction" to *Selected Letters of John Keats.* New York, 1951; reprinted in Trilling's *The Opposing Self,* Compass Books [paperback], 1959.

JOHNSON

Bate, Walter Jackson. *The Achievement of Samuel Johnson*. New York, 1955. Reprinted by Galaxy Books [paperback]. New York, 1961.

Hagstrum, Jean. *Samuel Johnson's Literary Criticism*. Minneapolis, 1952.

Leavis, F. R. "Johnson as Critic," *Scrutiny*, XII (1944), 187-204. Reprinted in *The Importance of Scrutiny*, ed. Eric Bentley. New York, 1949.

Tate, Allen. "Johnson on the Metaphysicals," *Kenyon Review*, XI (1949), 379-394.

LONGINUS

Brody, Jules. *Boileau and Longinus*. Geneva, 1958.

Grube, G. M. A. "Notes on the περι ὑψsους," *American Journal of Philology*, LXXVIII (1957), 355-374.

Henn, T. R. *Longinus and English Criticism*. Cambridge, 1934.

Monk, S. H. *The Sublime: A Study of Critical Theories in Eighteenth-Century England*. New York, 1935. Reprinted by Ann Arbor Paperbacks, 1961.

Tate, Allan. "Longinus," in *Lectures in Criticism*, ed. Eliott Coleman. Harper Torchbook [paperback]. New York, 1961. First printed in *Lectures in Criticism*, Pantheon Books, New York, 1949; reprinted in Tate's *The Forlorn Demon*, Chicago, 1953, as "Longinus and the New Criticism."

PLATO

Lodge, Rupert C. *Plato's Theory of Art*. London, 1953.

McKeon, Richard. "Literary Criticism and the Concept of Imitation in Antiquity," *Modern Philology*, XXXIV (August, 1936), 1-35. Reprinted in *Critics and Criticism*, ed. R. S. Crane, Phoenix Books [paperback], 1957.

Rau, Catherine. *Art and Society: a Reinterpretation of Plato*. New York, 1951.

Verdenius, Willem. *Mimesis; Plato's Doctrine of Artistic Imitation and Its Meaning to Us*. Leiden, 1949.

SIDNEY

Boas, Frederick S. *Sir Philip Sidney, Representative Elizabethan: His Life and Writings.* New York, 1955.

Myrick, Kenneth O. *Sir Philip Sidney as a Literary Craftsman.* Cambridge, Mass., 1935.

Thaler, Alwin. *Shakespeare and Sir Philip Sidney: The Influence of "The Defense of Poesy."* Cambridge, Mass., 1947.

WORDSWORTH

Barstow, Marjorie L. *Wordsworth's Theory of Poetic Diction.* New Haven, 1917.

Havens, R. D. *The Mind of a Poet: a Study of Wordsworth's Thought with Particular Reference to "The Prelude."* Baltimore, 1941.

James, D. G. *Scepticism and Poetry.* London, 1937. (pp. 141 ff; pp. 164 ff.)

Peacock, Markham L. *The Critical Opinions of William Wordsworth.* Baltimore, 1950.

Thorpe, C. D. "The Imagination: Coleridge Versus Wordsworth," *Philological Quarterly,* XVIII (1939), 1-18.